BACKWATER
WAR

Edwin P. Hoyt

BACKWATER WAR
THE ALLIED CAMPAIGN IN ITALY, 1943–1945

PRAEGER

Westport, Connecticut
London

Library of Congress Cataloging-in-Publication Data

Hoyt, Edwin Palmer.
    Backwater war : the Allied campaign in Italy, 1943–1945 / Edwin P. Hoyt.
        p.   cm.
    Includes bibliographical references and index.
    ISBN 0–275–97478–2 (alk. paper)
        1. World War, 1939–1945—Italy.   2. World War, 1939–1945—Campaigns—Italy.   3.
    Anzio Beachhead, 1944.   4. Italy—History—German occupation, 1943–1945.   5.
    Italy—History—Allied occupation, 1943–1947.   I. Title.
    D763.I8 H66   2002
    940.54'215—dc21   2002025328

British Library Cataloguing in Publication Data is available.

Library of Congress Catalog Card Number: 2002025328
ISBN: 0-275-97478-2

First published in 2002

Praeger Publishers, 88 Post Road West, Westport, CT 06881
An imprint of Greenwood Publishing Group, Inc.
www.praeger.com

Printed in the United States of America

The paper used in this book complies with the
Permanent Paper Standard issued by the National
Information Standards Organization (Z39.48–1984).

10 9 8 7 6 5 4 3 2 1

Contents

Contents

Photo essay follows page 79.

Preface

It has been more than half a century since the end of World War II, and the real story of the conflicts among the Allied high command still has not been thoroughly explored. In hindsight it seems a wonder that the great alliance between the British and Americans did not founder in 1943. The only thing that kept it together was Prime Minister Sir Winston Churchill's willingness to sacrifice the British strategy for winning the war to the exigencies of keeping the Americans in the European war.

It was a very near thing, as this book will show. The Americans felt from the beginning of their war effort that the solution in Europe called for a direct drive at the German heart. The British believed that the Germans should be nibbled into defeat, with a major effort made in the Balkans. General George C. Marshall, the U.S. army chief of staff, was particularly distrustful of Churchill, and all the way along, even after Normandy, he shot down one Churchill plan after another for action in the south. As late as September 1944, when the British prime minister plumped for an invasion of Trieste and Adriatic Italy, Marshall intervened to stop it.

It is quite obvious now that the British were right and Marshall and the Americans were wrong. The speed with which Adolf Hitler acted to shore up his southern defenses every time they were threatened is the proof of it. When the British threatened in Greece in 1941, he delayed the invasion of Russia for weeks to deal successfully with the threat. Again in 1943, when the Allies feinted an attack in the Balkans, Hitler rushed troops to the area. The result of the Allied strategy of the Cross

Channel Attack allowed Hitler to maintain his forces in the south, until very near the end.

As it turned out, the American campaigns in North Africa, Sicily, and Italy were unnecessary and costly, the result of confused Allied planning. The better course would have been for the Americans to keep their troops at home until they were better trained and to concentrate on the buildup for the Cross Channel Attack. This was not possible because President Franklin D. Roosevelt was eager to move after making the fateful decision to override his military advisers and concentrate on the war in Europe rather than the war in the Pacific. That decision caused the fall of the Philippines, and lengthened the war in the Pacific. Had General Douglas A. MacArthur received reinforcement from America, there is every reason to believe that he could have staved off the Japanese invasion of the Philippines, and the first American victory would have come there instead of at Guadalcanal. But in those first fateful weeks after Pearl Harbor, there were no reinforcements for the Pacific. Everything was being geared for the war against Hitler.

At the theater level, the conflicts between the British and the Americans began in North Africa and did not let up. After the first battles, the British began calling the Americans "our Italians," and their contempt for the American fighting ability did not cease until well into the Italian campaign. All the way through, the British underrated the American army and air forces, and since the war, a popular wave of anti-American sentiment has coursed through Britain, denying the competence of the World War II American fighting men on land or in the air.

This negativism was shared by American military commanders from General George S. Patton Jr., who once remarked that the best thing the Americans could do in England would be "to drive the British into the sea," to Admiral Chester W. Nimitz, who strongly resisted the demands of the British (not to be confused with the Australians and the New Zealanders) to participate in the Pacific war. It was only when higher authority decreed cooperation that British units were included in the Pacific Fleet operations.

In Italy, the conflicts between the British and the Americans were frequent, and sometimes expensive. British General Bernard L. Montgomery's narcissism is too well known to need elucidation. Time and again he balked or delayed Allied planning. Less well known is British Major General Richard L. McCreery's antipathy toward General Mark W. Clark, which finally erupted in McCreery's refusal to serve under Clark when he became theater commander. This resulted in an awkward command structure in which McCreery reported to another. This led to confusion and certainly did not advance the Allied cause in Italy.

The Germans in Sicily and Italy conducted a surprising retreat and defense. The Allies had expected the fall of Sicily and the collapse of the

Italian defenses to trigger a German retreat to northern Italy. Instead, after the Allies landed at Salerno, Field Marshal Albert Kesselring chose to first defend the Gustav Line in the south and thereafter to retreat slowly and stubbornly. General Heinrich von Vietinghoff conducted a masterful defense that has gone down in the annals of strategic warfare.

The tragedy of the Benedictine Abbey at Monte Cassino—the saturation bombing by the American air force that needlessly destroyed this historic landmark—has been described at length elsewhere. However, not so well known is the role played by a minor British commander, Lieutenant General Bernard C. Freyberg of the New Zealand Corps, who refused to attack on the ground unless the saturation bombing was carried out. After the bombing was over, Freyberg tried and failed to capture the abbey. This could have been predicted; Freyberg was the man who seized defeat from the jaws of victory on Crete, losing the island to an inferior force of German paratroopers because of his failure to attack at the strategic moment. General Clark, quite properly, took responsibility for the debacle at Monte Cassino, but the records only indicate the depth of the command quarrels that led to his decision about the bombing. It was a spectacular display of Allied disunity that marked the entire Mediterranean operations.

1

The Anglo–American Military Alliance

For two years Prime Minister Sir Winston Churchill worked feverishly to secure American support in the war against Germany, with growing evidence of success. Adolf Hitler believed that Churchill would be successful, and it was with great restraint that he did not declare war on the United States, particularly when America entered the de facto war by escorting British ships across the Atlantic and engaged German U-boats in battle.

Because Churchill felt an alliance was inevitable, he lost no time in going to Washington in December 1941, on the heels of the Japanese attack on Pearl Harbor. He anticipated that the American inclination would be to turn its face toward Japan. In his conferences with President Franklin D. Roosevelt, Churchill succeeded in persuading him to follow the course he had been previously traveling: to help Britain to the utmost to defeat Hitler. Roosevelt agreed and the Anglo–American military alliance was forged. America's military leaders were not in agreement with Roosevelt's decision; and although it became the American policy in the first few months after the United States entered the war, it was still being debated months later.

Roosevelt was anxious to take some action that would signal to the world America's commitment to the defeat of all the Axis countries: Germany, Italy, and Japan. He was specifically concerned that the Russians get this message and keep up their resistance against Hitler, which in the early months of 1942 seemed very precarious. Those who advocated Operation Torch—the invasion of French North Africa—said it would help the Russians, and would also give Americans some needed experience in combat before the Cross Channel Attack.

In its haste to get into action, the Americans acceded to a plan to join the British in what appeared to be a simple venture in French North Africa. It might even be possible, the British indicated, that French North Africa could be won over without firing a shot. But that did not happen. The war in French North Africa turned out to be real, and, thus, even before the Allied victory in Tunisia ended the Axis presence in Africa, the Anglo–American military alliance was experiencing difficulties. The American military planners were stunned into acceptance of the "Hitler First" strategy that Churchill brought to Washington on the heels of the Japanese attack on Pearl Harbor. The American military planners had not put their house in order by that time, and Roosevelt acceded to tactics and strategies that most of his advisers did not like.

First, the American military favored going to war against Japan. However, once the decision was made to fight the Germans first, the Americans wanted to go straight to the source. They wanted Operation Roundup—the Cross Channel Attack—and suggested that it could be carried out in 1943. Churchill seemed to agree enthusiastically, although there was no real enthusiasm for the plan in the British high command. After the end of the 1914–1918 War (World War I) the British dreaded the thought of another static war of that sort, in which millions of men had fallen as cannon fodder in endless capture and loss of the same tired territory. British strategy for the war indicated a drive in the Mediterranean to draw the Germans down in force and let them expend their war resources there. The first evidence of the strategy was Churchill's insistence on sending aid to the Greeks, who did not want it, thus forcing them to fight the Germans as well as the Italians, whom they were beating. By withdrawing the men and equipment from North Africa, where General Richard O'Connor had beaten the Italians to the point that one more drive would have expelled them from Africa altogether, Churchill paved the way for a campaign by Field Marshal Erwin J. E. Rommel that very nearly cost Britain Egypt and all of Africa.

By 1942, when the first breaches came in the endless series of German victories in Russia, and after the British had stopped Rommel at el-Alamein, Churchill could ignore his gaucherie. By the spring of 1942, it became apparent that talk of invading the north European continent in 1943 was foolish dreaming. The resources were not in England, and America could not get them there in time for such early action. In the search for some action that would put the final stamp on American participation in the war in Europe, Roosevelt was persuaded to approve Operation Torch. The motivations of the Americans and the British were quite different. For the British, Operation Torch cemented the Anglo–American military alliance. This was important enough to the British that they acceded, albeit reluctantly, to the overall American command of the operation and the provision that Americans would command the major operations against the Axis powers. They saw the operation as a part of the strategy of wearing down Hitler and forcing him to fragment his armies. The Americans expected to draw on their ancient amicable relationship with France and that the entrance to French North Africa would be a walk-in. They ignored the French mistrust and inimical feelings against an England the French charged had let them down in the defense of France, and had then sought to destroy the French fleet for purely British purposes. Thus the Americans were drawn, willy-nilly, into European politics once again.

When the Americans assessed the North African campaign, the planners wondered what they had been doing there. The pendulum began to swing in the summer of 1942. And the British were already single-handedly driving Rommel from Africa with the use of Commonwealth troops from Australia, New Zealand, and India. The American entry into the war caused no significant change in Hitler's allocation of troops, belying to the American mind the British contention that attacking in the "soft underbelly" of the Mediterranean was the way to Hitler's defeat.

By the middle of December 1942, General George C. Marshall was still hoping for a cross-channel attack the following year. He considered the North African adventure a detour and wanted to forget it as soon as possible. He felt that once the Germans and Italians had been eliminated from Africa, American troops and equipment should begin flowing to England in preparation for the Cross Channel Attack.

So as the North African war drew the Americans into Algeria, Morocco, and Tunisia during that winter, all the American objections to Operation Torch and American involvement in the Mediterranean were raised again. The hopes of a quick victory, and French acceptance of the invasion with rise to arms, proved faulty. Events in the east and the west moved very quickly by the beginning of 1943. The Americans, at Guadalcanal, had knocked the first hole in the hitherto impregnable Japanese perimeter. So American thoughts were very much in the Pacific. But this time there was a difference. The Americans were in the Mediterranean, and as such were held captive to the strategy that now must be evolved. There were murmurs in the American camp of dumping the whole enterprise and transferring American attention to the Pacific where Americans, Australians, and New Zealanders were marching up the Solomon Islands chain, preparing to isolate Rabaul, the major Japanese base in the South Pacific. Admiral Ernest J. King was very much of the opinion that the American effort started at Guadalcanal must press on with ever greater strength, lest the Japanese be given a chance to consolidate their defenses, which would certainly attenuate the war in the Pacific.

Roosevelt was still in the Churchill camp at this point, but his senior advisers were of unlike minds. They proposed the American buildup in England for the future invasion of the Continent, a major buildup of strategic bombing of Germany, and an equally powerful strategic bombing of Italy to knock Italy out of the war. They said nothing about future Mediterranean land operations. But in the British camp was also General Dwight D. Eisenhower, who having won command of the Allied forces was not going to give it up easily. He was looking for another operation in the Mediterranean, most hopefully against Sardinia, and he was supported in this by the British chiefs of staff, but not by the American chiefs of staff. The reason was that the Eisenhower proposal played to the British strategy of indirect approach to the defeat of Hitler, postponing as long as possible (and perhaps avoiding) the Cross Channel Attack that was so popular with the American leaders and so unpopular with the British.

In January 1943, it was apparent that the American leaders in Washington were willing to make only a limited effort in the Mediterranean. Churchill quite accurately pointed out that the North African campaign had caused the Germans to move 11 divisions from the 40-division force that guarded the coast from the channel to southern France. He said the Germans would have to move four to six divisions to Italy to guard against Sardinia. Other British leaders hoped for a major offensive in the Mediterranean to bring about the collapse of Italy, which would bring another 20 to 30 German divisions to Italy.

As it turned out, there are indications that they were right. Hitler's reaction to the uprising of Marshal Josep Broz Tito's partisans and his later reaction when the British invaded Greece show that a major Allied assault in the Balkans would have diverted a good share of Hitler's men and resources, and probably would have prevented the Russians from taking over Eastern Europe lock, stock, and barrel. But the Americans were never convinced of that.

So on the eve of the Casablanca Conference in mid-January, when Roosevelt asked his Joint Chiefs of Staff what they wanted, they were unanimous in stating that the Cross Channel Attack was the first consideration. None of them wanted to get involved in a major campaign in the Mediterranean. If they had to do something in the Mediterranean, then, General Marshall said, it should be Sicily. But the problem would be once Sicily was taken, where did they go from there? The Casablanca Conference opened with these questions very much up in the air.

By the time of the meeting, German resistance in Tunisia had stiffened, and Eisenhower's staff estimated that it would be summer before the Germans would be cleared from Africa. At the end of the campaign, there would be 250,000 Americans in Africa. What to do with them was a major dilemma.

The British, who wanted to take the Sicily course, estimated that by the summer of 1943 the buildup in England would be 13 British and 9 American divisions, which, Lieutenant General Alan F. Brooke said, would be sufficient to mount the Cross Channel Attack. Brooke spoke plainly against an occupation of Italy. This so relieved the Americans that it dispelled their fears about Mediterranean operations for the moment. A major consideration in the American acceptance of the Sicilian invasion was that it could be conducted with the troops already in the Mediterranean and, hopefully (from the American viewpoint), would not involve the use of a tremendous amount of American shipping, which the American chiefs wanted to share between the buildup for the Cross Channel Attack and their operations in the Pacific.

Therefore, it was decided at Casablanca to invade Sicily, with the hope of causing the fall of Benito Mussolini, the exit of the Italian government from the war, and the forcing on Germany of the whole commitment for the defense of Italy. No mention was made of invading Italy later.

One material military change came out of the conference. For the North African invasion, the Americans had demanded control, and it was given to them in the person of General Eisenhower as Supreme Commander of the Allied Forces. The British fretted about this arrangement and succeeded in getting it changed in the Sicilian adventure. Eisenhower was to command the Sicilian invasion but General Harold R.L.G. Alexander was to be commander of the ground forces and deputy commander; Admiral Andrew B. Cunningham was to command the naval forces; and Air Chief Marshal Sir Arthur W. Tedder was to command the air forces. Eisenhower was furious with this change. He said it put the British committee system in charge of operations. But Major General Walter B. Smith, his chief of staff, persuaded him that this was no time to argue about it, and, therefore, his protest was never officially registered. But Eisenhower's dislike of the established system remained.

Thus, the conference ended with the future strategy in the war undecided. The Americans left with the fervent hope that this would be the end of the Mediterranean adventure and that the future would shift to France, both north and south. The British did not change their minds even a little bit about wanting to approach Germany from the south rather than the north, and the only thing keeping them from talking about it was their understanding that the Americans were still insisting on the direct approach to Germany in the north. Their position was summed up by Air Chief Marshal Charles F. A. Portal, who hung on to the string of possibility: "It was impossible to say exactly where we should stop in the Mediterranean since we hoped to knock Italy out altogether."[1]

As the conference ended, British planners in London were thinking about the future. The collapse of the Italian government, they assumed, would force the Germans to withdraw their forces to the Pisa–Ravenna

Line, to cover the Po Valley, thus letting the Allies land in south and central Italy without any problems. They also envisaged activity in the Balkans.

As American authors Albert Garland and Howard McGaw Smyth put it in their official history of the Sicilian campaign: "The British were not thinking of deploying great armies on the continent, where the decisive strike would be made. They were thinking rather of the large scale employment of air power, of cutting the German economic lines of supply, of drawing in new allies such as Turkey or adding patriot forces in Yugoslavia or stimulating political revolt in Hungary. As a consequence logistical problems were no more important than any other factors of political strategic planning. Furthermore the British had no liking for far-reaching plans, they wished instead to retain a freedom of choice and the ability to adjust to new opportunities as they arose."

And as British General W.G.F. Jackson put it in his book *The Battle for Italy*: "The background of American strategic thinking was very different. They were far nearer in military experience and inclination to the Germans and the French than to the British in their assessment of the relative importance of the principles of war. They prized the careful selection and the ruthless maintenance of the strategic aim, the concentration of maximum effort at the decisive point and the strict limitation of diversionary operation. The principle of flexibility in strategic planning—a key feature of British thinking—came low on their list of priorities. Their experience in the first world war had confirmed them in their dislike for the indirect strategy preferred by the British. The Kaiser's Germany had been defeated by direct assault. Churchill's Gallipoli campaign had been a failure, and the Salonika expedition had led to nothing decisive and Allenby's victories over the Turks in Palestine, although brilliant in British eyes, had been little more than a manifestation of British imperialism. Just as the British wished to avoid a repetition of Ypres, the Somme, and Paschendaele, so the Americans tended to stop any waste of resources on diversionary operations."

Throughout, the Americans were conscious of an attempt by the British to drag them into support of their colonial operations, and the American military was determined not to take the American nation on this route. They were determined to avoid being sucked into the hole of European power politics.

The agreement on the invasion of Sicily did not stop British planners from considering the "soft underbelly" of Europe. The Americans continued to hold out for the Cross Channel Attack. They reconsidered all the options that spring of 1943, and concluded that nowhere else, as they had previously concluded, was there a direct way to strike the blows. If they had to go through the southern area, the best way was through Italy and southern France.

But their eyes were aimed on the Cross Channel Attack. One thing all of this maneuvering by the British did was to cause the Americans to demand a definite commitment and date for the Cross Channel Attack on which the British leaders appeared to be so slippery.

This became a major issue at the Trident Conference between the Combined Chiefs of Staff, held in Washington on May 25, 1943. As was now expected, Churchill arrived in Washington full of himself and British plans. All Allied resources, he proposed, were to be put into the Mediterranean in 1943, and the Cross Channel Attack was to be relegated to some indefinite future. This was precisely what General Marshall and the other American leaders had feared: Churchill's attempt once again to lead Roosevelt into plans of Churchill's making. But this time, the British found the Americans less tractable, and apparently willing to scale back their effort in Europe and concentrate their efforts in the Pacific. The Americans as much as said that the policy of nibbling around the edges of the German empire was tantamount to abandoning the strategy of "Hitler First" and thus would free the Americans to go their own way. General Marshall was becoming thoroughly disgusted with British caviling on the matter of the Cross Channel Attack, and suggested in conversation with Roosevelt that he indicate his own strong views, that if the British insisted on fighting in the Mediterranean, let them do so, and the Americans would withdraw their forces and send them to the Pacific. Only Roosevelt's refusal to let him be so bold kept Marshall from saying just that. But somehow the idea got through to the British that they had overstepped their bound and the Americans might change the focus of their war.

This alarming idea stimulated the British to reconsider somewhat their approach. The idea of demanding the abandonment of the Cross Channel Attack was quickly discarded by the British. They had to address themselves primarily to the problem the Americans posed: Cross Channel Attack, when and where?

They recovered sufficiently to keep their toe in the door by concentrating arguments on the elimination of Italy from the war as the next important step. The Americans, immediately suspicious that the British were not really converted to the Cross Channel Attack, specified that American ground and naval forces would not be used in the Mediterranean, east of Sicily.

The British changed the subject a little. A premature attack on France would certainly come to disaster, they said. The Americans saw through this ploy, which convinced them more than ever of British insincerity about Operation Overlord. They began to get testy. The British backed down and appeared to give full support to the Cross Channel Attack. With tongue in cheek the Americans accepted this, and turned their attention to the need, as the British saw it, for further Mediterranean operations beyond Sicily.

The British argued constantly for continuation in the Mediterranean. The Americans said the Cross Channel Attack should come in April 1944; the British agreed. Mediterranean operations before that time would lose the element of deception. The Americans accepted this and agreed to continue both buildups in the next few months, but only when the British said the buildup in the Mediterranean would not hamper the buildup in England.

The discussions ended without anyone being convinced, but their coming together on the immediate future was a matter of necessity. The Americans would countenance future operations in the Mediterranean, but the British must put more enthusiasm into the Cross Channel Attack. The last said on the subject was that Italy would be taken out of the war immediately and the Cross Channel Attack would come by May 1944.

Churchill, however, was determined to have his way. After the failure of the military leaders to secure American support for the war in Italy that he wanted, more and more, Churchill's real feelings were being exposed. He hated the idea of a cross channel attack. He said, and Lieutenant General Brooke supported him, that only Russia could yield definite results in war on the continent of Europe. This was a new admission by Churchill and a stunning one.

Churchill and the American and British military leaders went to Algiers to confer with Eisenhower. Nothing substantial came of the discussions, and Churchill, so far having revealed his hand and his determination to avoid the Cross Channel Attack, if at all possible, subsided for the moment. He had achieved Roosevelt's support of continued operations in the Mediterranean, after the invasion of Sicily, and he was wise enough to let it go at that.

2 _____

The Allies Prepare

The Allies decided in January 1943 to continue the indirect approach toward Germany by attacking Sicily; the reason, from the American point of view, was simply that there was no place else to go to utilize the forces that had been assembled in the Mediterranean. The Americans' eye, from the outset, had been on the Cross Channel Attack, and they refused to be diverted. Thus, from the defeat of the Axis powers in Africa, British and American war policy tended to diverge, with the Americans holding for direct assault on Germany, and the British hoping to wear down Hitler with a succession of attacks on the perimeter of his empire.

At the moment, however, there was no argument about the next objective: Sicily and the elimination of Italy from the war. Nor was there any open quarrel about the manner in which this should be done. The British military establishment was not happy with the selection of Eisenhower to head the North African operations, but Roosevelt convinced Churchill that the American people, having been attacked by Japan but not Germany, were, at best, lukewarm about the "Hitler First" strategy, and the only way to assure its success was to invoke American command leadership. For the Sicilian adventure, the British secured a major concession in the Combined Chiefs of Staff: the introduction of the British committee system of command. So while Eisenhower retained supreme command of the Sicilian operations, the actual command of land, sea, and air operations was all in British hands. Eisenhower was furious and drafted a hot cable to the Combined Chiefs of Staff protesting the undermining of his authority, but his chief of staff persuaded him that this was not the time to create a fuss, so he allowed himself to be diverted and tore up the cable. Thus, land operations were headed by General Alexander, naval operations by Admiral Cunningham, and air operations by Air Chief Marshal Tedder.

The British planners in London believed that when Italy collapsed, which they quite rightly envisaged after the fall of Sicily, Germany would withdraw its forces to the Po Valley in the north, thus making an invasion of Italy easy. They also envisaged operations in the Balkans. They were not thinking of employing great forces on the Continent, but, instead, using airpower to destroy Germany's economy and bringing in new allies such as Turkey and the anti-German forces of Yugoslavia and Hungary. In their mind the Cross Channel Attack was only one of many plans that might be executed and might not be.

General Alexander was not only ground force commander, he was also deputy to Eisenhower and charged with the planning of the ground operations, under a command that would be known as the Fifteenth Army Group. To carry out the ground operations, Eisenhower appointed General Montgomery to lead his British Eighth Army, and American Major General Patton (soon to be promoted to lieutenant general) to command the American troops. His command would be called the U.S. Seventh Army. The American forces would consist of an army headquarters, a corps headquarters, four infantry divisions, one armored division, and one airborne division.

Because the British Eighth Army was more experienced than the new U.S. Seventh Army, it was chosen to carry the brunt of the attack on Sicily, with the American forces in a backup position. The Eighth Army consisted of the 13th Corps and the 30th Corps, with a third corps—the 10th—held at Tripoli. The troops were six infantry divisions, one armored division, one airborne division, a tank brigade, and an infantry brigade.

The Americans would attack in the southeast corner of the triangular island, along the Gulf of Gela from Licata eastward to the Pachino Peninsula. The British would attack on the coastal sector from the Pachino Peninsula to Syracuse.

The assault would cover a very large front: more than 100 miles long. It would be preceded by landings of parts of two airborne divisions, and then 13 divisions would land. The British expected to have three ports almost immediately available, but the American sector had only two very small fishing ports and so they would have to depend on the newly developed two-and-a-half-ton amphibious trucks (DUKWs; called "ducks"). They could take men and material directly from the ship to a "dump" (assembly point) on the beach.

General Alexander had no firm plan for after the landings were made;

he wanted to get the troops safely ashore before worrying about where they were going. It was assumed that the major effort would be made by the British, and General Montgomery would drive swiftly through Catania to the Strait of Messina. When the plan was made, Alexander was aware that the Americans might be offended by being given a back-seat in this invasion, only being utilized to protect the flank of the British advance. But to him the Americans were very much an unproved force, and he did not think a great deal of what he had seen from them so far. After the American disaster at Kasserine Pass, the British had begun referring to them as "our Italians"; and in the early months of the war, they shared, with the Germans, a contempt for the American fighting ability.

The Americans did not think much of the British plan, which made their landings not only subsidiary to the British but far more difficult. But Patton refused to protest. His attitude was that he had been given orders to land where he did, and he would do his best to carry them out.

As for the airborne landings, which preceded the seaborne, the British planned to send in gliders carrying their troops, and the Americans would use parachute troops, dropping them to land in critical sectors ahead of the beachhead. The British 1st Airborne Division would make the landings in Catania, and a regiment of the U.S. 82nd Airborne Division would make the American first effort. The planes that would tow the gliders and carry the American troops were British and American, but the pilots were Americans of the 51st and 52nd Troop Carrier Wings.

The U.S. Seventh Army consisted of the II Corps, which was made up of the 1st, 3rd, and 45th Infantry Divisions; the 82nd Airborne Division; the 2nd Armored Division; and part of the 9th Infantry Division. Besides these elements, the Americans committed three Ranger battalions, four motorized chemical battalions, and a battalion of Moroccan Goums. Patton would command the army; II Corps was under the command of Brigadier General Omar N. Bradley. As to the infantry divisions: the 1st was commanded by Major General Terry de la Mesa Allen, the 3rd was commanded by Major General Lucian K. Truscott Jr., and the 45th was commanded by Major General Troy H. Middleton.

The British ground forces consisted of the 5th, 50th, and 78th Infantry Divisions; the 51st Highland Infantry Division; the 231st Infantry Brigade; the 1st Canadian Infantry Division; and a Canadian tank brigade.

Naval and air support would be provided by a mixed group of British and American warships and fighter planes. There would be no preliminary bombardment, but the warships would be ready to furnish fire support after the troops were ashore. The command was depending heavily on a deception plan that had thoroughly confused the Axis powers—it was known from Ultra intercepts. This plan had involved ejecting a dead body—which was carrying false papers to indicate the coming of an invasion in the Balkans—from a submarine off the Spanish coast. Obviously, the enemy had fallen for the ruse and had moved several divisions that might otherwise have been concentrated on the Italian shore. But the element of surprise was not as complete as the Allies had expected. Some German units were not fooled, nor, in the end, was General d'Armata Alfredo Guzzoni, commander of the Sicily defenses.

Air support, from the standpoint of the ground forces, was totally confusing and incomplete. The British view that airpower was a separate force and could not be tied to naval or land action prevailed because the British were in command of the effort. The air force, then, would make no promises of air support anywhere, but would rely on its own judgment regarding where the action was to be, with great concentration on knocking out Axis airpower. The air plan was described by one American officer as "the most masterful piece of uninformed prevarication, totally unrelated to the naval and military joint plan."[2] Ground and naval commanders had no idea of what support they would receive. The maximum air support furnished to the U.S. Seventh Army during the initial phases of operation consisted of 18 tactical reconnaissance missions per day, each mission lasting 30 minutes.

The British ground force units were widely dispersed and came from all angles. The first American units to sail were those of the 45th Infantry Division, which had come directly from America, loaded for action, and stopped at Oran. They sailed on July 4. The 1st Infantry Division sailed the next day from Algiers. Later, the 3rd Infantry Division sailed from Bizerte along with the field commanders and the 2nd Armored Division elements.

On July 9, when the units were at sea, a storm blew up and a number of ships lost their places in the columns. The LSTs (landing ships, tank) and the LCIs (landing craft, infantry) rolled heavily in the seas, and all the convoys were late in arriving at their assigned areas offshore. Generals Eisenhower and Alexander had gone to Malta to await reports on the invasion. There they considered postponing the operation for 24 hours; however, if they did postpone it, the whole effort would be thrown into confusion, because the naval forces said they needed at least four hours to transmit the information to all concerned. (As it turned out in the air drops, even this was not enough time nor was it satisfactory.) Luckily for the chances of success, Eisenhower decided against postponement.

On the evening of July 9, Eisenhower hoped to catch a glimpse of the troop carrier aircraft flying over Malta toward Sicily, and he did see a few planes. Rubbing the seven lucky coins he carried, he offered up a silent prayer for safety and success, then he went back to the palace of the governor of Malta and sent a wire to General Marshall to tell him that the invasion was on. After that he returned to Admiral Cunning-ham's underground headquarters to wait.

On Sicily, General Guzzoni was not fooled by the Allied deception plan. He learned from his intelligence organization early in July that 90 percent of the available Allied troops and 96 percent of the landing craft were concentrated in the central western Mediterranean, and he expected a landing in Sicily. The Germans still expected a landing in Greece and another in Sardinia, but in the future. On July 5, Italian reconnaissance aircraft noted the increase of Allied hospital ships from two to 16. By nightfall that day, they observed a convoy traveling under an umbrella of barrage balloons. By July 8, General Guzzoni was convinced that the landings would come on the 10th and ordered the ports of Licata, Porto Empedocle, and Sciacca prepared for demolition. On July 9, he received reports of 90 landing craft and transports off Pantelleria, and later of the approach of other convoys. On the evening of July 9, he ordered a partial alert, and later that night a full alert.

On the night of July 9, the air and waters off Sicily were as quiet as if there was no war. But it was a deception. Just offshore, the Italians knew, a huge Allied fleet was ready to pounce.

3

The Axis Defenses of Sicily

The Allied attack on the fortress island of Pantelleria had two effects. It signaled to the people of Italy that their country had lost the war, and that it was just a matter of time before the Allies would arrive in Italy. It signaled to the Germans the weakness of their Italian allies, whom they no longer believed could be counted on in the joint defense.

After the fall of Pantelleria, the Italians accepted five divisions of German troops to help with their defenses. Field Marshal Kesselring was willing to give them. He had a great deal of faith in the German ability to hold Italy, given reasonable cooperation from the Italians, and because he was an optimist, he expected this to happen. But Field Marshal Rommel, who had been fighting with the Italians at his side for two years, had no such optimism. He warned that the Italians were likely to come apart completely.

Kesselring went to Berlin and conferred with Hitler, who said he was willing to send any military aid that Mussolini asked for. This posed a problem for General Vittorio Ambrosio, the commander of the Italian armies, because Mussolini had been talking about breaking off with the Germans. If this happened, there should not be any more German troops in Italy than were there now. But if Mussolini chose to fight with the Germans against the Allies, then they needed more German help.

By the end of June, five German divisions were in Italy and two more were about to come. As far as Sicily was concerned, all the ground forces were under the command of General Mario Roatta, commander of the

15

Italian Sixth Army. The German naval and air units in Sicily remained under German control.

As General Roatta waited for the Allies that spring of 1943, he put his troops to work enlarging beach defenses and building a belt of fortifications about 12 miles behind the beaches to stop the Allied advance if the troops reached the shore. But Roatta did not trust the Sicilians, and he issued a proclamation that showed it. An uproar followed and Roatta was transferred to Rome and General Guzzoni took his place. Guzzoni surveyed the defenses and found them very much lacking. The coast battalions were full of old men and were strung out to cover sectors up to 25 miles. He had only one antitank gun for each five miles of coastline. He received about one-fourth of the supplies from Italy that he needed; he needed artillery and tanks even after the transfer of the Hermann Goering Panzer Division of German troops to Sicily.

The beaches were generally undefended, with no obstacles except here and there. A number of blockhouses and fortifications had been built, but most of them were unmanned. For example, on the highway from Licata to Campobello, a distance of 12 miles, the whole antitank defense was one 47-mm gun.

The three naval bases had anti-naval and antiaircraft guns, but little defense against land attack; and the airfields needed a lot of work. Guzzoni began to complete them. The airstrips were mined so they could be blown to slow down Allied use. The airfields were surrounded with obstacles and would be defended by infantry personnel that would come from the Italian Sixth Army, which consisted of six coastal divisions, two coastal brigades, and four mobile divisions. After the end of June, Guzzoni had two German divisions in Sicily. On paper it was quite a strong force, numbering some 200,000 Italians and 30,000 Germans. But the Italian arms were inadequate and deficient, and their training had been badly neglected. Only one Italian division, the 4th Livorno Division, was at full strength. But the German divisions were something else: well trained, well commanded, and ready for action.

The Italian navy had no carriers and could operate effectively only if it had good land-based air support, which was not available. Further, it was 24 hours away from Sicily.

The Italian air force was now a paper tiger, with obsolete and inferior aircraft. After the Allied aircraft attacks on Sicily that spring, the Italian and German bombers were withdrawn to the mainland. General Hans Jeschonnek, the chief of staff of the Luftwaffe, came to Italy that spring and found the German air forces there inferior to what they could expect from the Allies. But Reichsmarshall Hermann Goering stubbornly refused to admit it, even though, in a series of air battles from May through July, the Germans had sustained heavy losses against British and American aircraft.

Thus, the defense of Sicily rested on the shoulders of the Italian and German ground forces. Kesselring had so little confidence in the ability of the Italians to stop the Allies at the water's edge that he instructed the German commander, without waiting for orders from Guzzoni, to counterattack as soon as he saw the burden of the Allied attacks.

This German suspicion had been growing for some time. In May, Hitler had offered Mussolini five new German divisions to help the Italian defense, but Mussolini, who had grown very restless under growing German domination, declined the offer. This put the wind up in Berlin. Hitler appointed Rommel as his special adviser on the Mediterranean, and Rommel still felt that the Italians were incapable of a sustained military effort. Hitler was concerned because he wanted to keep Italy in the war; otherwise, he would have to give the Mediterranean front more priority. His thinking was much the same as that of the British. Therefore, Hitler kept encouraging Mussolini with weapons and men during the spring of 1943.

Speculation in the German high command about Mussolini and Italy was running very strong. Joseph Goebbels, the head of German propaganda, remarked that Mussolini had become an old, tired man and that Hitler was not at all convinced of his reliability, although he remained loyal to the man who had been his mentor in days gone by.

In May, the Oberkommandowehrmacht (OKW) report on the defense of Italy was very discouraging. What was needed, from a purely military point of view, was a German high command for Italy and enough German troops to work as "corset stays" and hold the fabric of the Italian army together. At a long conference on Italy, Hitler commented to Field Marshal Wilhelm Keitel, his chief of staff of the OKW, that it would be wise to have Rommel ready to step in and take over in Italy if Mussolini fell apart. A few days later, the OKW came forth with an emergency plan—Plan Alarich—that called for the Germans to occupy northern Italy and evacuate the rest of Italy, if Fascism collapsed. The German force would be placed under the command of Rommel and would withdraw six or seven divisions from the Eastern Front. Eventually, he would have 13 or 14 divisions.

The Germans were also wise enough to organize their own services of supply across the Strait of Messina. Their armed forces command there was unified under Colonel Ernst G. Baade, who was responsible for ferry service and antiaircraft defenses.

General Guzzoni's headquarters were near Enna, in the middle of Sicily. The Hermann Goering Panzer division was in the southeast part of the island, and the 15th Panzer Grenadier Division was near Catania. The plan agreed upon by the Germans and the Italians was that the battle was to be fought at the coastline by the local units and coastal troops and the four mobile Italian divisions, and the Germans were in reserve to clean up. They expected the Allies to land in several different places and intended to give them no time to consolidate.

So, as the Allies prepared to invade, the western Italian corps was located near Palermo, the eastern corps near Syracuse, and the 4th Livorno Division on the high ground above Licata; the Hermann Goering Panzer Division was on the high ground behind Gela. The greater part of the 15th Panzer Grenadier Division was in the west.

On June 26, Kesselring and Guzzoni held a final coordinating conference. Kesselring summarized his theory of defense: The local troops must oppose the landings. The Italian mobile divisions must attack as soon as they knew where the Allies were heading, and the German divisions would follow to finish the job. Kesselring thought the Allies would land on a wide front at many different points. The aim was to wipe out the beachheads one by one before they could link up. He felt that the Allies had missed their big chance by not following up quickly and coming to Sicily just after the capture of Tunis. The Axis powers had now made the defenses of Sicily much stronger. The Allies would probably come around the middle of July. The defenses of Sicily were as strong as they could be, with the materials at hand.

Early in July, Guzzoni's intelligence told him that 90 percent of available Allied troops, 60 percent of the air forces, and 96 percent of the landing craft were concentrating in the center of the western Mediterranean. Information from German and Italian intelligence sources warned of invasion attempts in the first ten days of July, either against Sicily or Sardinia, but mostly Sicily.

Then, on July 4, Guzzoni had news of an Allied convoy of 25 merchant vessels with naval escorts in North African waters. He noted the substantial increase in fighter planes on Malta and came to the conclusion that the danger was to Sicily. The Germans thought the Allies would launch simultaneous invasions of Sardinia, Sicily, and Greece, but not just yet. Guzzoni was not convinced, and on the next day, when he learned that the Allied hospital ships in the area had been increased from two to 16, he was certain that invasion was imminent.

By July 8, Guzzoni ordered the ports of Licata, Porto Empedocle, and Sciacca prepared for demolition. Trapani and Marsala were rendered useless by dumping dirt into the harbors. When this did not work completely, the Italians demolished the docks.

On the evening of July 9, Guzzoni received more messages about approaching convoys. That night he issued orders for a preliminary alert, and three hours later, he ordered a full alert. And on that night of July 9, Allied air forces bombed the headquarters of the three divisions on Sicily.

The Allies were coming. All the Italians and Germans could do was sit and wait.

4

Invasion

Late on the afternoon of July 9, the Red Devils of Britain's 1st Airborne Division began climbing into gliders at six airfields around Karouan. The 1st Landing Brigade, under the command of Brigadier P.H. Hicks, was about to set off on Operation Ladbroke—the glider operation that was to seize the crucial Ponte Grande bridge outside Syracuse. Shortly, 144 tow planes would take 136 American-made Waco gliders and eight big British Horsa gliders to Sicily. One hundred and nine C-47s and 28 Albemarle and 7 Halifax bombers were the tow planes. All the glider pilots were experienced British pilots, although 19 Americans were about to get some experience as copilots. But the British pilots were very short on experience in flying the American-made gliders.

Six of the Horsas were to land nearly on the Ponte Grande bridge, and the other gliders would crash-land in several zones nearby. Operations would be led by Major General B.F. Hopkinson, who had persuaded General Montgomery that his unit could help immeasurably in the reduction of the enemy defenses. Soon the tow planes and the gliders (300 feet behind) were taking off and preparing to head for Sicily. By 8:20 P.M. they were in the air and heading on course for the island. Soon thereafter gliders and tow planes (five of them) began to turn back for various reasons, but the others went on, buffered by crosswinds that blew several tow planes and gliders off course, causing them to miss the beacon on Malta and find their way to Sicily.

The winds continued, and by the time the gliders were in the Sicily area, they had reached 45 miles per hour. The casualties began. One tow rope broke, and a Horsa plunged into the sea, carrying 28 Red Devils and two pilots to their watery doom. A few minutes later, one of the Wacos broke loose and 15 more men plunged into the sea. Just off the Sicilian shore, they passed over the big convoy that carried General Montgomery's British Eighth Army to the beaches. There were tense moments when the men above wondered if the men below would recognize them, or if they would open fire thinking they were the enemy. But a few minutes later, the tow planes and gliders began an 18-mile run to the glider release point near Syracuse. Light suddenly blinded several pilots. The enemy had discovered them and was manning searchlights, and flak guns, and flak began to explode around the air armada.

As the pilots approached the Syracuse area, their vision was obscured by smoke from fires set by Allied bombers. The formation broke up as tow pilots took the action they thought best to bring their charges over the target. The confusion was complete when the communications failed and the tow pilots were unable to advise their charges about the release points. Thus, most of the gliders flew past the release point, and the gliders were cut loose at random, and began to seek landing places. Five gliders landed near Cape Passero, 15 miles south of the landing zones. Seven others plunged into the water in the Cape Passero area. One glider crash-landed near Augusta, 18 miles from the bridge. Sixty-seven of the Waco gliders plunged into the sea, drowning 200 airborne troops and pilots. Others dropped into the water near the shore; the survivors clung to the wreckage and waited for rescue by boats and ships of the invasion armada. Among those who fell into the sea was General Hopkinson, who emerged spluttering and cursing the American tow pilots of the 51st Troop Carrier Wing, who he blamed for the predicament and the obvious failure of his mission.

One Horsa was cut loose near the landing zone, but the glider was hit by machine-gun fire as it came down. It blew up, exploding the bangalore torpedoes and explosives it was carrying, killing Major Thomas Ballinger and the others who were heading for the bridge.

Dozens of crashed gliders littered the Sicilian countryside. One glider flew into the face of a cliff; miraculously the 13 glidermen survived, and when they had pulled themselves together, they began heading for the Ponte Grande bridge.

Lieutenant Louis Withers and his 27 men landed safely. The lieutenant looked around for others, but all he could find were his men. If the Ponte Grande bridge was going to be seized, they would have to do it, and so they set out.

Five men went with Withers to swim the Apana River and the canal beside it that ran under the bridge. They were spotted by defenders in a pillbox, and fire broke out. They responded with automatic weapons and grenades. The others of the platoon struck at the bridge from the south. After a short firefight, the defenders disappeared in the darkness. They had failed to blow the bridge, and the lieutenant and his men found the charges that had been laid, tore them away, and threw them into the water. Lieutenant Withers and his men had taken the primary objective of Operation Ladbroke. But could they hold the bridge against the opposition that had to be coming soon in force?

That night, Withers was reinforced by a detachment of airborne troops that had landed a half mile away, and more survivors of the air mission began to straggle in. By dawn of July 10, the bridge was held by eight officers and 65 enlisted men. About 150 other airborne troopers had landed on the Maddalena Peninsula, four miles southeast of the bridge. They attacked and captured the Cape Morro radio station but not before the alarm had been given by the staff that gliders were swarming around the island.

That warning got to General Enrico Rossi, commander of the Italian 16th Corps, who was responsible for the defense of southern Sicily. He ordered four combat groups to rush to the defense, but his orders got lost somehow and nobody moved.

Although General Hopkinson was still cursing the tow pilots that morning, the airborne survivors were active in tiny groups, cutting telephone wires and creating confusion among the defenders. This action had disrupted communications and was the reason General Rossi's orders never arrived.

Shortly after dawn, Brigadier Hicks established a headquarters on the island. He, too, had landed in the water and had had a hard time getting to shore, but he had made it. He organized the men he could find and began to plan for action.

Without orders from the high command, several units of Italian defenders began to move that morning. They approached the bridge and began a mortar assault, with a deadly effect on the airborne troops. They brought up a field gun. By midafternoon, they overran the Red Devils on the north bank of the canal, and when the fighting ended, a small band of survivors surrendered. By 3:15 P.M. the bridge was back in the hands of the Italian defenders, who marched their prisoners to Syracuse. However, near the outskirts, they ran into a British captain and one man with automatic weapons who opened fire on the Italians, and soon the Italians surrendered. The Red Devils left alive from the bridge were freed again.

Shortly after the British glidermen had taken off from African fields, the Americans in 266 transports began to take off for their parachute drop in the area around Gela, 60 miles west of the British landings zones. At 8:35 that night they were off. Immediately they had bad news: the wind was blowing at 35 miles per hour, west to east, which meant they would have difficulty at their drop zone. But there was nothing to be done about it at this point. The planes assembled over Tunisia, and then set course for Sicily three-and-a-half hours away.

On the way, many of the planes missed the checkpoint at Malta and flew blindly ahead. By the time Brigadier General James M. Gavin (known as the "Jumping General") and his planeload of paratroopers began to drop, he could see no landmarks, and did not have the slightest idea where he was. Where were the other 3,400 paratroopers? After a few minutes, Gavin made contact with 19 officers and men and started off cross-country to try to find the place they should have been dropped. They encountered a drunken Italian soldier, who promptly escaped from them. They began walking, not really knowing where they were going. Behind them the others that were on their plane dropped one by one and as the last man got out, the plane was hit by gunfire and crashed.

One by one the aircraft disgorged their human loads, scattering them all the way from Niscemi at the western end of the drop zone to San Croce Camerina, on the eastern edge, with 23 loads of men dropped in the British sector. Some of the troops jumped too soon and landed in the sea, to be dragged under and drowned by their heavy equipment. But some of the men came down in groups. One such group, of about 80, reached the two-lane Ponte Dirillo bridge across the Acate River. They engaged in a firefight with Italian defenders and captured the bridge, which was an essential point in the plans of the 45th Infantry Division. They drove the defenders out of the pillboxes around the bridge. Other small groups got into firefights and captured some prisoners, and some were killed.

The Germans were getting ready for the air drop as it arrived. At 10 o'clock that night, long before the planes reached Sicily, General Conrath ordered his Hermann Goering Panzer Division to move toward the beaches of Gela and Scoglitti, conforming to Field Marshal Kesselring's order to him not to wait for the Italians to alert him but as soon as he heard the Allies coming to roar to counterattack.

The American paratroopers were badly scattered. By dawn, General Gavin managed to make contact with only five of his men. Others engaged in fighting and searching all over the drop zone and outside it, in the British zone. But about 100 of the Americans had dropped on Liano Lupo, the high ground that was supposed to have been the center of the drop of 3,400 troopers and was known as "Objective Y." It dominated a key road intersection seven miles northeast of Gela. At about 7 o'clock, the Germans launched a counterattack with about 300 infantrymen supported by tanks, which the Americans met and stopped. Then the Germans began firing on the American position with an 88-mm gun. In the confused fighting, the Germans captured a number of the paratroopers, but the result was that the drive to the beach at Gela was stopped. One group occupied an ancient castle and held it against German attacks that day and the next. The antitank men with their bazookas knocked out several tanks. Everywhere little groups of paratroopers were locked in combat with the enemy; the result was that General Conrath's drive on the beach at Gela never got under way.

The 2nd Battalion of the 505th Parachute Infantry Division dropped almost intact but 25 miles southeast of their drop zone on Liano Lupo, unfortunately into a complex of Italian pillboxes that cost a lot of casualties. In about four hours they captured four major pillboxes.

By morning of the day the sea assault began, the paratroopers were mingled with the men of the assault force, but others were roaming through the rear areas of the coastal defense units, interrupting communications and creating confusion. Perhaps it was not what the Allied high command had wanted, but it was serving a useful purpose, a handful of effectives—British and American—were more than carrying their share of the invasion. The most important service was to confuse the German and Italian commands regarding where the paratroopers and airborne landings were actually headed.

General Guzzoni, the Italian Sixth Army commander, received word of the airborne landings just after midnight. He ordered the Gela pier destroyed and alerted the German and Italian troops. The Germans were already going into action when they got the alert (a few minutes before 2:00 A.M. on July 10). An hour later, the initial waves of the assault groups began to come ashore, and the real battle was enjoined. As light came so did the Allied aircraft, which had been spread wide, but thin, over the assault beaches.

The British seaborne landings were uniformly successful. The first assault waves achieved tactical surprise. Supporting naval gunfire was very effective in wiping out enemy assault groups and strong points.

At 4:00 A.M. at Enna, General Guzzoni received word that British troops were ashore and fighting at the seaplane base at Syracuse. Guzzoni had two defense groups in the area: the Schmalz Group of Germans, a highly mobile assault force, and the 54th Napoli Division of Italians.

Those Britons who had captured the Ponte Grande bridge held it all day against almost constant assault, but by 3 o'clock in the afternoon there were only 15 men on their feet; a half hour later, they were overrun. Eight of them managed to make their way south to meet a column of the 5th Infantry Division, which came rushing up and with tanks and artillery captured the bridge again intact, and the column forced its way into Syracuse and headed for Augusta. But then Group Schmalz got into the picture and stopped the British advance of the 13th Corps. General Guzzoni then ordered the Hermann Goering Panzer Division to strike the Americans near Gela, which the Germans were already in motion to do. Guzzoni also ordered the 15th Panzer Grenadier Division to come from the west to a central position near Ennato and await orders.

In the east, the 54th Napoli Division was ineffective in stopping General Montgomery. The Schmalz Group stopped the 13th Corps but could do no more. The garrison of Syracuse surrendered without firing a shot, and the garrison of Augusta started destroying equipment and guns and making ready to evacuate before the British appeared. But the 4th Livorno and Hermann Goering Panzer Divisions launched several strong attacks on the American 1st Infantry Division beaches east of Gela. As mentioned, the Americans of this division fought stoutly and were supported by gunfire from their naval vessels offshore. The little lost units of the 82nd Airborne Division also proved noteworthy here, holding up the German and Italians in odd places and preventing any sustained attack. By the end of D Day, the Axis divisions were bruised but not broken and were preparing to attack again the next day.

During the night of D Day, Guzzoni recognized that the British threat was the larger, and that Messina was in danger. He would let the Italian 16th Corps carry the fight against the Americans, and he called on the Hermann Goering Panzer Division to strike the American 45th Infantry Division on the east flank, and then to link up with the Schmalz Group against the major British threat. The 4th Livorno Division was ordered to swing west toward Licata and meet the 15th Panzer Grenadier Division, and take on the American 3rd Infantry Division beachhead. The Luftwaffe was ordered to fly missions against the American beaches.

The Hermann Goering Panzer and 4th Livorno Divisions moved early in the morning and made good progress as long as they were out of the range of the American naval guns. But as they came down near the beaches, the American ships' guns began to make a difference. By noon the Panzer units were within striking distance of the American beach parties. A premature report from the Hermann Goering Panzer Division indicated that the Americans were being forced to embark; and that news electrified Rome. But it was short-lived. The 1st Infantry Division made a determined stand, fully supported by the naval guns, and the Hermann Goering Panzer Division thrust was stopped. By day's end, the division lost about one-third of its tanks.

The 4th Livorno Division also came up against the American naval guns and the American Rangers in the town of Gela. Many Italian units, fighting bravely, were cut to pieces. By evening, both Axis divisions were pulling back to their morning start lines. They had failed to breach the American beachheads.

That night Field Marshal Kesselring expressed his dissatisfaction with the operations of the Hermann Goering Panzer Division, and General Conrath replaced a number of senior officers. But the truth was that Kesselring's policy of defense at the water's edge, and an attempt to throw the invader back into the sea, had failed. Guzzoni had used his reserves and had no fresh troops to throw into the attacks. The British had begun to move northward, opening, not closing, the gap between the Schmalz Group and the Hermann Goering Panzer Division. Guzzoni now had to rely on the reserves in Italy, and be thankful for the very efficient German ferry service across the Strait of Messina. He knew that the thrust of the Allied attack was now in the British sector, toward Messina, and he could concentrate his resources on stopping the British.

That night, General Patton's Americans were nearly exhausted. The thrust of the Axis attack all day had been against them. He, too, had no reserves, and his closest help was the 82nd Airborne Division, the bulk of which was still in North Africa. He decided to bring in part of the division that night the fastest way: by air drop. The 50th Regiment, the 376th Artillery, and one Engineer Battalion would come in to reinforce the beachhead. The drop was supposed to start at 10:45 P.M. All the ships of both fleets and the army units were told that "friendly" planes would be flying overhead. General Matthew B. Ridgway, commander of the 82nd Airborne Division, was on the beachhead that day, and he personally checked six antiaircraft sites to see if they had "gotten the word." One had not gotten the word, so the warnings were given all over again.

During the day, the Luftwaffe had been doing its job, attacking the ships at sea. An ammunition ship had been bombed and exploded with a series of fireworks that amazed everyone who saw them. Just before 10:00 P.M., another Luftwaffe attack damaged several American ships. The antiaircraft fire died away then, and the 144 American troop-carrier planes began their approach over the fleets. The first echelon passed over and dropped its troops. The second flight was in sight of its objective. Then one antiaircraft gun opened fire, and soon almost every ship—British and American—was firing at the armada overhead. The carnage was fearful; some pilots turned back and flew to Africa with their loads of troops. Some exploded in midair. Many went down in the sea. Many virtually jettisoned their troops anywhere they could.

Admiral Cunningham defended his sailors with the claim that the British had been being bombed so long that they now shot first and asked questions later. That may have accounted for the British part of the mayhem, but it did not account for the American part. It was a matter of "trigger happiness" that affected the soldiers at their antiaircraft guns as well as the ships. It was an immense foul-up at the highest level of Allied command, and there was no gainsaying it. Only that one first flight, which had actually been ahead of schedule, missed the fury. As one of the paratroopers under fire said later: "It was . . . most uncomfortable . . . knowing that our own troops were [firing] at us. Planes dropped out of formation and crashed into the sea. Others . . . wheeled and attempted to get beyond the flak, which rose in fountains of fire, lighting the stricken faces [staring out] the windows."[3]

Of the 144 planes that had left Tunisia, 23 never got back, and 37 were badly damaged. The loss of aircraft was 16 percent. The 505th Parachute Infantry Division suffered 229 casualties that night. But worse than that, the attack on the air drop completely disorganized the unit; and by late the next afternoon, only 37 officers and 518 men were united and ready for duty. The reinforcement was almost a total failure. As one pilot put it, "The safest place . . . would have been over enemy territory."[4]

No blame was ever fixed, and the excuses continued. Ultimately, General Ridgway said that as far as he could see, the disaster could not have been averted, and he hoped that the high command had learned something from it. That was all that could be said.

5

The British Eighth Army's Drive

The Germans and the Italians had suffered that first day of the Allied invasion, but that night they pulled themselves together and displayed a remarkable unity of action in their plans for the second day. General Guzzoni's efforts now would be to contain the Allied bridgeheads and preserve the escape route through Messina as a last resort. The troop dispositions were made to that end, holding the high ground overlooking the Allied beachheads and covering the Catania plain, with the Gerbini airfields. When he was forced to give up this line, he retreated slowly to his main line of resistance running from the mouth of the Simeti River just south of Catania, along the Dittaino River to Leonforte, and then to the north coast at San Stefano. This would be known as the San Stefano Line.

But first the wide gap between the Hermann Goering Panzer Division and the Schmalz Group must be closed. Second, the areas around Enna and Leonforte must be held until the divisions in the west had withdrawn to the San Stefano Line. On July 12, Field Marshal Kesselring visited General Guzzoni and agreed with his plans. The Axis morale was raised during that visit, when a regiment of German paratroopers came in and dropped with great precision in zones south of Catania. It was as if the Germans were showing the Allies how it should be done. On the negative side, the Hermann Goering Panzer Division was not living up to its advance billing; it was moving far too slowly to comfort the Axis high command. It did not reach the Schmalz Group until Guzzoni was forced to order the withdrawal to the San Stefano Line on July 13.

And in the background, the Germans were moving swiftly. Hitler decided to take personal charge of Sicilian operations. He stopped an offensive that had just been started against the Russians, and told Chief of Staff Kurt Zeitzler to be ready to release troops to the west. He ordered Kesselring to hold the San Stefano Line and delay the Allied advance. He began to detach troops and aircraft of the Luftwaffe to send to Sicily and secretly ordered his command chiefs to begin taking over control of the defenses from the Italians.

The Axis defense now had the inestimable assistance of General Montgomery, who decided that he was going to win the battle of Sicily single-handedly. His first move was to ignore General Alexander and his American Allies, and to that end, on July 13, he ordered the 51st Highland Infantry Division on the left of the British line to clear the town of Vizzini, which Alexander had given to the American zone of operation. No conference with anyone; no word to Patton; Montgomery just moved.

He sent 13th Corps, as expected, along the coast road. He reinforced that movement by a commando attack from the sea behind the German line and a parachute drop of a brigade on the Prima Sole bridge just south of Catania. But he also had the inspiration to send a wide flanking movement of the 30th Corps along Route 124 to Caltagirone, and toward Enna to outflank 11 German positions on the Catania plain. It was apparent that he was bent on winning the war in Sicily in one stroke. Unfortunately, the general did not count on the fact that he had allies and enemies to deal with, not just points on a map. General Patton had planned the same maneuver along Route 124 and had pointed out his maneuver to General Alexander who had visited his headquarters that morning, only in the evening to send a message to Patton to hand over Route 124 to the British. Obviously, Montgomery had gotten to Alexander during the day, and neither of them seemed to have any sense of the sensitivity of the Americans, who were already chafing at playing second fiddle. This matter came to a head that evening when Brigadier General Bradley pointed out to Patton that the way things were going the British would soon emerge in splendor at Messina, while the Americans were forbidden to make any real attacks, to keep the British flank protected, and let the British have all the victories and all the glory. Had this been a German operation it would have been simple enough: the "allies" did what the German generals said. But the British had gone to great pains to reassure their American allies of the "partnership" in those weeks when the Americans were half-inclined to withdraw troop participation from Europe and concentrate their resources in the Pacific. This was what the Americans regarded as a genuine breach of faith by people they did not like very much anyhow.

British historians have explained this contretemps in terms of gamesmanship, indicating that generals are like children, fighting primarily for personal glory. Certainly, both Montgomery and Patton were glory seekers, but Bradley was anything but, and he was the most annoyed.

But not only did Montgomery try to hog the action, in his usual fashion, having laid the claim, he moved with the speed of a turtle. One reason was his loading of the ships: priority had been given to guns, tanks, and ammunition, and so these all had to be gotten off before the infantry could move. Although the Augusta garrison had evacuated on July 11, the British 5th Infantry Division did not enter the town until the next day. Montgomery was now also held up by the reinforced Schmalz Group, and more of the German 1st Parachute Division. His attack by the commandos on the Leonardo bridge behind the German lines failed. His attack with the parachute troops on the Prima Sole bridge failed, the latter because of trigger-happy naval gunners. By this time, Admiral Cunningham's excuse that his gunners had been too nervous did not wash. It was simply a case of inadequate communication between airborne and seaborne, and it was compounded when the army antiaircraft gunners also fired at their own airborne troops. Because of the confusion, only 200 paratroopers with three antitank guns reached their target. They were met by a savage reception, the much better organized German 3rd Parachute Regiment had dropped in the same area 36 hours before. The British managed to take and hold the bridge for a few hours on July 14, but then were forced to withdraw. They stayed on the perimeter until the 50th Infantry Division reached them and the division finally captured the bridge on July 16, but was then exhausted, and the Germans had formed up their main line of resistance. The British were stalled on the road to Catania by first-class German and Italian troops.

The 30th Corps, which had supplanted the American 45th Infantry Division on Route 124, did not manage its wide sweep around the German flank but instead was stalled at Vizzini and only managed to take the town with the assistance of the 45th. The 1st Canadian Infantry Division then took the lead, but they did not get very far. The movement was too slow and failed in its objective. Guzzoni had done a very good job of delaying the troops with rear-guard actions and demolitions. Thus, all that Montgomery's grandstand play accomplished was to delay matters and infuriate the Americans. His army bogged down after the first three days. The Canadians captured Caltagirone and went on to Leonforte and Agira, bypassing Enna, without telling Bradley, which left him the responsibility for clearing this obstacle, which was in the British zone. The British were unable to rectify their mistake and take Enna, and Bradley had to use his 1st Infantry Division for the job.

At this point, Alexander was showing his innate distrust of the Americans (which would continue long into the Italian campaign and cause much confusion and ill will). He trusted the British Eighth Army, and basically ended up giving them all the roads in central and eastern Sicily, thus relegating the Americans to the southwest part of the island. His intent was to get the Eighth Army firmly established on the line from Catania to Enna, before pausing any longer.

But Montgomery encountered very strong resistance because Hitler ordered the reinforcement of the German troops in the eastern sector of Sicily. Their new role was to delay the Allies as much as possible and hold eastern Sicily.

Patton accepted Alexander's directive of July 13, which gave the roads to the British, and set for himself a new goal: He would capture Palermo in the west. Thus, he reorganized the U.S. Seventh Army and set about that task, taking care to meet Alexander's orders, and stay out of the way of the British, while guarding their flank. But a "reconnaissance in force" by the 45th Infantry Division went through the Italian defenders of Arigento like a warm knife through butter, and Patton speeded his movements to the west. By July 18, it was apparent that Palermo was all but open to the Seventh Army, with only a few Italian troops to be bested on Route 121. But now Patton faced a new problem: Alexander had not sensed any of the American feelings about being relegated to a backseat role, and the general also had badly underestimated the quality of the Seventh Army. He was trying to use it as the Germans used the Italians: to back up their positions, and that only. On July 16, Alexander compounded the injury by stipulating that Montgomery would break into the Messina Peninsula while Patton continued to protect Montgomery's rear. He said nothing about Palermo.

This time Patton acted. He had not objected to Alexander's previous changes of mission, but at this point, he felt U.S. forces were being deliberately slighted. Given Alexander's feelings about the Americans, this obviously had more than a grain of truth. Patton flew to Alexander's headquarters in Tunisia and complained. Alexander expressed surprise that the Americans were annoyed by the position in which they had been put, and he gave his blessing to the U.S. attack on Palermo. So while the British drive was stopped in the east by vigorous German and Italian defense, with the approval of General Alexander, General Patton's Seventh Army was preparing to make a lightning thrust to the west and take Palermo.

Meanwhile in Algiers, General John P. Lucas arrived at Eisenhower's headquarters to tell the general about the difficulties with the British. Eisenhower was his most chameleon self. He told Lucas he had never had any real trouble with the British and did not believe they were trying to demean the Americans, but he also told Lucas that Patton had to stand up to Alexander or Eisenhower would relieve him of command. So the issue of British–American unity was left to simmer.

The Germans and Italians were now amassing their defense along the

Etna Line. By July 17, Hitler had judged that Sicily could not be held, although he was still sending reinforcements. He had intended to send the 29th Panzer Grenadier Division, but this order was countermanded and the division remained in Italy, where it was ready for the collapse of the Italian government, at which time the Germans would implement Plan Alarich—German control of Italy's defenses. Still, Sicily was to be held as long as possible, and to that end a strong German–Italian defense line was being built at the northeast end of the island. If the Germans could consolidate their positions across the Messina Peninsula, they might be able to reinforce Sicily and stage a counterattack on the Allies.

That night Patton returned to his headquarters and the next day spelled out Palermo as the Seventh Army's objective.

6

The U.S. Seventh Army's Drive

The Americans were eager to stop playing defense and go on the offensive, and the German–Italian movement of their basic defense line to the east opened up the possibility for a quick capture of Palermo by the Americans. The British maneuvering had caused the 30th Corps to alter its plans, including the capture of Enna in their sector and to bypass Enna. They did not inform the Americans, and Brigadier General Bradley suddenly learned that his flank was being left open. He then announced to the British that he was going to capture Enna, and close it. The British, having made a serious error, had no choice but to accede to this.

While Bradley moved north, the other corps of the U.S. Seventh Army—the Provisional Corps—sent the 82nd Airborne and 3rd Infantry Divisions to the west. General Geoffrey Keyes, of the Provisional Corps, committed the 2nd Armored Division, with Patton's acquiescence. On the morning of July 21, they were moving fast on the way to Palermo. All the way, the Italians were surrendering by the hundreds. In the one day, the task force collected some 4,000 prisoners. By the evening of the 22nd, the 3rd Infantry and the 2nd Armored Divisions were in position to assault Palermo. But there was to be no last-ditch fight. On that afternoon, a delegation from the city came to the 3rd Infantry Division headquarters and offered to surrender the city. The offer was declined for reasons of propriety; General Keyes was supposed to accept the surrender of the city. In the end it was a comedy of errors, and General Giuseppi Molinero, commander of the Port Defense of Palermo, ran into a patrol from Combat Command of the 2nd Armored Division and promptly offered to surrender the city to Keyes. Since this was the right general to accept the surrender, they all went into Palermo together; and at the royal palace at about 7 o'clock in the evening, the Americans accepted the formal surrender. Patton ordered the troops to occupy, and at 8 o'clock that evening, two American divisions walked into Palermo and were greeted as conquering heroes.

After the capture of Palermo, only the isolated ports of western Sicily remained to be invested. On the 23rd, Patton sent General Ridgway's 82nd Airborne Division to Trapani at the extreme western end of the island. Combat command of the 2nd Armored Division was sent along the northern shore to the east, to pick up the towns and cities there. That was done the same day. On July 23, the Americans moved out toward Marsala. They were held up by a demolished bridge over the Marsala River. As the engineers moved up to fix the crossing, enemy guns began to shell the position, so the advance was delayed overnight. On the 24th, Colonel Tolley, commander of the 39th Regimental Task Force, sent two battalions across the river under covering fire from the 26th Field Artillery and overran the city. Meanwhile the 505th Parachute Infantry Division was moving toward Trapani in what turned out to be a pleasant parade; they were greeted by the local population with fruit, bread, and chocolate. But as the column reached the outskirts of Trapani, things changed. Here, the first vehicles ran into a defended roadblock and minefields. As the advance guard delayed returning the fire the road came under concentrated artillery fire from the Italian troops that were defending it.

For three hours the Italians shelled, and the paratroopers battered against the roadblock. The paratroopers brought up the 367th Parachute Field Artillery and returned the fire, and suddenly Rear Admiral Giuseppi Manfredi, commander of the Trapani Naval District, appeared to surrender and give up his sword. At that point, the paratroopers sent their trucks back to pick up the 504th Regiment to take them to Alcamo and Castellammare.

That was the end of the Provisional Corps' combat operations. At a cost of 272 casualties, they had captured 53,000 and killed or wounded another 2,900. They had defeated the Hermann Goering Panzer Division at Gela. They had captured a grab bag of guns, vehicles, and tanks. For the rest of the campaign, the Provisional Corps would garrison western Sicily. Palermo became the center of the Seventh Army operations. By July 19, the 1st Engineer Special Brigade had taken over the operations of the roads and beaches. For the first time, the army had a deep-water port capable of handling ships direct from the United States. On July 24, the engineers opened Palermo port, and on July 28, the first ships entered the harbor. On July 27, the Seventh Army transferred supply operations from the southern beaches to Palermo. By this time the 727th Railway Operating Battalion had come in and was running trains in southern and central Sicily. The line was open as far as the Enna loop. Patton could now put his mind to something that Alexander and Montgomery had not envisaged; the American capture of Messina. But now, reluctantly, Alexander really had to authorize the use of the Americans to this end because there was nothing else left for them to do except for sit idly by until Montgomery decided to move.

In the meantime, Bradley's II Corps had been engaged in some very hard fighting against the Germans as they headed north to protect Montgomery's rear and cut the north coast road. The 1st Infantry Division moved up in step with the 2nd Canadian Infantry Division. They had to fight the rear guard of the 15th Panzer Grenadier Division who were keeping the escape route to Messina open for the 28th Aosta and 26th Assieta Divisions. It was only after strenuous fighting that the 1st Infantry Division reached Petralia on Route 120 on July 23. This was as far north as it would go. The 45th Infantry Division moved faster because it was on the flank of the Germans and opposed by the Italians. It cut the north coast road east of Termini Imerese on July 23 and then turned east along the coast road. Promptly it ran into a battle group of the 29th Panzer Grenadier Division, which had just arrived, subsequent to Hitler's orders.

While Patton had been moving like the wind, Montgomery had hardly been moving at all because he was facing the cream of the German troops, and they were not giving any ground. Thirteenth Corps got nowhere in its efforts in the Catania sector. Thirtieth Corps was barely moving. The 51st Highland Infantry Division took Gerbini airfield on July 20 but lost it to counterattacks from the Hermann Goering Panzer Division. The Canadians had tough going against the 15th Panzer Grenadier Division on the road to Leonforte. Between those two units, the Malta Brigade was stopped three miles south of Agira.

On July 21, Montgomery finally admitted that he had taken on more than he could handle. He ordered 13th Corps onto the defensive in front of Catania, and shifted the attack to the 30th Corps. It did not make much difference because he had no fresh troops to throw into the battle to break Guzzoni's defense line. It was hard for him to admit that he was stymied, and when he did, he called the 78th Infantry Division from North Africa. But it was not as easy as that because the division could not arrive until the end of the month. In the meantime, Montgomery sent the Canadians to turn east and attack Agira, with the assistance of the Malta Brigade. This change of direction and emphasis meant that Montgomery could no longer claim exclusive use of the two northern roads on the island: Route 120 and Route 113. They were freed for Patton to use in his drive that now headed toward Messina. He was itching to move, the stifling of the past weeks had infected the whole American command, and they were eager to do anything to beat Montgomery to the capture of Messina.

7

The Fall of Mussolini

On July 13, after a trip to Sicily to observe the course of events there, Field Marshal Kesselring met with Mussolini and reported on the development of the Allied offensives. Mussolini was shocked to learn that his Italian forces had almost completely disintegrated under fire. The two mobile divisions—4th Livorno and 54th Napoli—had shown some good fighting qualities, but as soon as they came under fire by the Allied naval guns, they had halted their attacks and retreated. The naval bases at Augusta and Syracuse had completely disintegrated. What was being proved to the Germans was Field Marshal Rommel's negative contention that the Italians would be of no use in defending Italy from the Allied attack.

This bad news increased the friction between the German and the Italian high commands and discussions quickly went beyond Sicily to the state of the defenses of Italy. The Commando Supremo had also surveyed the defenses. Because the land defenses had failed to stop the Allies, it was decided that the only possible defense now was in the air by attacking them at sea and disarranging their supply system. But to achieve this they needed airpower. The Italian air force was in such a state that the airpower must come from Germany. If German planes arrived promptly, Mussolini saw hope for the defense. "If we do not throw out the invaders right now, it will be too late," he said.

On July 14, Mussolini was so upset by the situation on Sicily that he worried about it all day, but still he did not find it irretrievable. That day he demanded from the Commando Supremo a careful update on the situation, with estimates on the remaining potential and how the potential could be increased.

Mussolini was optimistic, but the Commando Supremo was ready to quit. On July 14, General Ambrosio told Mussolini that the fate of Sicily was sealed. He urged Mussolini to end the war, to spare the Italian people any further waste and destruction.

In Germany, Hitler's initial reaction to the Allied invasion was to send the 1st Parachute Division to Sicily, but after that he asked for a review of the situation, in view of the Italian failure to make any progress in the defenses. Field Marshal Kesselring said the best thing to do was fight for time. He did not think that all was yet lost. He proposed to move the remainder of the German 1st Parachute Division and all of the 29th Panzer Grenadier Division to Sicily to reinforce the Luftwaffe and to increase the number of submarines and small craft operating against the allied convoys. Hitler called off his new offensive in Russia—Operation Zitadelle—and prepared to send an SS Panzer corps to Italy.

General Alfred Jodl felt that Italy was about to fall. He decided that the moment had come to change the defense plan, to regroup in Italy and prepare for the defense of the German homeland. He did not want to send any German forces south of the Appenine Mountains for fear they might be cut off by a change in the Italian political situation. But Kesselring opted to defend Sicily and this fit with Hitler's feeling that he should not give up a single foot of ground that German troops had occupied. Thus, Jodl was overridden and the decision was made by Hitler to help as long as Mussolini remained in power. But he redefined the task of the Germans, which now was to delay the enemy advance as much as possible, and to bring it to a halt in a defense line that ran from San Stefano via Adrano to Catania. Only eastern Sicily would be held; western Sicily was to be abandoned.

The 29th Panzer Grenadier Division was to be ready to move at any time, but the actual movement was delayed until it could be known that the German supply situation in Sicily would support this division. The Luftwaffe was to get three new bomb groups. A fourth bomb group and a torpedo squadron would be added later. Hitler also sent eight 210-mm guns and German personnel to defend the Strait of Messina.

Privately, Hitler issued instructions to his chief commanders. In the future, they were to exclude the Italians from their planning and assume complete control of operations in Sicily and Italy. Jodl took this further and instructed the field commanders to conduct operations in Sicily with an eye to saving as much of the German forces as possible. General H. V. Hube was to be transferred to Sicily to head the operations of the German forces there.

On July 15, Mussolini, Kesselring, Ambrosio, and German General Enno van Rintelen met in Rome. Many topics were discussed, including the defense of Italy generally, but nothing was decided. The trend of German thinking was revealed by Kesselring, who spoke to General Roatta about the best place to defend Italy: Sicily or on the northern Appenines. Kesselring said Sicily. They talked about resuming the offensive around Mount Etna. Kesselring assured the Italians that General Guzzoni would remain in overall command of the Axis forces, but he suggested that German and Italian units be intermingled. The Italians deferred the decision on that idea.

So by July 15, Kesselring and Guzzoni were still expressing the belief that, at last, part of Sicily could be held. This was contrary to General Ambrosio's feeling that all was lost in Sicily. He now wanted to separate Italy from Germany. Mussolini was of a like mind, but he felt the need of a tactical success before he could do it and make a peace move. Hitler stood firm; he proposed to continue to fight in Italy and to support Mussolini as long as there was anything to support.

On the night of July 13, the Germans and the Italians in eastern Sicily withdrew to a new defense line south of Mount Etna. They, at least the Germans, were prepared to continue the defensive effort and they still had hopes of ultimate victory. But the next day the OKW brought Plan Alarich up-to-date. The plan called for the occupation of northern Italy by Rommel and Army Group B and the reinforcement of German troops in the Balkans and Greece.

On the following day, Jodl and Rommel submitted a memo to Hitler asking him to make certain demands of Mussolini. For full command under Mussolini, they wanted a supreme commander—a German to be appointed to that position—and the Italian Commando Supremo be changed to include only officers the Germans trusted. Also, the air forces should all be placed under the command of Field Marshal Wolfram Freiherr von Richthofen.

On July 17, Hitler met with Keitel, Jodl, Rommel, and Grossadmiral Karl Doenitz and admitted that Sicily could not be held. They would do everything they could, Hitler said. (In the end they had to withdraw.) So the 29th Panzer Grenadier Division was not to be moved to Sicily. If Italy collapsed, Plan Alarich would follow immediately.

The Germans were indulging in a little "king-making," in these wild dreams. One of them suggested that they encourage a political revolution that would eliminate the monarchy and keep Mussolini in full power. That showed how little the leading German military figures understood the feelings of the Italian people at this point. General Ambrosio was closer to them than any of the others, and he felt the cause was lost.

For several days the German and Italians engaged in bickering, about the causes of the problem. Ambrosio knew what they were: "It is useless to search for the causes of this state of affairs. They are the result of three years of war begun with scanty means and in which the few resources have been burned up in Africa, in Russia, in the Balkans."[5]

A meeting was hastily arranged between Hitler and Mussolini and held at Feltre in northern Italy. Hitler wanted to put Mussolini back on track, so he ignored the advice of those who wanted him to issue ultimatums.

The first session consisted of a long harangue by Hitler that exhausted all the others in attendance. The burden of the speech was that the failure of the Italians alone was responsible for the situation they now faced, particularly plane losses, which represented the growing power of the Allied air forces. Hitler attributed this to the Italian crews on the ground.

As to Sicily, Hitler was of two minds. If the supply line could be assured, he would invest the men and material to fight on and convert the defense into attack. Reichsmarschall Goering was prepared to send in a number of flak batteries to guard the Strait of Messina.

Mussolini was silent. After the meeting Generals Ambrosio and Guiseppe Bastianini reproached Mussolini for not speaking up and explaining the true situation in Italy: the people wanted out of the war. During the auto trips from and to the airfield, Ambrosio and Keitel had two talks. Keitel asked how things were going in Sicily, and Ambrosio asked how things were going in Russia. Ambrosio observed that Keitel's answer—that they were wearing the Russians down—was not the road to victory. The Axis was losing the war, he observed. On the journey back to the airport, Keitel summed up Hitler's offer: two divisions, if the Italians would put up two more divisions, pledge to continue the war to the end, and guarantee the supply line to Sicily. Ambrosio could only say that these things would be brought up with Mussolini.

During the last few days of July, events in Sicily and Italy moved rapidly. After the meeting at Feltre, Mussolini told Ambrosio that he intended to write a letter to Hitler breaking off the Italian alliance with Germany. But he had waited too long. The officers of the Italian high command were already planning the end of the Italian dictator as the essential step to get Italy out of the war.

On the surface, the alliance was unchanged. On July 21, Ambrosio informed the Germans of Italy's decision to fight the war to the finish and asked for the two German divisions Hitler had promised plus the other help. The Germans replied that they were sending it. They named the 305th and the 76th Infantry Divisions, which were in France. General Roatta had already decided where they would go.

Three separate groups were plotting Mussolini's demise: the dissident Fascists, the anti-Fascist opposition, and the military conspiracy. The dissident Fascists were led by Dino Grandi and Mussolini's son-in-law Count Ciano. They were in touch with the king's private secretary and through him with the king. They hoped to replace Mussolini but retain the Fascist system of government. The anti-Fascist parties were holding out for a complete elimination of Fascism and a return to the parliamentary system of government. The military conspirators were led by General G. Castellano. They wanted the king to be returned as commander of the armed forces. All three wanted a quick approach made to the Allies to end the war.

The king knew what was going on around him, but he was not very well satisfied with the alternatives he faced, which seemed to be a military dictatorship either by Field Marshal Pietro Badoglio or Field Marshal Enrico Caviglia; he did not trust either man. He did not want Fascism to be overthrown immediately but to be changed gradually.

These various groups advocating change were not in agreement on how to achieve it, but on July 15, Badoglio had an audience with the king in which he proposed a new government with himself at the head of it and some politicians as members. The king opposed this absolutely; he did not want any politicians involved in the change.

Two days later the king let it be known that he was prepared to act against Mussolini, but he wanted a cabinet of civil servants who would not upset any apple carts. Several of the leaders of the conspiracy then pointed out to the king that as soon as action was taken the Germans would know, and any delay in taking the reins of state would help the Germans prepare a faction against the new government.

Finally the conspirators agreed that Mussolini had to be arrested and the regular army had to be used to neutralize the force of the Fascist militia.

On July 20, the king made up his mind to act. He then tried to persuade Mussolini to resign voluntarily, but Mussolini refused to understand that he was the impediment to progress. He obviously did not know the depth of public sentiment against him because he ordered a meeting of the Fascist Grand Council, without realizing that most of them now opposed him.

The Grand Council, which numbered 28 members, met on the afternoon of Saturday, July 24. The members debated the war and the questions of power for hours. After nine hours, at around three o'clock in the morning, they voted 19 to 9 against the continuation of Mussolini in power. Mussolini then went to see the king and told him that the vote did not mean that he had to step down. The king told him coldly that it did, he must step down, in favor of Badoglio. Mussolini then went to leave the palace and could not find his car. After some confusion, he was escorted into an ambulance, and the door was shut with an ominous thud. He was a prisoner. When the public learned of his imprisonment, they danced in the streets, and mobs attacked Fascist party officers and tore down the Fascist symbols. The air of defeat and disappointment was suddenly electrified with hope. The people waited for news that the war was over and the Germans were gone. In fact, they seemed to be gone, because the Germans suddenly took a very low profile in Italy. And, like the people of Italy, they waited.

Although the Allies had been speculating for weeks on the effects of the invasion of Sicily, they were taken by surprise by the overthrow of Mussolini. Earlier the Americans had argued that bombing and the capture of Sicily might throw the Italians out of the war, but the British had dismissed this argument as vacuous. Only an attack on the Italian mainland, said the British, would accomplish this purpose. The Americans had given in and the wheels were turning for the next move: an attack on Italy proper. Now, one of the great strategic errors of the Allies suddenly loomed large on their horizon: Unconditional Surrender.

They were powerful words. When uttered first by President Roosevelt, they served notice on the Axis powers that the Allies were in the war to stay and intended to pursue the war vigorously. But when reality loomed, and it appeared that the Italians were very eager to get out of the war, the words suddenly acquired a harsh and unforgiving sound that tended to make capitulation impossible, unless the Italians were ready to say "Do what you want with us." Everyone, Roosevelt included, realized that this was not an enticing dish to set before the Italian people, and everyone scurried to try to overcome the obstacle the Allies had created for themselves.

The Allies at this point were not even in agreement on the terms of Italian surrender. "Unconditional Surrender" meant no terms. But that is not what the Allies wished to convey. The Americans were sticking by the "Unconditional Surrender" statement but were trying to come up with conditions that would make this seem to be true. The British were much less doctrinaire, but they had put together a long list of conditions for a surrender. One basic difference was that the Americans had no qualms about junking the House of Savoy as the Italian ruling institutor, while the British hesitated to depose yet another monarchy in this era of popular government. Despite the apparently harsh nature of the American position and the easier aspect of the British, the situations were the opposite. The British sought revenge against the Italians, and the Americans, cognizant of a large Italian–American electorate at home, were much more inclined to go easy on Italy.

General Eisenhower drafted a set of armistice terms in which he completely avoided what was now the embarrassing issue of "Unconditional Surrender," which once and for all proved the absurdity of the "Unconditional Surrender" thesis.

The first condition was the immediate cessation of hostilities, and guarantees by the Italians that the Germans would observe the terms of armistice. Second was the freeing of all prisoners of war and internees. Third was the transfer of the Italian fleet to places designated by the

British Royal Navy, which would supervise its disarmament. Fourth was the evacuation from Italy of the German air force. Fifth was the evacuation of all Germans from Italy, which was to be completed in a month. German forces in Sicily would surrender or be destroyed. Sixth was the surrender of Corsica. Seventh was the acceptance of a military government by the Allies. Eighth was the guarantee of the use of all Italian ports by the Allies even as the Germans were getting out. Ninth was the immediate withdrawal of all army units from the war front. Tenth was a guarantee by the Italian government that it would move to implement these provisions.

Prime Minister Churchill issued a similar directive calling for Italians to cooperate, but then he reconsidered and retreated to the "Unconditional Surrender" settlement, in which he was joined by Roosevelt.

As General Marshall put it, this was a nice political luxury. "Our terms for Italy are still the same as our terms for Germany and Japan, 'Unconditional Surrender.' We will have no truck with Fascism in any way, shape or manner. We will permit no vestige of fascism to remain."[6]

Very nice and concise. But did Roosevelt and Churchill want the Italians to surrender or not? Political bombast at this time was hardly helpful in a situation in which the Allied soldiers who were doing the fighting were trying to persuade the Italians to surrender.

Soon Washington and London had the matter so bollixed up that General Eisenhower asked the two governments for general terms he could quote.

Then the British foreign office told Washington that they considered the king of Italy a perfectly acceptable instrument for the surrender. The combined Civil Affairs Committee of the two governments took up the surrender matter but could not solve all the problems the two governments had posed. Roosevelt then reversed his field and accepted Eisenhower's draft terms. He did not back off from the idea of unconditional surrender, he just did not mention it anymore.

By the end of July, both governments had realized what a mess they had created and were trying to squirm out of it. The propagandists now began to tell the Italian people that everything would be fine if they would just get rid of the Germans. They could have peace under honorable conditions. The Allies were coming to them as liberators. That does not sound much like unconditional surrender, does it?

Whatever it was, it worked. The Italian government forbade the publication of the Allied message. However, within hours it was on the streets in mimeographed form and was circulated throughout Italy.

Of course the real problem was that the Allies did not really mean what they said. As the official *U.S. Army History* of the struggle for Sicily states, "As Churchill and Roosevelt clearly wished, the psychological warfare beamed to Italy from the allied headquarters in Algiers was sharply differentiated from the problem of agreeing on [a] suitable article of capitulation."[7] Nothing was said about war crimes.

But by hook or by crook Eisenhower now had a draft of armistice terms that made surrender possible and one that had been accepted by both Allied governments, and this was no mean feat. The Joint Chiefs of Staff suggested that Eisenhower be permitted to act to meet situations as they arose without too much reference to what was written down. British and Americans leaders were still worrying about the comprehensive statements of terms that the British had prepared, but it did not seem that anybody else was paying too much attention. To confound matters, on August 6, the Combined Chiefs of Staff told Eisenhower that if he employed the draft terms he had, he was to make it clear that they were purely military and that political, economic, and financial conditions would follow. So Eisenhower was to persuade the Italians to surrender on one basis, and then the Allies would come down on them with a whole new set of conditions. It seemed hardly likely that the "meal" set before the Italians would prove palatable.

During the last days of July, the Allies had suspended aerial bombardment of the Italian mainland, but they resumed it again early in August—again broadcasting to the Italians that things would get worse if the Badoglio government did nothing to end the war. In the first week of August, British and American bombers raided Naples half a dozen times.

The British said that one could not separate the military from the political and economic conditions. Roosevelt had talked earlier about Mussolini as a war criminal, but that suddenly stopped when he realized that insisting on such a proposal might junk the whole negotiation. But he could not refrain from telling the press that neutral nations should be warned against sheltering Axis war criminals. The trouble was that the politicians talked too much. They had now talked themselves into a situation in which they had to secure the capitulation of Italy before deciding what to do next.

8

Confusion

Because the July suspension of Allied bombing of Italian cities had not convinced the Italians to surrender by the first week of August, General Eisenhower ordered the resumption of the bombing. Raids were carried out against Naples and were planned for Rome. But suddenly on August 2 came word through the Vatican that the Badoglio government of Italy wanted to know what conditions the Allies would demand to declare Rome an open city.

At this, in the belief that the Allies were not far from capturing Rome in any case, Churchill started talking about unconditional surrender again. The Allies gave a noncommittal answer to the Italians that they were free to declare Rome an open city if they wished, and that was the end of it. On August 14, the Italian government declared Rome an open city, but the Allies reserved the right to continue bombing targets in the area. So the Allies, trapped in their "Unconditional Surrender" policy, were making it as difficult as possible for Italy to get out of the war.

At this time, the Italian government that had emerged after the fall of Mussolini was divided in its responsibility. Field Marshal Badoglio was the head of the government, but he did not control the military. King Victor Emmanuel III took over command of the armed forces himself. General Ambrosio continued as chief of the Commando Supreme and General Roatta as chief of the Army General Staff.

Badoglio then made two proclamations: one assuring the world that the war continued, and the other to the Italian people warning against agitating for political change or for peace. These were clearly reaffirmations of the alliance with Germany, and the king made it clear that he wanted to avoid conflict with the Germans.

After the Feltre conference with Mussolini, Hitler felt more at ease with the Italian situation. Rommel was poised to take command of troops that would occupy Italy, but he was dismissed from this job and sent to Greece to command the German forces there, an indication of the German recognition of Churchill's preoccupation with the Balkans.

When Hitler learned that Mussolini had been forced to resign and was imprisoned, he was furious and made all sorts of threats about kidnaping the king and Field Marshal Badoglio, seizing Rome with the 3rd Panzer Grenadier Division located 35 miles from Rome, and even of seizing the Vatican. But he quieted down. Still, he thought some sort of action would restore Fascism.

Rommel urged caution, lest the German reaction prompt the Allies to invade Italy. He thought the Germans should retire from Sardinia, Sicily, and southern Italy but hold northern Italy. But on July 26, the OKW issued orders recalling him from Salonika to command Army Group B at Munich and troops were moved to the Italian border. Other contingency plans were made for the occupation of northern Italy, for Rommel to occupy northern Italy, for General Kurt Student to fly to Rome to take personal command of two divisions there and seize the capital and leading political figures and liberate Mussolini, and for Colonel Otto Skorzeny, who had been personally selected by Hitler, to discover the whereabouts of Mussolini and free him.

Field Marshal Kesselring, who was more optimistic than Hitler or Rommel, called on Badoglio and General Ambrosio and was assured of Italy's adherence to the alliance with Germany. Kesselring then reported back to Germany that he felt he could hold Italy and the Balkans. When the OKW heard what Kesselring had to say, the frenzy suddenly went out of their actions. The Skorzeny and Student missions were suspended, but by that time they and a parachute group had already arrived at an airfield near Frascati. The Italians wondered what the parachute troops were doing there, but accepted Kesselring's assurances that they were reinforcements for the 1st Parachute Division in Sicily.

On July 27, Badoglio and the king agreed to seek a joint peace with the Germans and sent an emissary to Hitler. That same day Kesselring met with Hitler to reassure him about the Italians. Hitler seemed to accept what he said, but actually was planning strong action and using the "Italophiles"—Kesselring, General Rintelen, and the German ambassador to Rome—to pacify the Italians until he was ready to act. He believed the Italians were planning to surrender to the Allies. Later in the day, Hitler refused the suggestion that he meet with the king, and instead proposed a conference of foreign ministers and chiefs of staff at Tarvis just across the border from Italy. He did not want to face the decision of whether to make peace with the Allies. Badoglio refused to initiate any approach to the Allies until he had conferred with Hitler.

Amid all the confusion, Hitler had drawn up a new plan for the German takeover of Italy by force. At the touch of a button, Plan Achse would be initiated.

Early in August, the Germans were moving Army Group B into Italy, preparing to take over. The Italians began to make overtures to the Allies, worried about the stranglehold the Germans now had on Italy. On July 30, the new foreign minister, Raffaele Guariglia, went to the Vatican and asked for help in contacting the British. But the Vatican did not have any safe means of communicating with the Allies. The next day the council decided to separate Italy from the alliance with Germany, and an emissary was sent to neutral Portugal. On August 3, that envoy flew to Lisbon and made an appointment to see the British ambassador. He told the ambassador that the Italian government wanted to break off with Germany but was under great military pressure and that the Germans had begun the occupation of the country. He gave the exact location of the German troops. He asked for the end of the propaganda attack from the Allies against the king and Badoglio and the halting of the bombing of Italian cities. Then the Italian government waited for a reply to this overture. None came.

The Italians made another attempt. They sent an emissary to Tangier, with the instructions to let the Allies know they should attack in the Balkans to draw German troops from Italy, and that they should continue the propaganda campaign against Badoglio to confuse the Germans. He also suggested that the Allies plan a landing in Italy as far north as possible, as soon as possible. The envoy then waited. There was no reply.

9

The Race for Messina

As the Italians were desperately seeking a way out of their dilemma, and now moving as far from the Germans as possible, the struggle in Sicily continued. The field of battle had shifted from the southern lowlands to the mountainous Messina Peninsula, and the standing of the British and American armies had been subtly changed. In the beginning the Americans had been relegated by General Alexander to a strictly subordinate role, which they had fulfilled, albeit reluctantly. But with the bogging down of General Montgomery's British Eighth Army, because it had taken on more responsibility than it could handle, and the capture of Palermo and the clearing of the western part of the island, the Americans had now positioned themselves to make their own drive against Messina.

Major General Allen's 1st Infantry Division moved to the north coast of Sicily. On July 20, Alexander issued new instructions to General Patton that reflected his decision to use the Americans in the general advance east. Alexander had received an admission from Montgomery that he needed the assistance of the U.S. Seventh Army because he had bogged down in the face of stout German and Italian resistance. But the new instructions were tentative. Two days later, it was apparent to Alexander that the British drive had failed when Montgomery called for the 78th Infantry Division to come from Africa, and called off attacks by 13th Corps on the Catania plain. On July 23, Alexander took the wraps off the U.S. Seventh Army and gave it equal footing with the British Eighth Army for the first time. Patton was told to employ maximum strength along Route 117 and Route 120. That meant Messina was open to the Americans if they could capture it.

Patton's reaction was to tell Brigadier General Bradley, "The British have the bear by the tail in the Messina Peninsula and we may have to go in and help."[8] So he strengthened II Corps by giving them the Moroccan Goums, who had fought very well with the 3rd and the 36th Infantry Divisions, the 34th Field Artillery Battalion, and some other artillery units. He called for the remainder of the 9th Infantry Division from North Africa and prepared to drive on Messina.

Meanwhile, the political events in Rome had a direct effect on events in Sicily. As previously mentioned, when Hitler learned of the dismissal and imprisonment of Mussolini, he was furious and set in motion changes that threatened the Italians with German takeover. Even when he saw a letter from Mussolini to Field Marshal Badoglio thanking him for good treatment, he was not mollified, and was determined to free Mussolini at the first moment. However, he also decided that the German troops would have to be withdrawn from Sicily; and about this he had no second thoughts. What they did agree to do was keep future German moves secret with the caveat that they would have to continue the game as if they believed the Italians when they said they would continue to fight, but Hitler did not believe a word of it. General Jodl agreed with this.

That night of July 25, Jodl sent a message to Field Marshal Kesselring ordering him to evacuate the Germans from Sicily, and he sent a personal envoy to Rome to brief Kesselring on the new German plans. But almost immediately Hitler changed his mind, deciding to delay the evacuation of German troops as long as possible.

In Sicily, General Guzzoni decided that the Allies would not invade Italy until the fate of Sicily had been decided, and he proposed to delay the loss of Messina as long as possible. If he could get reinforcements, he would go on the offensive, he decided. But now the Germans brought in reinforcements. General Hube had the 29th Panzer Grenadier Division, which was put in position to stop the American II Corps; otherwise, the Americans would have a clear shot at Messina.

Guzzoni wanted to defend, and if he got reinforcements, he talked about going on the offensive. Hube had no such illusions. His orders were to conduct an orderly retreat of the Germans from Sicily and that is what he intended to do. Hube had actually taken control of the fighting on the ground in Sicily.

Now the U.S. II Corps was prepared to advance on Messina along two routes: Route 113 along the north coast and Route 120 through Nicosia, Troina, Cesaro, and Randazzo. Between the two roads ran the Caronia Mountain chain almost as far as Messina—mountains that were rugged. The north coast—Route 113—was full of short streams that flowed down from the mountain crests to the sea. The streams were obstacles but between ran much more formidable ones: very steep ridges ideally suited for defense.

The road along the north shore followed a narrow belt of flat between the high ground of the ridges and the beaches. Where there was no beach, the road was dug into the cliff, directly above the surf. The twists and turns of this coast road gave the defenders many good positions.

Route 120 passed along the southern slopes of the Caronia Mountains. It was narrow and crooked, with steep grades and hairpin turns. Often, heavy vehicles had to stop and back up to make the turns. The mountains dominated Route 120 on both sides.

There was one other factor that would help the Axis troops because of the rugged terrain. The American forces advancing along the two roads would not be able to support each other, and supply problems were going to be twofold.

The Americans began to move with the 26th Regimental Combat Team, which captured Gangi and moved toward Cosia. On July 25, they ran into heavy German artillery fire. One bit of real estate, known as Hill 937, was captured by the Americans, recaptured by the Germans, and then recaptured by the Americans in one day. It was the same with another eminence: Hill 962.

Bradley released two battalions of the 16th Infantry Division from corps reserve to enable General Allen to capture Nicosia, which he moved to do by development. It was hard going all the way, with the Germans resisting stubbornly as a very natural point of defense. Using tanks, the Americans moved along the road to Nicosia, and the Germans withdrew on the night of July 27. Hube was beginning to withdraw to the Etna Line. The Americans began to advance.

Along the north coast, the 45th Infantry Division moved swiftly on the night of July 23 and the next day and one element reached the town of Castelbuono eight miles north of Petralia. At that point the 45th and the 1st Infantry Divisions were on line in their advance.

The ridge fighting meant scaling steep cliffs and climbing from sea level—almost 3,000 feet—in less than 1,000 yards under rifle fire, machine-gun fire, mortar fire, and artillery fire. The Germans could roll their hand grenades down the slopes. Late on the afternoon of July 26, the Americans were stopped by Germans in strong positions. But the Germans were retreating, doggedly, and with many firefights.

On July 25, Alexander met with Patton and Montgomery south of Syracuse. Here they drew up the plan for the expulsion of the Axis forces from the Messina Peninsula. The Seventh Army was to continue east; the Eighth Army would move on the left and go around the eastern side of Mount Etna.

Even with all their difficulties on the ground because of the terrain and the stubborn defense of the Germans, the Allies had one advantage: control of the skies. Allied planes roved the air, seldom seeing opposition, and the planes gave many close support air missions to the troops. Allied fighters, fighter bombers, and light bombers were operating from captured airfields. By July 30, most of the U.S. 64th Fighter Wing had moved to Sicily.

The Americans also had the support of "General Patton's Navy"—Task Force 88, which comprised two cruisers, 14 destroyers, PT boats, and other small craft. On the east coast, Admiral Cunningham had a large force available to support British land operations and even to launch an amphibious operation if need be.

On July 27, Kesselring sent instructions to Hube to prepare for the evacuation of all German troops on Sicily. The next day the Germans pulled back abruptly into the main San Stefano positions, sometimes without telling their Italian allies, and thus leaving them exposed.

Hube's master plan of withdrawal called for movement in five phases. The first two phases were a continuation of Guzzoni's defense battle, to the San Fratello Line, and then to a new and shorter line, running from Cape Orlando on the north coast through Tortorici and Randazzo to Riposto on the east coast. The evacuation would take place over eight nights. As each division retired from one line to the next, one-third of its strength would board one of the five special ferries operated by the Germans. Heavy guns and equipment were to be abandoned, on Hitler's specific orders. The Italians had a similar plan and four ferries at Messina.

On the night of July 29–30, the Eighth Army opened its offensive. In four days, the extremely competent 78th Infantry Division along with a Canadian brigade attacked over the Dittaino River. The Germans fell back as planned to the Tortorici Line. On August 5, 13th Corps entered a narrow front between Mount Etna and the sea, which the Germans blocked with mines and demolition. The 30th Corps went around the western side of Mount Etna and found itself in the same position. The fighting fronts were so narrow that the British had more divisions than they could use, so Montgomery withdrew the Canadians and the 5th Infantry Division into reserve so they could prepare for the invasion of Italy, which was soon to come.

In the Seventh Army sector, Bradley drove ahead with one regiment leapfrogging another. The U.S. 1st Infantry Division had a very hard fight at Troina, which took six days to win. They broke the 15th Panzer Grenadier Division's hold on that town with artillery and the support of the air force. The U.S. 9th Infantry Division moved on Cesaro, but Patton was becoming agitated by the slowness of the American advance. His objective was to beat Montgomery to the capture of Messina. So Patton began launching an end run, using amphibious landing craft to get behind the Germans and hasten their withdrawal, but the landings got confused and delayed and came to very little, hardly affecting the rate of the German withdrawal.

By the time the Germans had lost Catania, Adrano, Troina, and San Fratello, they were convinced that the time had come for the general withdrawal from Sicily. General Fridel von Senger visited Kesselring and advised that it would be dangerous to wait any longer. He ordered the evacuation of the Germans—Operation Lehrgang—to begin on August 11.

General Alexander suspected a German evacuation was coming by the manner of their defenses and asked Admiral Cunningham and Air Chief Marshal Tedder to coordinate plans. But the navy could not operate in the restricted waters unless the coastal batteries that Hitler had sent in to cover the strait were destroyed, so it was agreed that the air forces would carry the load of trying to interfere with the German evacuation. The plan was to maintain constant air surveillance, day and night, of the waters, and then American strategic bombers would be available for daylight attack and the British Wellingtons for night bombing.

But the Germans had planned very well. On August 12, Hube ordered the evacuation of the Tortorici Line and pulled back the 15th Panzer Grenadier Division from Randazzo Strait to the ferries that night. That left the 29th Panzer Grenadier and Hermann Goering Panzer Divisions to make up the rear guard. Patton made this difficult by trying a second end run on the night of August 11–12, landing a battalion behind the 29th Panzer Grenadier Division's positions on the north coast road. But the battalion was not strong enough to cut off the German battle group and was soon in difficulties. It called for fire from ships at sea, and got it. The fracas speeded up the German withdrawal of the 29th Panzer Grenadier Division.

On the other coast, the Hermann Goering Panzer Division and the 1st Parachute Division had no trouble in the rough terrain in fending off the Eighth Army attack with mining and demolition. Montgomery had to bring the 5th Infantry Division back into the line alongside the 50th Infantry Division to make any progress at all. As he was preparing for attack, orders came that set the date of September 1 for an attack across the Strait of Messina; and he had to relieve the 5th Infantry Division and withdraw 13th Corps headquarters to prepare for the invasion of Italy. The Germans withdrew rapidly, and both Montgomery's and Patton's attempts to cut them off failed on August 15.

The race to Messina was almost a dead heat, but Montgomery ran into more trouble than Patton did, and so Patton was ahead in the race. The U.S. 3rd Infantry Division's 7th Infantry Regiment entered the city on the evening of August 16 and was there to greet the British commandos the next morning as they came in. To the Americans, it was a historic moment. Starting out in the campaign as a distinctly inferior force being used to guard the flanks of the British advance, the Seventh Army had developed a strong fighting power and had taught the British something of the difficulty of underestimating your allies as well as your enemies. But in the greater scheme of the war, the question of who captured Messina was totally unimportant. The important fact was that the Axis powers had brought out their best fighting men from Sicily.

In the first two days of the evacuation, they moved everything by night, as the Allies had expected. But the heavy bombing by the Wellingtons and the difficulties of directing units in the dark made for slow progress, and so on August 13, they decided to risk daylight bombing to speed up the evacuation. Losses were extremely light, which was a pleasant surprise to the Germans. The superb antiaircraft batteries kept the tactical air forces at bay. The American "Flying Fortresses" were not called. The Germans switched to a daylight ferrying operation.

The Allies were unaware of the evacuation for three days, and after that it was too late to switch the American heavy bombers from other tasks. It was a remarkably inept performance of the Allied air forces and a very skillful performance by the Germans and Italians. Not only did Hube get all the Germans off, but he proved Hitler wrong by saving almost all their equipment and still had time and space to spare to give substantial help to the Italians. But the changing nature of the war was indicated when the Germans commandeered most of the heavy equipment of the Italians once they got to the Italian side of the strait. Thus, the German units returned to Italy with more equipment than they had when they left for Sicily months earlier.

The last of the German defenders crossed to the Italian mainland very early on the morning of August 17, and Hube reported that Operation Lehrgang was completed. The last Axis troops to leave Sicily were eight men of an Italian patrol picked up by a German assault boat.

That morning, on the ridge line overlooking the city, General Truscott received the city's officials at 7 o'clock. An hour later, the senior Italian officer offered to make a formal surrender. Truscott sent an officer into the city with the Italian to prepare for a formal surrender to General Patton and "to be sure that the British did not capture the city from us after we had taken it."

Patton showed up at about 10 o'clock, took his place in a car at the end of a motorcade, and roared into the city, accompanied by the fire of the enemy artillery from the Italian mainland. The British armored column entered the city and arrived at the big park in the center just after Patton had accepted the city's surrender. The senior British officer of the column walked over to Patton, shook hands, and congratulated him: "It was a jolly good race," he said. "I congratulate you."[9]

And there in Messina that day, the artillery fire from the Germans across the strait continued, to remind the British and the Americans that in the final analysis it was the Germans who won the race for Messina.

The campaign for Sicily was over. The island had been conquered in 38 days, and the original objectives of the Allies had been accomplished. They had cleared the Mediterranean Sea lanes of Axis forces. They had taken some of the pressure off Stalin on the Russian front as Hitler's cancellation of Operation Zitadelle showed. It had caused the fall of Mussolini, as some had predicted it would, but it had not taken Italy out of the war, largely because the Allies were not sufficiently quick or aware to take advantage of the political advantages offered them and had made no provision for Italian surrender. Thus, they stumbled over their interpretations of unconditional surrender.

But the Allies were now poised on the southern gateway to Europe. All this had been accomplished at a cost of fewer than 20,000 men: 7,400 Americans and 11,800 British. They had killed 12,000 men and taken 147,000 prisoners.

From the American point of view, the Seventh Army had distinguished itself and retrieved the reputation of the American fighting man after a dismal beginning in Tunisia, although this was still not apparent to the British. It had landed on the most difficult terrain—open beaches—it had faced the bulk of the German defenders, its airborne operations had been a liability rather than an asset, but within 72 hours after landing, the troops had established a firm beachhead, and although relegated to a secondary role had refused to sit and wait for the British conquest of the island.

The invasion plan for Sicily, as amended, was originally a British affair, at the time of the landing, with the Americans relegated to a secondary position. But when Montgomery bogged down, Patton had his chance and he took it, and performed brilliantly. He was the first "romantic" military figure to emerge as an American hero in the war. He was flamboyant, reminiscent of the cowboys of the Old West, with his slender figure and the twin pistols on his hips, his brusque manner, and his obvious bravery. Personally, Patton showed, in Sicily, his fatal character flaw—the inability to deal with soldiers—and thus lost his chance for high command. After incidents involving the slapping of young American soldiers who were in a state of shock after action, Patton was very nearly relieved of command, he got very bad press in America, and one reporter in Sicily said there were 50,000 American soldiers who would like to shoot General Patton. General Eisenhower made the decision then that Patton would never rise above army command, and he was soon eclipsed by his deputy—Brigadier General Omar N. Bradley—in the American chain of command.

General Montgomery had displayed his prickly character as well, beginning with his insistence on changing the plan for Sicily to his own ends and (hopefully) glory, his eagerness to accept the glory for any of the accomplishments of his units, and his constant demand for more power and strength in the field before he would move.

From the British point of view, the most important development was the success of the amphibious landings, which erased the unpleasant recollections of the failure at Gallipoli in World War I. They had learned in North Africa and here to land troops, equipment, and supplies and to keep them coming. They, as much as the Americans, had suffered from the bad coordination of airborne operations.

From the mistakes and errors and chafing on each other's nerves, the Allies had begun to learn to work together. What they still had to learn was the skill of the Germans in defense and withdrawal.

10

The Surrender of Italy and the Surprise That Wasn't

The end of the Sicilian Operation found the Allies in basic disagreement about what to do next. The British wanted to avoid the invasion of Europe across the English Channel if possible, and the Americans could scarcely wait for that invasion. The argument was only settled when the Americans made it quite clear that if the Cross Channel Attack was off, then they would thereafter devote their major resources to the Pacific. The British referred to this as blackmail, but it was decisive; and thereafter the British learned to live with Operation Overlord—the Cross Channel Attack—which was scheduled for 1944.

Still, the British enthusiasm for some sort of activity in the Mediterranean caused General Eisenhower to set up several planning offices. One explored the idea of an invasion of Sardinia, one dealt with Corsica, one dealt with a landing on the "toe" of Italy, and one dealt with a landing on the "ball of the Italian foot." In all, nine different plans were made. The atmosphere at the planning offices grew more positive after the landings in Sicily were successful. A few days after the landings, General Montgomery predicted that he would capture Messina around mid-July. However, when Montgomery bogged down in front of Catania, the optimism was sharply tempered. Talk about Christmas in Rome died down.

By July 17, Eisenhower had opted for an invasion of the Italian mainland, but no one knew where or when. In Washington, General Marshall was very suspicious of an Italian mainland landing because he felt that it would develop into another quarrel with Prime Minister Churchill about keeping the resources in the Mediterranean when he felt they could go to England for Operation Overlord. So the Americans stood fast on the number of divisions that would be made available for continued Mediterranean operations. It was the end of July before the name "Salerno" began to crop up in the planning, largely because of the steep beaches that were ideal for landing men, tanks, and vehicles. The disadvantage that the beaches were overlooked by hills seemed to be overcome by the fact that there were no German divisions in those hills. And the deciding factor for Salerno was air cover. Two-thirds of the Allied fighting force were British aircraft, with very limited range. When fitted out with drop tanks, the Spitfires and Mustangs had a range of 180–200 miles. Chief Air Marshal Tedder advised that he could not cover the beaches north of Naples, which were also under consideration, but that he could cover Salerno.

Montgomery did not like the Salerno plan, but his bog-down in Sicily had muddied his credentials, and this time his objections were heard but not honored, and, thus, Salerno was chosen for the Allies' first foray into Hitler's *Festung* Europe. The decision was affirmed on August 16, the day before General Hube completed the German evacuation of troops from Sicily.

Meanwhile, the Allies had planned a new strategic conference—called "Quadrant"—in Quebec City on August 14. President Roosevelt and Prime Minister Churchill were there when the reports of the two separate peace missions of the Italians at Lisbon and Tangier arrived. The two Allied leaders did not look on the feelers warmly because they were still struggling with the problem of "Unconditional Surrender."

The Italians waited for news, supremely aware of the new speed with which German troops were surging across the northern borders into Italy. The tension grew so great that General Castellano persuaded his peers in the Commando Supremo to let him go to Madrid. But he did not have the power to sign for the government because the king would not give it until he was sure the Allies would intervene enough to prevent Italy from being overrun by the Germans. He told the British ambassador that he thought unconditional surrender could be made acceptable if the Allies would act. Castellano then went on to Lisbon.

The Allies still did not have any surrender terms ready and were still arguing. They agreed to confuse the Italians by offering them terms that did not spell out unconditional surrender, and bringing that in later. American General Walter B. Smith and British Brigadier General W. D. Strong went to Lisbon and met with Castellano on August 19. There they learned that their delays in these negotiations had permitted the Germans to bring in division after division and that the number of Germans in Italy was enormously increased.

Castellano went back to Rome on August 27. He had been gone so long that the Italians sent a second representative. More delay. The Allies at Quebec decided to stick with "Unconditional Surrender," and in Africa, Eisenhower knew that this would be unacceptable, so he persuaded the Combined Chiefs of Staff to try to fool the Italians. They held the second representative hostage and sent his interpreter back to Rome with a letter urging acceptance of the Allies' terms, which no one in Rome really knew, and promising that the Allies would adjust "Unconditional Surrender" if the Italians cooperated.

The Italian government was not entranced with the goings on. Field Marshal Badoglio made one last attempt, saying the Allies must first land at least 15 divisions near Rome. The Allies rejected these terms, and put it hard to the Italians: Yes or No?

General Alexander, who was present at these meetings, was now concerned about the Salerno landings. The Germans were getting too strong. The whole surrender plan could work only if the Italians surrendered and created enough confusion to throw the Germans off balance. The Italians said the Allies had to make a concession—not Yes or No. The Allies promised to drop an airborne division near Rome, and on that note, the meetings broke up.

In Rome, the Italians did not think much of the concession made. The task of defending the government against the Germans was impossible. The king said to negotiate a surrender. Castellano went back to Sicily and was confronted with an instrument of surrender and told to sign it. At 5:00 P.M. on September 3, Castellano signed the surrender as Badoglio's representative.

Feverish movement was made to try to get the surrender to the troops before the Salerno landings. But the parachute landing near Rome was called off as suicidal. The Allies would not tell the Italians when they were going to land at Salerno, and the Italians deduced that it would be between September 10 and 15.

The Allies now had General Montgomery's army ashore just opposite Messina. They had started crossing the Strait of Messina at 4:30 A.M., accompanied by naval bombardment, air bombardment, and a barrage from the field artillery. Thirteenth Corps landed just north of Reggio de Calabria with the 5th Infantry Division on the left and the 1st Canadian Infantry Division on the right.

It was an easy advance. The British did not meet any Germans, and the Italians did not resist. The German 29th Panzer Grenadier Division had retired two days earlier north of Reggio. The people of Calabria cheered the British and Canadian troops as they came.

But the British Eighth Army was delayed by German demolition and mines. The first contact with the 29th Panzer Grenadier Division came on the night of September 3, and by September 9, 13th Corps was approaching its first major objective: the Catanzaro Isthmus.

General Clark was to land at Salerno. The British 1st Airborne Division was to drop on the Italian naval base at Taranto. The airborne landing near Rome was called off because it was impractical. So the Italians had not gotten anything they wanted in exchange for the surrender.

It was unfortunate that the Allies did not elect to give the Italians any information because the Italians believed that the invasion would come on September 12, and thus did nothing on September 9, the day the Allies landed at Salerno. Rather, the day before, they sent a message to the Allies saying they would not be able to accept the armistice, because the Germans in Rome were far too strong. So the Allies called off the air drop of the 82nd Airborne Division that was supposed to fall in conjunction with uprisings in Rome.

When Badoglio's message that the armistice could not be implemented reached Algiers, Eisenhower was away at his advance headquarters in Bizerte. The staff signaled the Joint Chiefs of Staff for instructions, and sent Eisenhower copies. Eisenhower was so angry that he drafted a curt note to Badoglio that said he was going to announce the armistice as planned. He did so at 6:30 that night over Radio Algiers. But from Rome came silence. It was more than an hour later that Rome broadcast the news.

The Italians had hesitated because they were virtually paralyzed by events and had made no plans to resist a German takeover. The king, Badoglio, and all the high-ranking military leaders abandoned their headquarters and escaped in a convoy of autos to Pescara on the Adriatic coast, leaving no instructions and no one in charge in Rome. The royal party embarked on an Italian warship and sailed for safety behind the Allied lines. In Rome, there was no government and no military leadership.

As all this was going on, the Germans had amassed for the defense of Italy, more strongly than the Allies expected. Field Marshal Rommel moved his headquarters to Lake Garda close to transportation links to Germany. He appointed General von Vietinghoff to command the new Tenth Army, which would control the German troops in lower Italy. Now the German forces in Italy comprised 17 divisions, five of them from the Eastern Front. The British were pleased to note that the prospects of the Allied invasion were already drawing troops from the east, in proof of their contention that this was the way to win the war. (The disposition of the German troops in Italy on September 3 is shown in Appendix B.) The German defense system was set. Rommel's Army Group B was to serve as the protective force holding a grip on northern Italy. The aim of the defensive position was on the Appenine Mountains between Pisa and Rimini, which would be known as the Gothic Line. Behind that line, Rommel was to build a defense for a long battle.

The Germans had learned in Sicily that it was futile to try to stop the invasion forces once they had a foothold. The thing to do was attack before the enemy was organized in its beachheads. If this failed, then it was best to withdraw to ground of German choosing and fight a land battle away from the covering fire of battleships and cruisers at the water's edge. This way the choice of terrain and military skill of the Germans tended to compensate for the enormous resources of the Allies.

The Germans considered that the Allies would land in one of five places, but soon they narrowed it down to three: the "toe" of Italy, the Naples area, or Rome. Each area was made the responsibility of a German corps commander who was to cooperate with Italian troops as far as possible. The "toe" and "heel" were given to General Herr's 76th Panzer Corps. He had three divisions: the 29th Panzer Grenadier Division, the 16th Panzer Division, and the 1st Parachute Division (which was down to one fighting regiment). But the country was so mountainous and difficult that by using engineers to blow up the bridge and mine the roads, a handful of men could (and already had) hold up the enemy army, in this case Montgomery's Eighth Army.

The Naples area was the responsibility of General Hube's 14th Panzer Corps when it escaped from Sicily. His primary responsibility was the port of Naples, which he defended with the Hermann Goering Panzer Division and the 15th Panzer Grenadier Division, both experienced in the Sicilian fighting. The 16th Panzer Division was already stationed near Foggia. There were three approaches to Naples: from the Gulf of Gaeta, through the Bay of Naples, and from Salerno. The northern approach—the Bay of Naples—seemed most likely; the southern approach—from Salerno—seemed the least likely because it was so easily defendable that if it were attempted, an Allied landing could be quickly blocked. So Hube left Salerno to the Italians and disposed his two divisions to the north of Naples. In Rome, General Student was made responsible for preventing or thwarting any attempted uprising by the Italians.

If the Germans failed to stop the Allies on the beaches, they would withdraw to a series of defensive lines stretched across the Italian peninsula from which they could launch counterattacks when opportunity arose. They would try to hold south of Naples and the Foggia airfields. The next line ran from Gaeta to Isernia, and then to the Adriatic Sea. It would be known as the Gustav Line, with Cassino at the center.

North of Rome ran a line from Grossetto to Ancona. And finally there was the Gothic Line in the northern Appenines. The Allies did not yet know it but the German policy was to give up nothing until forced to do so, and to gradually withdraw northward, abandoning southern and central Italy. This plan was drawn up because the Germans overestimated the military strength the Allies (Americans) were willing to throw into Italy, and they underestimated the German ability to deal with an Italy that decided to abandon the Axis alliance.

As for dealing with the Italians, Plan Achse was issued by the OKW on August 30. If the Italians defected, as the Germans expected, the Italian army would be disarmed and the soldiers given the choice of fighting with the Germans or going home. The navy would be seized by the German navy, and the Italian aircraft would be seized by the Luftwaffe. Rommel took a fierce view; in his orders to his army group, he said the Italian soldiers who did not want to fight with the Germans were to be taken prisoner and transferred to Germany as slave labor.

The news of the Italian surrender reached the Germans from the Algiers broadcast in English. Field Marshal Kesselring was conferring with Italian General Roatta when General Jodl rang up from the OKW to ask about the broadcast. Roatta said it must be a trick, and for an hour Kesselring believed that. Then he ordered the implementation of Plan Achse.

It was obvious to the Germans all day that the Allies had something big going on. Their headquarters at Frascati was bombed and for a time communications with the outside were lost. That bombing had shown them that there was Italian treachery afoot: someone had given away the location of their headquarters.

With the realization that the Italian surrender was real, the Germans put Plan Achse into immediate action. In the north, Rommel's forces disarmed the Italians and took them prisoner, much to Kesselring's annoyance. The Italian fleet escaped because the Italian chief of staff had convinced the Germans the day before that they should sail out to attack the Allies. They tried to join the Allies at the point mentioned but were attacked by Luftwaffe planes, and the flagship *Roma* was sunk, taking down an admiral and most of his officers. The rest of the fleet escaped and joined the rest of the fleet to surrender to the British at Malta.

Three hundred Italian air force pilots took their planes to Allied airfields. The rest went home or were taken prisoner by the Germans.

In the south, the Italian Seventh Army surrendered without a whimper to the Germans and turned over equipment, weapons, and supplies to the German Tenth Army. General von Vietinghoff sent all the soldiers home; he had no time to be taking prisoners and using German soldiers as guards.

Kesselring was now on his own. But Hitler had been so sure that he would not be able to save the Tenth Army that he had given no orders. So Kesselring was free to support von Vietinghoff at Salerno, and he saw no reason to abandon southern Italy, as Hitler was willing to do.

In Rome, General Student moved swiftly to put Plan Achse into force. The German ambassador and his staff left for the north. The 1st Parachute Division dropped on the Italian headquarters at Monterotondo, outside Rome, but was too late to catch Roatta. The 2nd Parachute Division and the 3rd Panzer Grenadier Division advanced on Rome, asking the Italians not to fire on them. Some Italians opposed the Germans and fought fiercely. Others gave up without a whimper. By evening, the Germans were negotiating for a cease-fire, and General Siegfried Westphal, Kesselring's chief of staff, used every method from argument to bullets to inducing surrender. There was no one in charge of the Italians, until Field Marshal Caviglia, who did not like Badoglio, took charge and authorized the surrender of Rome to the Germans. By nightfall of September 10, Kesselring was the master of Rome and his communications with Rommel in the north and von Vietinghoff in the south were in perfect condition. He could now concentrate on defeating the Allies and proving Rommel wrong in his contention that the Germans had to abandon all but northern Italy.

So the Americans and British prepared to invade Italy proper with only three divisions in the assault wave on Salerno and two divisions in reserve to follow up. Coming from Messina, Montgomery would bring another two divisions, but this gave the Allies only seven divisions to operate with against the eight German divisions in Kesselring's command. Obviously, there had been a slipup of major proportions somewhere.

It went back to the shoddy planning in the shadow of the Trident Conference and the basic disagreement between the Americans and the British that was never really settled. Even before the Sicily operations, the Americans were convinced that Churchill and the British wanted to subvert the attack across the English Channel, and everything they did was viewed in that context. General Marshall insisted on cannibalizing the U.S. Seventh Army, sending some of the divisions back to England to prepare for the invasion of France and some to participate in the Italian campaign. General Patton felt that the Seventh Army was now only a shadow of its former self, and he became a propaganda foil, to fool the Germans into believing that he might strike somewhere. However, the actual plan was to abolish the Seventh Army altogether. Operation Avalanche was planned to operate on a shoestring, and it would have been worse if Admiral Cunningham had not sent back ten troopships from the Mediterranean after they arrived in Britain, and allowed the retention in the Mediterranean assault craft, which should have been sent back. The U.S. Fifth Army was about to start its war faced with a stronger force than its own.

In the air it was the same. Eisenhower had to give up three medium bomber groups to northwest Europe. Tedder had asked for more Flying Fortresses and P-38 fighters, but the request was refused because the Eighth Air Force was planning to launch its strategic bombing campaign against Germany and needed more fighters and more bombers. The fact was that the Allied planning was premature, and the resources were not available to build up both the Mediterranean and the North Atlantic theaters as quickly as the planned operations demanded. The Mediterranean command suffered the deprivation. Thus, the airpower of the Allies at the time of the invasion of Italy was weaker than it had been at the time of the Sicilian invasion. The Germans now had many more air bases within the range of ground operations. If it had not been for naval coverage of the invasion beaches with carrier planes, the air show might even have been worse than it was.

The plan for Operation Avalanche was anything but neat. First, there were too many alternate plans floating about, taking possession of people's minds and creating uncertainties. The manner in which units were yanked out of Sicily and sent back to England and the use of shipping and what shipping was left for the operation were all confused, almost until the last. General Clark did not help matters by changing the plan several times, such as advancing H Hour by 30 minutes, which he did on August 14, thus upsetting the detailed timing of the assault waves and convoys.

Clark's plan was to land General McCreery's 46th and 56th Infantry Divisions of the British 10th Corps on the northern half of the Salerno beaches, and General E. J. Dawley's American 6th Corps, with only the 36th Infantry Division in the assault wave, on the southern beaches. Two regimental combat teams of the American 45th Infantry Division were in the floating reserve and the British 7th Armoured Division would follow 10th Corps after D plus 4 and participate in the assault on Naples.

The northern flank of the beachhead was to be secured by three battalions of American Rangers and two British Commandos who were to land first on the beaches and block the passes on the two roads leading south from Naples. These were the roads the Germans were expected to use for reinforcement.

After establishing their initial beachheads, the American and the British corps were to go forward and establish a perimeter on the arc of low hills that overlooked the beaches. The boundary between the Americans and the British was to be the Sele River, and the Ponte Sele bridge on Route 19 was to be the junction point. The 10th Corps also had the specific task of taking the small Salerno port and the Montecorvino airfield from which Tedder hoped to launch planes by D plus 1. Later, 10th Corps was to break out to the north and seize Naples by September 21 and have it in hand when the first convoy of reserves and supplies was scheduled to arrive.

The naval plan was iffy. If the Italians did not surrender their fleet, then a covering force would be necessary. Admiral Willis' Force H had four battleships, two fleet carriers, and four cruisers. Two other battleships would watch the naval base of Taranto. Three cruisers would give fire support to the British plus two other ships, and four cruisers would support the American operations. American Vice Admiral Henry K. Hewitt was in command of the naval assault force, and he had his flag in the headquarters ship *Alcon*, on which General Clark also would be riding.

Since submarines had found the Gulf of Salerno mined, minesweepers would move in first to clear the lanes and beaches.

The air plan called for neutralizing the Luftwaffe, driving it from the forward airfields. Bombing was to reduce the German ability to bring up reinforcements; and fighter cover was to be provided until the time when the army broke out from its beaches. There was to be no preliminary bombardment or bombing. General Clark wanted to rely on surprise. Not taking a very bright view of surprise, General McCreery arranged privately for a close naval support program in case the enemy was not surprised. But the Americans took no such precautions.

At the end of August, General Hube seemed to have smelled a rat because he brought the 16th Panzer Division from the Adriatic side of the peninsula to strengthen the defenses at Salerno. This was a division dating back to Stalingrad days that had 4,000 survivors of the division who had fought in Poland, France, and Russia. Its morale was very high and relied on strong mobile patrols of tanks, self-propelled guns, and the infantry to cover the gaps.

On the afternoon of September 8, the Germans received reports of enemy shipping in force 25 miles south of Capri. The whole 14th Panzer Corps was flashed into the highest state of readiness, and all troops were told to expect a major landing almost immediately. Preparations to meet the landing were going on, when at 8:00 P.M. came the code for Plan Achse—"*Ernte Einbring*"—and the Germans began to disarm the Italians. The commander of the 222nd Coastal Division was asked to surrender but he refused, whereupon the German major who had made the demand shot him dead. But generally the Italians were only too glad to surrender, give up their arms, and begin heading for home. The Germans had completed the disarmament when the American Rangers and the British Commandos headed in for shore. There would be no surprise.

11

Unrest at Quadrant

At the end of July, the Joint War Plans Committee of the U.S. Joint Chiefs of Staff had some serious reservations about General Marshall's insistence on sticking with the concept of the Cross Channel Attack. They pointed to the turnaround in Russia, where the Soviet Union had wrested the initiative from the Germans, and the Anglo–American superiority established in the air and on the sea. It was obvious that Germany was no longer capable of defeating the Soviet armies and was on the defensive in the east. Therefore, the prime reason for Operation Overlord had evaporated. They decided that the inflexible adherence to the Cross Channel Attack was wrong. Taking the wherewithal from the Mediterranean for the launching of a major offensive might cause a loss of momentum; and if the Germans decided to defend the Italian peninsula, it could mean the bogging down of the Allies. The committee was critical of Marshall's insistence on bringing seven divisions from the Mediterranean back to England to prepare for Operation Overlord when they could make all the difference in the Italian campaign.

But Marshall was inflexible. He believed that the defeat of Germany depended on the Cross Channel Attack. He was also becoming disturbed because he saw in the British attitude an attempt to subvert Operation Overlord, no matter how much lip service they might pay to it. He was well aware that the British felt they had been dragooned into accepting Operation Overlord to keep the Americans from carrying out their threat to move the center of their operations to the Pacific.

Marshall did not have any use for the contention that much could be achieved by hitting the Germans in the Balkans. A campaign on the Danube River held no magic for him. Marshall wanted Operation Overlord and an invasion of southern France, and he was quite willing to accept a laborious campaign in Italy—basically a waste of time—as the cost of it. So, when the British and some Americans talked of the dangers of a slow campaign in Italy, he was unimpressed.

Between the end of the Trident Conference, and the next conference—called "Quadrant"—in Quebec in August 1943, various British leaders continued to express their reluctance to proceed with Operation Overlord. Prime Minister Churchill told American General Albert C. Wedemeyer that he would much rather attack the Balkans in the south and Norway in the north than go up against the strength of the Germans in France. General Brooke told General Eisenhower that he would not at all mind dropping the Cross Channel Attack entirely.

All during the Sicilian campaign, the British had pressed the Combined Chiefs of Staff to allot more resources to the Mediterranean. One result of this situation was the American feeling, from President Roosevelt down, that the British attitude toward the Cross Channel Attack was so negative that it could never succeed under a British commander. So, the American minds closed on that issue. Another result was a deep suspicion by the Americans of the British and their motives in everything they did that related to the Mediterranean. Therefore, the Americans blinded themselves to the realities of what was happening in Italy. Hitler had decided to defend Italy no matter the cost and was setting out to do so.

The Quadrant Conference was the stickiest yet held between the British and Americans, and the issue all the way through was Operation Overlord. In the end, the Marshall position prevailed, but it was apparent that the reluctance of the British was unabated. The conference ended with a partial agreement that Operation Overlord was still paramount. It did not address the basic problem of what would happen if the Germans devoted major resources to the defense of Italy, and it was obvious that Marshall was willing to let Italy become a backwater theater; he was not willing for it to become a primary theater. In the major attention devoted by the Americans to achieving the Italian surrender, little thought was given to the possibility that the Italian surrender might be meaningless because of German seizure of power in Italy.

Bemused by consideration of the help they were going to get from the Italians, Eisenhower and his staff declared themselves satisfied with the resources that Marshall agreed should be retained in the Mediterranean, and did not worry about the seven lost divisions. In Washington, Roosevelt worried more about that than Eisenhower did in Algiers. Roosevelt suggested that the seven divisions be replaced by seven new American divisions. Marshall would not agree. To him everything had to be predicated on the buildup of resources for Operation Overlord. He allayed Roosevelt's worries by telling him that Eisenhower said he had plenty of resources. He also pointed out his concern that by hook or by crook, if resources were left in the Mediterranean, Churchill would contrive to entertain his Balkan adventure. So distrustful were the Americans of Churchill's intentions and statements in this regard that the Marshall position carried the day.

So the Quadrant Conference ended with no one happy. The Americans were still not positive of the British commitment to Operation Overlord. The British agreed to the withdrawal of the seven divisions, but feared that many opportunities to shorten the war would be lost in the Mediterranean. So the Allies went into the Italian campaign without the resources to ensure victory, and not even knowing that this was so, or paying adequate attention to the comparative logistics.

After the Quadrant Conference, Eisenhower had new instructions from the Combined Chiefs of Staff: He was to eliminate Italy from the war, which he thought was in the works with the Italian surrender. The Allies deluded themselves into believing that in their own country the Italians would be able to control the Germans.

Now Eisenhower was to capture Corsica and Sardinia, operations that were already under way but being carried out by the French. He was to keep the pressure on the Germans to create conditions that would enable the Allies to carry out the Operation Overlord adventure and the eventual invasion of southern France as well.

But the questions were, would the Germans allow themselves to be contained and static? Or would the Allies find themselves bogged down in Italy, taking heavy material losses and the Germans sapping their strength instead of it being the other way around?

In the planning for the Italian campaign, the Allies failed to understand what the Germans intended, and failed to make plans based on the realities of the situation, as it developed in Italy, or for the contingencies that might be involved. This was how it was as they approached the landings at Salerno.

12

Salerno

On September 7, 1943, the Germans sent the alert for Plan Achse—the takeover of Italy. On that day General von Senger arrived in Sardinia with secret orders to prepare for the German evacuation of the islands so they would not lose the 90th Panzer Grenadier Division, which was occupying them, and waiting for Allied attack. Also involved would be the evacuation of Corsica by the SS Reichsführer Brigade. So the 90th withdrew to Corsica that next day. But, there, the Italians refused to cooperate with the Germans, and the French community rose up in rebellion and von Senger had to fight a withdrawal action to a bridgehead at Bastia from which he organized an evacuation during the last two weeks of September. On September 20, French General Henri-Honoré Giraud arrived on Corsica with Free French soldiers, and the Germans had to fight them as well. It was October 30 before von Senger managed to get away from Corsica with his rear guard. So, as the battle for Italy began, two of the option targets for action in the Mediterranean were also falling to the Allies.

Meanwhile, in the confusion of the Italian surrender and the takeover of Italy by the Germans, Mussolini was rescued by a daring German maneuver. The former dictator had been moved from a jail in Rome to a ski lodge at the Campo Imperiatre on the Gran Sasso. On September 8, Colonel Skorzeny, who had been selected personally by Hitler to rescue Mussolini, located the ski lodge and a possible landing site for a small plane. He took photos and sent a German staff doctor to visit the ski lodge on the pretext of planning to use it for German troops. The doctor returned to say that he had not been allowed to go to the ski lodge because a detachment of Italian soldiers guarded the funicular railway station that led to the top. Then, Skorzeny learned that other troops guarded the top. But they could not learn whether Mussolini was being held there. Skorzeny discussed the problem with General Student, and they decided that Mussolini must be there and that they must hurry before the Italians could transfer Mussolini to Allied custody. So Skorzeny set out on the afternoon of September 12 with a company of glider-borne troops. Skorzeny's glider was the first on the ground, crash-landing 50 yards from the lodge. He and his men ran to the hotel and scrambled through a second-story window. Inside was Mussolini. The Italian guards offered no resistance, and the paratroopers captured all of them, on the bottom of the mountain at the funicular station, and on top. A Storch aircraft landed on the mountain, and Mussolini was airlifted out with Skorzeny. The pilot flew to Pratica di Mare, where three Heinkel 111 planes were waiting to take Mussolini to Germany. Shortly after 7:30 that evening they were in Vienna, and the next day they flew to Munich. On September 15, they arrived at Hitler's headquarters in East Prussia.

As soon as it had been made clear that the Italian fleet was going to surrender as called for in the agreement between the Italian government and the Allies, Admiral Cunningham had released the 12th Cruiser Squadron to pick up the British 1st Airborne Division for the attack on the naval base at Taranto, called "Operation Slapstick." The paratroopers were embarked, and on September 8, as the Allied forces moved in on Salerno, the paratroopers were at sea. They arrived on the following day, and landed unopposed. There was one casualty: the minelayer *Abidel*, loaded with paratroopers, hit a mine while anchoring. She exploded, with heavy loss of life.

As the Allied convoys approached Salerno on the night of September 8, the sea was calm and the night was clear. The American and British troops suffered none of the usual tension the night before an invasion. It would be, as the cockneys liked to say, "a piece of cake." The announcement of the Italian surrender was in the air, and anyone who had been in Sicily could only too easily recall the sensation of being greeted as conquering heroes by the people of Sicily. The troops were arriving in an almost festive air.

The minesweepers came in and did their job without arousing the troops on shore. The invasion fleets assembled in the landing areas. The ships of the fleets performed with much more precision than they had in the Sicily landings, the result of experience.

But there the dream ended. In the northern sector, the British were detected before they could get started into the landing craft. The shore batteries, manned by Germans who had just taken over from the Italians, opened fire with great accuracy on the ships carrying the Rangers and the Commandos. Five minutes after they landed, the destroyers in the British assault area opened an intensive 15-minute barrage of gun and rocket fire to support the landings. Fortunately, the commanders in the north had made contingency arrangements for full fire support. The British warships fired back on each coastal battery, and the supporting destroyers moved in behind the assault waves to give close-fire support. The Rangers and Commandos landed against light opposition and secured their objectives, with few accidents. One landing craft did land on the wrong beach, creating some confusion.

The troops on shore did not just walk in. The Commandos suffered some casualties but managed to hold their positions. The British 46th Infantry Division was fortunate to land away from any German strong points, but the 56th Infantry Division ran into heavy opposition. By the end of the day, the dream of an easy time had ended. Neither division had achieved its objectives and the 56th had suffered heavy losses. The port of Salerno was not far, but the 46th had not captured it. The 56th reached the edge of Montecorvino airfield but could not go any farther.

In the American sector, there was surprise; they received a hot welcome, not just a warm one. The beaches were silent as the landing craft went in, but when the men hit the beach, they were met by heavy fire from concealed positions. Much of the fire was too high to do much harm, but it soon steadied down and the losses began. After landing safely, on the extreme right, the 1st Battalion of the 141st Infantry Division began to work its way to the railroad station near the Solofrone River. But the third wave of boats met German fire so intense that it and the following waves were immobilized on the beach. The fact that no plan for fire support from the ships had been arranged was almost the undoing of the landing. The 3rd Battalion on Yellow Beach ran into German fire from the beginning, 400 yards from the shore.

Following are the words of the official U.S. Army historian describing the scene:

> From the massive heights that loomed over all the beaches, and from Monta Sopprano in particular, came the flashes and sounds of the enemy fire. Flares of all colours illuminated the sky, while the crisscrossing tracers of machine guns flashed over the beaches, the heaviest concentrations coming from the right near Agropoli. Some boat pilots who judged the fire too strong for them to land their troops turned around and headed back toward the ships, until intercepted by control vessels and sent again to shore.[10]

Landing craft foundered and some burned near the shore or drifted in the waves. Lost equipment floated on the surface and communications equipment was lost. Boats sank and men swam for the beach. As one mortar squad debarked, the gunner tripped on the ramp and dropped the mortar into the water. Machine-gun fire scattered that platoon, and the men who hit the shore joined whatever unit they were near. Some mortars came ashore without any ammunition. The Americans were finding this a much tougher landing than anything they had ever experienced before.

Casualties were very heavy but the 36th Infantry Division, a National Guard Unit, had been well trained and managed to win most of its D-Day objectives. By dusk, it was holding a narrow beachhead around the Roman ruins of Paestum.

The British and the Americans had met the German 16th Panzer Division, which had 17,000 men, 100 tanks, and 36 assault guns. At the end of the first day, it was apparent that the invasion was already in trouble. The Italians had been counted on for support by the Allies but had produced none. The Germans were very strong and could now concentrate all the weight of their Tenth Army against the U.S. Fifth Army before the British Eighth Army could come up from the south. The Americans still did not know it, but they were facing a numerically superior force, and one very skilled in the art of war.

Now one of the problems over which General Eisenhower had glissaded so easily arose to haunt the Allies: the serious shortage of shipping. The beachheads needed reinforcement immediately.

When dawn came on D plus one, the seriousness of the Allied position began to become apparent. They occupied two corners of the beach. Every action could be observed by the Germans on the hills around Salerno.

Shortly after dawn in the American sector, German tanks came into action working in small groups, supported by their infantry in platoon units. A lone tank reached the beach shortly after dawn and fired on the landing craft approaching. Antiaircraft guns on the LSTs and machine guns on the landing craft took the tank under fire and soon drove it off. Without any naval support fire, it was individual American infantrymen who kept the German tanks at bay in the south during these early hours. Corporal Roy C. Davis, a bazookaman, crawled under machine-gun bursts up the beach until he got to a point near a tank. With one round, he pierced the tank's armor, then crept up to the disabled vehicle and thrust a grenade through the hole, killing the crew. Sergeant John Y. McGill jumped onto a tank and dropped a grenade through the open turret hatch. Even men without useful weapons helped. Private First Class Harry Harpel kept one group of tanks from reaching the beach by moving the loose planking of a bridge across an irrigation canal. These untried American troops moved with the efficiency of veterans.

But they were badly hampered by the lack of naval fire, and the American tanks, in particular, were disorganized and slow to get ashore. Many of the tanks did not get ashore until afternoon and some not until after nightfall. Six LSTs carrying tanks of the 191st Tank Battalion, moving toward Blue Beach at 6:30 in the morning, were hit by enemy shell fire; four received direct hits and one tank was burning. For five hours the LSTs circled aimlessly, and at 11:00 A.M. finally approached the shore. With neither artillery nor tanks in support during the first four hours, the infantry depended to a great extent on a few 40-mm antiaircraft guns that came ashore at daylight.

At the end of D Day, the Allied troops were ashore, with the British controlling the north entrance to the beaches; the Americans controlled the south. But the Germans controlled the center where Route 19 and Route 94 arrived at a gap in the hills and from which the Germans could bombard the beaches with their artillery and bring their tanks down when they wished.

So although the landings were an official success, they placed the troops in peril. Immediate reinforcement, which they could not get, was needed, as well as the speedy arrival of the Eighth Army from the south.

Almost from the beginning, General Alexander recognized the problem. He ordered the Eighth Army to race for Salerno even though Montgomery argued that to hurry was to take risks. Sometimes, said Alexander, even Montgomery had to take risks. Eighteen American LSTs, which had been assigned to other theaters, were still in African ports, and the Combined Chiefs of Staff ordered their release to build up the force at Salerno.

General von Vietinghoff now recognized his opportunity. If he could bring up reinforcements and destroy the Allied landings at Salerno, he could then turn his efforts against the Eighth Army in the south and destroy that force methodically. It was a race against time. The Germans had the advantage of proximity and numbers, and the use of rail and road transport to bring up their troops. Von Vietinghoff ordered General Herr, in the south, to break off contact with the Eighth Army and move the 76th Panzer Corps toward Salerno. The 26th Panzer Division and the 29th Panzer Grenadier Division were to leave only rear guard behind and move at its best speed over the 125 miles of mountain road to the beachhead. General Hube's 14th Panzer Corps was ordered away from the Gulf of Gaeta to send the 15th Panzer Grenadier and the Hermann Goering Panzer Divisions south to block any advance of the Allies north to take Naples. Field Marshal Kesselring ordered General Student to release the 3rd Panzer Grenadier Division from Rome and asked the OKW for Field Marshal Rommel's two Panzer divisions, a request that was denied, but still five divisions could come to the aid of the German troops at Salerno. That meant von Vietinghoff could move enough troops to have six divisions to contest the four that General Clark had available. The Allies had air superiority, but it was not very strong.

On the morning of September 10, the Americans landed part of their floating reserve: the 45th Infantry Division. Clark visited the beachhead and was pleased with the conditions in the 6th Corps area. He visited General McCreery and learned what resistance the British were meeting in the north. McCreery indicated it would be difficult for the British to advance to the point where they were to rendezvous with 6th Corps. So, Clark ordered reinforcements to the 10th Corps area in view of the preponderance of German strength located there. Clark was very optimistic. He told General Alexander that he expected to be able to attack north toward Naples. So favorable did the situation seem that the Northwest African Tactical Air Force proposed to reduce the fighter cover over the beaches. Just at this point the Germans were planning to step up their air attacks.

On September 10 and 11, both sides did their best to build up their forces and contain the enemy. The German effort was directed first against the British 10th Corps, which threatened Naples. The Commandos, Rangers, and the 46th Infantry Division were hit by the 15th Panzer Grenadier Division and the Hermann Goering Panzer Division. The 46th managed to capture Salerno, but the Germans had the high ground and kept the harbor under observation and fire.

The confusion between commands continued. The forces off Salerno saw that the number of Allied air sorties was decreasing and protested to the air force, but the air force saw that the air opposition over the beaches was light on September 9 and, thus, cut back the number of fighter sorties as the Germans were increasing theirs. On September 10, the number of Allied fighters was definitely decreased, as more Germans came in. By the 11th, American Admiral Hewitt radioed Eisenhower that the status of the beachhead was growing critical because of the lack of air support. He was told that the only help that was coming was from Admiral Philip Vian, commander of the carrier force.

The Germans continued to hold the Montecorvino airfield and stopped the 56th Infantry Division, which was trying to get to Monte Eboli. Because of the concentration of the Germans on the British 10th Corps, the American 6th Corps was left alone to expand its bridgehead and secure key points overlooking the Ponte Sele bridge. However, that left a huge gap between the British and the American forces, so Clark landed his floating reserve to fill it.

Ashore once again on September 11 Clark was impressed by the way German pressure was building against the British area in the Battapaglia area, where they had pushed into the outskirts of Vietri and were within 12 miles of Salerno. On that day the Germans had captured 1,500 prisoners, most of them in the British sector. That night American troops were moved into the gap between the two forces.

By this time the air situation was indeed serious. The Germans launched 450 sorties by fighters and bombers and 100 sorties by heavy bombers in the first three days of the battle; and they sank four transports, one heavy cruiser, and seven landing craft and made many hits on the Allied fleet. On September 11, a near miss damaged the cruiser *Philadelphia*, another damaged a Dutch gunboat, and a direct hit on the cruiser *Savannah* put it out of action. Admiral Hewitt had to declare his situation critical to Admiral Cunningham, who sent the cruisers *Aurora* and *Penelope* from Malta.

Clark came ashore again on September 12 and found the British 46th Infantry Division badly bruised and the German strength increasing and pointing toward the center of the beachhead. He had evidence that the Germans were preparing to launch an attack in the near future, and his forces were spread very thin.

After four days, the Allied beachhead was still dangerously shallow and the number of troops to man the perimeter was very small. Clark decided that day to bring his headquarters ashore, as a way to preserve and enhance troop morale.

The first signs of German counterattack came on the evening of September 11. That day, General Clark had ordered his floating reserve to land on the bank of the Sele River to close the wide gap between the American and the British landings. One regimental combat team was to go up the south bank and seize the Ponte Sele bridge; the other combat team was to advance along the north bank to 10th Corps in the Battapaglia–Eboli area. But these moves had not been made that evening of the 11th when the German counterstrike caught Clark off balance.

At the first signal of German attack, the 56th Infantry Division was hit by the leading elements of the 26th Panzer Division, which arrived in the area up Route 19 and attacked virtually without pause. The Royal Fusilier Battalion in Battapaglia was surrounded by the Germans and 450 men were taken prisoner. At the same time, the U.S. 45th Infantry Division thrusting toward the Ponte Sele bridge was stopped by the 29th Panzer Grenadier Division. Overhead the Luftwaffe flew more sorties and damaged one British cruiser and two American cruisers. The German aircraft were up at 18,000 feet, too high for any Allied fighters except the P-38s, but most of these had been sent back to England.

The Germans had planned their countermove carefully. They would attack the 10th Corps from the north while moving their reinforcements around the Ponte Sele bridge into the Battapaglia area. Then they would attack along Route 19 to the west, to crush 10th Corps against the anvil of the northern force. Then they would move southwest along the Sele River and break through to the sea between 6th Corps and 10th Corps.

Then the two corps would have to either escape by sea or face destruction.

During the next two days they nearly succeeded. The 10th Corps lost heavily in fighting around Battapaglia and the Montecorvino airfield, but managed to hold on because of excellent air support and naval gunfire.

The American 36th Infantry Division was forced off Altavilla and Point 424 (a strategic defense point) on September 12. On September 13, the critical point of the battle came. A mixed force of tanks, self-propelled guns, and infantry from the 16th Panzer Division rushed through the American 45th Infantry Division positions along the Sele River and reached a point two miles from the beaches. It was the American artillery that stopped them, firing almost point-blank into the tanks and infantry. There were no American reserves left, and that night of September 13–14 General Dawley had to draw his perimeter back to a point not far from his D-Day beachhead line.

The situation looked so bad on September 14 that General Clark ordered his staff to draw up a contingency plan to reembark one of the two corps to reinforce the beachhead of the other, but his naval commanders pointed out that the plan was totally impractical. It would involve getting men from shore to ship under constant enemy artillery fire. The plan was dropped when General McCreery and Admiral Cunningham argued against it, and the next day General Alexander opposed it.

But by September 14, the Allied position was getting stronger because a regimental combat team from the 82nd Airborne Division had been dropped in the American sector of the beachhead. This time the Allied navies made sure that no one disrupted the landings. Although a Luftwaffe air raid came just before the troops dropped, the gunners held their fire and did not shoot down their own troops.

Back in his forward headquarters at Bizerte, General Eisenhower secured permission from the Joint Chiefs of Staff to use the strategic air forces to help in the battle. Admiral Cunningham brought the battleships *Warspite* and *Valiant* from Malta to use their 15-inch guns in support of the landings. Churchill signaled General Alexander that he could ask for anything and it would get the highest priority, but Churchill could not resist fighting the Battle of Gallipoli over again. He gave some advice: He urged Alexander to get to the front because the Battle of Suva Bay had been lost when Sir Ian Hamilton stayed far from the front on the advice of his staff at Gallipoli. Alexander was wise enough to ignore the Churchillian wisdom. Alexander was not in the rear; he was at Salerno watching the effect of reinforcing moves he had made two days before.

The British 7th Armoured Division started to land units in the 10th Corps sector on September 14. The 3rd Regimental Combat Team of the U.S. 45th Infantry Division arrived in the American sector. The U.S. 3rd Infantry Division was en route from Sicily, and a second regiment of the

82nd Airborne Division landed on the beachhead that evening and another dropped at Avellino. That drop was not very successful because of the mountainous nature of the area. The paratroopers were scattered all over the area. Most of them had to hole up in farms and mountain villages until the Allied advance liberated them from the fear of capture. But the beach drops were successful.

During September 14–16, the Fifth Army received massive naval and air support. The battleships with their 15-inch guns were particularly accurate in firing and in demoralizing the Germans. The strategic bombers did carpet bombing in the Battapaglia–Eboli–Ponte Sele area, and the Eighth Army began to come up. On September 16, a leading patrol met a patrol from 6th Corps 20 miles south of Paestum. The Luftwaffe managed to hit the battleship *Warspite* with a glider bomb, forcing it back to Malta for repairs, but the Allied reinforcements had come up in time to save the beachhead. It had been a very narrow escape, but the Allies had won the race.

After that linkup, von Vietinghoff advised Kesselring that the Allies were too firmly established to be thrown back into the sea or destroyed. He recommended disengagement so he could redeploy before the Eighth Army threatened his rear. So Kesselring authorized a slow withdrawal to the Volturno River north of Naples. Here the Germans were to stop and hold until the engineers could fortify the Gustav Line.

Von Vietinghoff made one more attack on September 17 against 10th Corps. Hube's and Herr's corps were sent to catch 10th Corps between them to try to crush it. But both attacks came under heavy bombardment that soon brought them to a halt. The Germans switched to the defensive as they had intended to do, and began to disengage on the south. The Battle of Salerno ended in a stalemate.

M-4 tank set on fire by enemy artillery in the vicinity of Cassino, Italy,
February 4, 1944. (Signal Corps Photo)

View of Anzio, Italy, from the air, September 13, 1945. (USAF Photo Anzio,
Italy)

President Roosevelt decorates General Clark: At an airfield in Sicily, President Franklin D. Roosevelt of the U.S. (right) congratulates U.S. Lieutenant General Mark W. Clark (left), commander of the Allied Fifth Army, during ceremonies at which General Clark was decorated with the U.S. Distinguished Service Cross for "extraordinary heroism in action" in the battle for Italy. U.S. General Dwight D. Eisenhower, Allied Commander in Chief in the Western Mediterranean area, is in the center. President Roosevelt inspected American soldiers in Sicily after the conclusion of historic Allied conferences in the Middle East. (Signal Corps Photo)

On December 13, President Franklin D. Roosevelt decorates General Mark
Clark with the Distinguished Service Cross during the president's visit to
Sicily. (Signal Corps Photo)

Dwight D. Eisenhower and Franklin D. Roosevelt in Sicily. (Signal Corps Photo)

Winston Churchill visits the Italian front: Left to right, Captain Pendell, Lieutenant General Mark W. Clark, Commanding General of the Fifth Army, and Winston Churchill troop the line of honor guard at Fifth Army Headquarters during the Prime Minister's tour in Italy. (U.S. Army Photo)

Fifth Army, Radicosa, Italy: G.I. vehicles on side road from highway 65 to II Corps command post during light snowfall, December 14, 1944. (War Department Photo)

Fifth Army, Castel Delrio area, Italy: Mules are being loaded with ammunition to take up to a battery of 155-mm Howitzers high on the side of a mountain, a location not accessible to trucks. (War Department Photo)

Pozzilli area, Italy: Medium tank of 755th tank battalion moves along mountain road near Demanio after a snow storm, January 2, 1944. (Signal Corps Photo)

Castiglioncello area, Italy: Winston Churchill and Lieutenant General Mark W. Clark (second from left) Commanding General, Fifth Army, chat with officers of the 34th Division just before lunch, which they enjoyed during the Prime Minister's tour of inspection of Fifth Army area. (Signal Corps Photo)

Cassino, Italy, monastery in ruins: Approach to Monte Cassino showing the excellent line of fire the Germans had. Picture taken from in front of Monte Cairo and hills 593 and 569. The trees were parched by shell fire and bombings. (War Department Photo)

Fifth Army, Castel Delrio area, Italy: "Cat" of 313th Engineers pulling jeep out of mud. (War Department Photo)

Rapido River area, Italy, the plains northwest of Cassino: Smoke can be seen on the horizon. In the foreground is the Rapido River. On the right is route 6 to Rome. (Signal Corps Photo)

Rapido River area, Italy: The famous St. Benedictine Monastery is easily discernible on the hill hiding Cassino. (Signal Corps Photo)

Rapido River area, Italy: Smoke from the shells of German "Nebelwerfers" partially obscures Cassino. Above the town is the Cassino Monastery, which U.S. artillerymen have orders not to shell. (Signal Corps Photo)

Aerial bombing of Anzio harbor, Italy. (Library of Congress Photo)

Fifth Army, Porretta Area, Italy: Lieutenant General Mark W. Clark (center), with Major General Joao Batista De Mascarenhas, Commanding General Bef, at his right, looking over enemy-held terrain from an observation point located above the town of Porretta. They could observe enemy movement through the scopes set up beyond them. (Signal Corps Photo)

"Ducks" of the Fifth Army coming ashore and moving inland, as more and more Fifth Army troops come into the beachhead. LST's are unloading other troops and equipment. Fifth Army beachhead near Anzio, Italy, January 28, 1944. (Signal Corps Photo)

Medium tank of a tank battalion moves along a mountain road near Demanio, Italy, after snow storm, January 2, 1944. (Signal Corps Photo)

Explosions from a second wave of dive bombers in the three-day attack on Monte Cassino Monastery, Rapido River area, Italy, February 17, 1944. (Signal Corps Photo)

A week after the destruction of the St. Benedictine Monastery by the Allies, it is still being used by the Germans for gun position and observation. Allied shells range in on a position, Rapido River area, Italy, February 14, 1944. (Signal Corps Photo)

Rapido River area, Italy, January 22, 1944: T-24 light cargo carrier stuck in the frozen mud. (Signal Corps Photo)

Anzio beachhead area, Italy, March 1944: After receiving first-aid, the infantryman is loaded into the ambulance that will take him to the hospital on the beach. (Signal Corps Photo)

Offshore of the Fifth Army beachhead near Anzio, Italy, January 22, 1944: One LCI burns while troops and equipment come ashore at the new Fifth Army beachhead, near Anzio, Italy. (Signal Corps Photo)

President Franklin D. Roosevelt is shown at a conference in December 1943 in Cairo, with President Innonis of Turkey and Prime Minister Winston Churchill. (Signal Corps Photo)

Cassino area, Italy, February 2, 1944: American M-4 tank laying helpless in a ditch after knocking out pill boxes and getting behind the Gustar line at the base of Monte Cassino. (Signal Corps Photo)

13

The Strategic Trap

The German withdrawal to the Volturno River attracted the Allies like a beehive attracts a bear. It had been superbly organized. The 14th Panzer Corps held the Sorrento Peninsula, which stopped the advance of the British 10th Corps on Naples. The 76th Panzer Corps moved back with the 1st Parachute Division, which was delaying the advance of the British 1st Airborne Division coming from Taranto. The whole German line moved from around the Fifth Army beachhead and then pivoted on Sorrento and swung back to form a line from the Gulf of Sorrento to the Adriatic.

At the end of one week, the Germans occupied a line from Sorrento to Malfi to the Ofanto River, and behind them, German engineers were blowing up Naples. Every ship berth was destroyed, cranes and shore gear were destroyed, pipelines and cables were ripped up, power stations were blown up, block ships were sunk in the landing area, and tugs and harbor craft were sunk in the harbor where they would prove the most difficult for the Allies. The harbor was heavily planted with mines. Ashore, booby traps and time bombs were planted in the important buildings, such as the post office. Hotels and barracks were mined. Some of the fuses had a 42-day run.

After the Germans pulled out of the northern beachhead area, it took 10th Corps two days to reorganize before it could start to attack northward toward Naples. Meanwhile, General Alexander issued his first directive to the U.S. Fifth and British Eighth Armies on September 21. The war would now go into four phases in Italy: the consolidation of the area from Salerno to Bari, the seizure of the port of Naples and the airfields at Foggia, the capture of Rome and the road and rail center of Terni, and the occupation of Leghorn and Florence and Arezzo. So the Allies had achieved one aim, to get Italy out of the war, but it seemed to have made very little difference. With Alexander's directive, it appeared that the Allies were locked in to the Italian campaign for as long as it took them to achieve these ends, with the constraint that General Eisenhower must operate with the troops and heavy equipment that he had. General Marshall was content with this program; it did not seem to interfere overly with his buildup for the Cross Channel Attack; and as long as Prime Minister Churchill could be restrained from plunging the Allies into the Balkans, Marshall had no objection. It was apparent that in Washington the whole Italian campaign was regarded as a way of marking time until the buildup and the assault on France could be prepared. No one seemed to pay much attention to the fact that the Allies were being drawn into an overland campaign in the mountainous peninsula of Italy where the defenders had all the advantages.

The change in the war became evident very soon. When the 10th Corps was ready to move on September 23, it was stopped cold by the Herman Goering Panzer Division and parts of two other German divisions. The 3rd and the 15th Panzer Grenadier Divisions were moving to the Volturno River to prepare the defenses there, but elements joined the Hermann Goering Panzer Division in a rear guard.

In the American sector, General Dawley was relieved by General Clark, who had been unhappy with him from the beginning. First, Clark appointed General Ridgway as deputy commander of 6th Corps; then on September 20, Dawley was replaced by General Lucas. The Americans tried a two-prong attack directly north through the ruins of Battapaglia and over the mountains toward Avellino by the 3rd Infantry Division while the 45th Infantry Division began a movement from the Ponte Sele bridge toward Teora, but they were really heading for Benevento.

The Germans opposed with rear guards of the 16th Panzer Division, while the 26th Panzer Division and the 29th Panzer Grenadier Division made their way northeast to stabilize the German line across the peninsula. As soon as the continuous line was firm, the 16th Panzer Division would be withdrawn for a rest because it had been fighting since the beginning of the Salerno invasion.

Now more Allied troops were coming in. The 78th Infantry Division and the 8th Indian Division of the British 5th Corps now began to land in the "heel of the boot" ports. The Eighth Army was moving slowly. Montgomery sent the 1st Canadian Infantry Division and the British 78th Infantry Division to the Foggia area. By September 29, the Germans had retreated out of the Gargarno Peninsula, but farther up the resistance was beginning to stiffen.

The Germans understood what the Allies were trying to do—take Rome—although they did not understand how low the project was on the overall Allied priority list and how limited the resources devoted to the task would be. So, on October 1, Hitler ordered Field Marshal Kesselring to base his plans on holding a front south of Rome. It might not be the Volturno Line but the Allies must be delayed in order to give the Todt Organization time to complete the defenses of the Gustav Line. As for the Gustav Line, it was the ideal defense position because the Italian peninsula was at its narrowest. By holding the Gustav Line, Kesselring would be keeping the Allies far from Germany, and Rome and its airfields would be safe. The weakness of the Gustav Line was its susceptibility to amphibious attack, but the Germans were sure that would not have to be dealt with in the winter months.

The Gustav Line ran along the Garigliano River and its tributary, the Rapido River, to Cassino and then up and over the steep Appenine Mountains until it reached the Sangro River on the coast of the Adriatic Sea. The main defensive positions were being built on the reverse slopes of the hills overlooking the river valleys. The riverbanks would be laced with minefields held by covering forces, with artillery sited to cover from behind the hills. In the Liri Valley, which stands in the shadow of Cassino, there were strong defenses on the low ground, too.

There were four possible approaches that the Allies might use to take Rome in the winter months. The first was Route 7, which ran up the west coast of Italy. It was easily blocked where it passed around the Aurunci Mountains near Gaeta, or in the Pontine marshes. The second was Route 6, past Cassino and up the valley of the Liri River to Frosinone and then to Rome. Here was the weakest sector of the Gustav Line, in the wide mouth of the Liri Valley, but it was protected by the Rapido River. Although that river was small in the winter, it could be fierce, and it was overlooked by two superb observation points: Monte Cassino to the north and Mount Majo to the south. Route 6 also possessed a number of natural defense positions closer to Naples.

The third approach was was up the Adriatic coast on Route 16. However, if the Allies went this way, they would have to get off the road at Pescara and then fight overland through the mountains on Route 5 to Avezzano and then to Rome. The fourth approach was by amphibious landing at the mouth of the Tiber River or farther north.

Kesselring believed that the Allies would choose the approach up the Liri Valley, though there was a chance they would move up Route 7 through the west-coast sector and then make an amphibious assault.

The German effort in October went into blocking Route 6 and Route 7 as the Todt Organization built the Gustav Line. The German Tenth Army had a delaying line, called the "Barbara Line," which ran along the ridge of the high ground between the Volturno and Garigliano Rivers and then over the Appenine Mountains to the Trigno River. General Hube had also found a covering position called the "Bernhardt Line," based on Mignano. This position was very strong, but it was too far forward and could not be worked in conjunction with the rest of the Gustav Line. The 14th Panzer Corps built that position into a series of strong points of considerable depth.

After the Battle of Salerno, it was time for the Hermann Goering Panzer Division to retreat through Naples, which it did, burning and wrecking the city as it went. By the time the British 7th Armoured Division moved into the city on October 1, its port, which once handled 8,000 tons of supply a day, could not handle 1,000 tons.

The Germans made no attempt to make a stand between Naples and the Volturno River. The first units of the 10th Corps reached the river on October 5. The British 46th Infantry Division moved into the coastal sector. The British 7th Armoured Division entered the center at Grazzanisi, and the British 56th Infantry Division entered Capua on 10th Corps' flank.

The American 6th Corps had tougher going through the hills to the east of Naples. The Germans were moving back slowly and setting many demolitions. The U.S. 3rd Infantry Division was first, and set up alongside the British 56th Infantry Division on October 7. The U.S. 34th Infantry Division, which had just arrived from North Africa, joined the American attack on Benevento on October 2 and then moved up the Calore River to its junction with the Volturno. The U.S. 45th Infantry Division moved up the east bank of the Calore until it was stopped by German defenses, which were designed as part of the extension of the Volturno Line.

The British Eighth Army resumed its advance up the Adriatic coast, led by the 13th Corps on Route 16 and the 1st Canadian Infantry Division on Route 17. The British 5th Corps was right behind them. The British 1st Airborne Division had gone into reserve, and its brigades were about to go back to England.

On the night of October 2–3, 13th Corps was assisted by a special landing at Termoli, in which the British surprised the German garrison and captured the headquarters, taking the town and port before it could be destroyed. By early afternoon, the landing force had linked up with the 78th Infantry Division and secured a crossing over the Biferno River. But the next day the Germans reacted severely because Kesselring had decided to hold Termini and the line to the Volturno until October 15. Thus developed the first major action since Salerno.

General von Vietinghoff sent the 16th Panzer Division out of reserve on a 95-mile march, and it came into action on October 4. Heavy attacks were made on the British 78th Infantry Division's bridgehead across the Biferno. The Luftwaffe was called to help, and for several hours the issue was in doubt. But during the night of October 5–6, a second brigade of the 78th landed in the port and a tank crossing was completed across the Biferno. The fighting resumed and the British drove the Germans out, and they retreated to the next river line: the Trigno.

On Route 17 the Canadians had to fight all the way in their advance on Vinchiaturo. By October 15, the gap between Montgomery's two divisions had grown so wide that he stopped and regrouped. The next objective of the Eighth Army was a road on the far side of the Trigno River, but Montgomery had to wait to start until his supplies were built up. He was then going to try a river crossing under fire. The Americans were already doing the same over the Volturno.

The dream of sunny southern weather was rudely shattered already. As the British moved around Mount Vesuvius, the autumn rains began to come down, and soon their tracks were marked in yellow mud. This meant real trouble in moving tanks and ammunition along the long route from Taranto. With the combination of mud and the damage wrought to the roads by German demolition of bridges and culverts, the roads became virtually impassable. The wise move would have been to wait until the rains stopped, but the Allies were in a hurry, and they churned on through the sticky mud until they bogged down. Then they had to wait to dry out, and they started all over again.

Four major roads ran north from Naples toward Rome: Routes 6 and 7 on the west and Routes 16 and 17 on the Adriatic coast. They were linked by three important lateral roads. The Allies headed for these.

During the first ten days of October, the Germans deployed all their divisions along the Volturno–Trigno Line; the only reserve Kesselring kept was the 2nd Parachute Division near Rome. Hitler was now intrigued by Kesselring's success in slowing the Allies, and so two more divisions were about to be committed from Rommel's force.

The U.S. Fifth Army reached the Volturno with six divisions abreast. Only the 36th Infantry and the 82nd Airborne Divisions were in reserve. On the night of October 12–13, General Clark ordered a simultaneous attack along the whole Fifth Army front. The Allied commanders were united in their belief that the Germans would not tarry at the Volturno but, instead, would hurry northward to Rome and the Appenine Line.

The river itself at this time of year was 200–300 feet across with no apparent fords. The countryside was so flooded and muddy that the convoys had to stay on the roads. Where there was a possible ford and room for assault, the Germans were strongly entrenched. After many surveys, the British opted for an assault across the river between the river mouth and Cancello. This way the army could make use of the naval artillery from offshore. The 46th Infantry Division would attack with two brigades. The 7th Armoured Division would cross at Grazzanisi and the 56th Infantry Division would cross at Capua. The 7th and the

56th would make feint attacks, but would be prepared to pursue them if the opportunity arose.

In the U.S. sector, the advance offered easier going. The river was narrower and the ground drier. The 3rd Panzer Division was not as strong as the Hermann Goering Panzer Division and the 15th Panzer Division that the British faced. It was composed of *Grossdeutschlanders*—men from the Eastern European countries—who, Hitler held, were all Germans. But many of them did not think so, and so the division had already gained a reputation for instability. The American crossings would be considerably easier than the British, running from Triflisco north.

The crossings began on the night of October 12, just after dark. The American 34th and 3rd Infantry Divisions established bridgeheads, which they expanded during the next 48 hours. But in the British sector only the 46th Infantry Division got its two brigades safely across and established. The 7th Armoured and the 56th Infantry Divisions then ceased their efforts, and the effort was devoted to the 46th area, where the equipment for movement across the river was limited. Fields full of nonmetallic mines, which had to be individually handled, slowed up the British advance for two days. On October 14, the division was making slow progress against the 15th Panzer Grenadier Division, but the Americans had made a more spectacular success and were building a 30-ton bridge at Triflisco. They moved the boundary east so the British 56th could cross this bridge and come up on the U.S. 3rd's left flank.

By this time the date was October 15, and the German troops had fulfilled Kesselring's orders to hold the Volturno until that date. So the situation eased and the British began to move more quickly, and by October 19, the Germans had withdrawn skillfully and the whole Volturno battle position was in Allied hands. Further, the fighting was brisk and the Germans resisted every foot of the way west of the Appenines. On the eastern side, the British Eighth Army was having the same experience. They could make no substantial progress against the 16th Panzer Grenadier Division, which was holding them up at Trigno. Montgomery would have to make a major effort, which he was not prepared to do until more troops and more supplies came to him, and that meant the end of October. It was apparent to Clark and Alexander that the Germans were going to continue this line-by-line resistance, and that they were much stronger than anyone involved in the Allied planning had expected. The first results of the Trident Conference decision to withdraw those seven divisions from the Mediterranean were now being fully felt. The Allies had chosen to march up the Italian "boot," and here, on the Volturno, they could see that they did not have the resources available to do so. They threatened to bog down altogether for the winter, which was precisely what the Germans wanted.

14

A Series of Delaying Actions

The main objective of the German Tenth Army was to gain time, to fight a series of delaying actions, using men and materials sparingly, and to inflict maximum casualties on the Allies and delay their passage until the German winter line was set up. The main purpose of the Allies was to reach the German defensive positions before they could be completed and organized for battle.

Three roads immediately beyond the Volturno River decided the tactics of the American 6th Corps. Each division had its own road: the 3rd Infantry Division a dirt track that wound around the mountains to Dragoni; The 34th Infantry Division a road that also led to Dragoni; and the 45th Infantry Division a road on the eastern side of the Upper Volturno that led to the Piedimonte d'Alife. The Germans had already strewn these roads with mines and booby traps and had blown all the bridges and culverts.

The Americans began to move on October 14, with the 3rd Infantry Division heading in a new direction, to the northeast. The 3rd sent troops to capture Liberi, which was four miles from the position that day. The ultimate objective at this point was Dragoni. The troops moved out and, in less than a mile, encountered resistance stiff enough to stop their tanks at the village of Cisterna. Colonel Harry Sherman sent another battalion, which moved that night, and by the morning of October 15 had reached a point a mile north of Cisterna. Sherman committed his 1st Battalion that morning on the right, and it tore through the village of Strangola-galli, then attacked to outflank the Germans at Cisterna. But the Germans, having delayed the advance for a day, were gone. Sherman then sent his 1st Battalion against Liberi, but it was stopped by intense fire. On the left the 2nd Battalion moved ahead until it was stopped after midnight outside Villa, not yet reaching its objective. The 3rd Battalion then was committed again on the left, but it ran into strong fire and then was counterattacked, as were the other two battalions.

This situation demanded reinforcement, which Sherman got from the 3rd Battalion of the 15th Infantry Division by General Truscott's order, and he prepared to attack. When he attacked that morning, there was no opposition; and at 10 A.M., they were in Liberi. Again the Germans were ahead of him, having withdrawn from Liberi to another defensive position. So, he released the reinforcing battalion.

On they went toward Dragoni. Just before noon the troops of the 1st Battalion hit rifle, machine-gun, tank, and artillery fire: another German-prepared position of defense. The battalion was pinned down the rest of the day. The 2nd Battalion moved into the hills to bypass the Germans, which they did, and returned to the road. They moved forward but struck another strong point and took to the hills again to avoid this roadblock. Later in the afternoon, Truscott told Sherman he expected Sherman's troops to be in Dragoni by dawn on October 18.

The 3rd Battalion of the 7th Infantry Division then attacked just before dark and by midnight reached high ground overlooking Dragoni. Patrols went into the village. At dawn on October 18, they moved across the Liberi–Dragoni Road. The 2nd Battalion came up to high ground west of Dragoni. The 1st Battalion came up and General Lucas instructed the regiment to remain where they were. Truscott protested but Sherman was ordered to wait for the 34th Infantry Division to come up abreast of his position. Truscott complimented Sherman on his leapfrogging, which had been very effective. But it was hard, and the men were worn out after four days of fighting to get a few miles of territory along their road. On their left, the 15th Infantry Division had much the same experience, in advancing ten miles against small groups of Germans who had defended very skillfully, forcing them to outflanking movements. By the time the Americans had established fields of fire and arranged for mortars and artillery, the Germans had moved on to the next position, and it all had to be done over again.

So who was containing whom? The Allies had set out to contain the Germans and draw many units south, as their job in connection with the overall strategy of getting through the winter, taking Rome, and then moving the center of military operations to the beaches of Normandy and the south of France. But the Germans were making a strong defense of the south, with the troops at hand, which was not altogether how the Allies had planned it. And the casualties were high for what they were getting. In the short advance that took five days, the 3rd Infantry Division suffered 500 casualties. Next to them, the 34th Infantry Division had the same sort of experience to capture the neighboring road center of Alvignano, two miles away. On another road, the 34th Infantry Division's 123rd Infantry Regiment made a run to try to entrap some German units crossing the Upper Volturno. They could hear the Germans moving. On October 18, they were ordered to seize the bridge near the town. The 2nd and 3rd Battalions attacked and the 1st Battalion covered their flank along the river. When sounds of firing indicated a firefight up ahead, the 1st Battalion commander decided to cross to the east bank of the river and bypass the fight and drive to the objective. But in crossing, the men ran into fast deep water, which slowed them down; only half of the battalion made it across. A patrol was sent to find a shallow ford and did, but it was near dark before they got across and began pushing toward the Dragoni bridge. It was midnight when they reached the bridge, and at that point the Germans set off their prepared charges and destroyed the structure. The Americans then improvised a roadway, and brought up their antitank guns and jeeps and the three-quarter-ton trucks loaded with ammunition. They met the other two battalions. But they had not trapped any German troops in this difficult maneuver. On the night of October 19, the 34th Infantry Division reached Piedimonte d'Alife, which had been bombed by B-25s a week earlier. It was a forest of ruin, carefully booby-trapped by the Germans.

Meanwhile, the 45th Infantry Division captured Monte Acero near the confluence of the Volturno and the Calore Rivers, and had driven up the eastern part of the Upper Volturno. But progress was slowed by the same sort of stubborn German resistance. General Middleton asked for air support missions several times, but the weather was so bad the planes could not manage them. They wanted to take Faiccio, which dominated the ground beyond Monte Acero, but German tanks and Luftwaffe attacks prevented it. Only when the Germans abandoned Faiccio on October 15 did the Americans move. It took the division four more days to reach Piedimonte d'Alife, and there the planned advance of the division ended.

The 133rd Infantry Battalion was then sent into the narrowing Volturno Valley toward Sant'Angelo d'Alife, five miles farther. But then the 100th Infantry Battalion (the Nisei Japanese–Americans, who would become the most decorated unit in the U.S. Army) started, they were caught in open flats not far from Piedimonte d'Alife. From prepared positions in the foothills of the Matese Mountains, the Germans opened fire with rifles, machine guns, artillery, and *Nebelwerfer* rockets—a new weapon to the Americans that they called "screaming meemies." The heavy fire disorganized the battalion, which erupted in temporary panic, and the regimental advance stopped right there.

Two artillery and mortar battalions were brought up and they tried to return the fire. However, they could not pinpoint the German positions, and no matter how hard they fought, the German guns were not stopped. The Germans had tanks as well, and they could not be dislodged. The 122nd Infantry Regiment tried for three days, without any success at all. Then on the fourth day, they started again. The Germans had pulled out, and they walked into Sant'Angelo d'Alife and Raviscanina, without opposition. But in a week, the 34th Infantry Division suffered 350 casualties.

Meanwhile, the British 10th Corps was fighting in the coastal area—an area of grainfields, orchards, vineyards, and olive groves, which was cut by drainage ditches, streams, deep ravines, and sunken roads. A dozen miles north of the Volturno a hill mass rises from the coastal plain topped by Monte Massico and Monte Santa Croce. This high ground commanded the approach of the corps from the south. To the northeast were greater eminences: Monte Camino, Monte de la Difensa, and Monte Maggiore.

The British 46th Infantry Division, working north, reached a canal four miles north of the Volturno but was stopped there by strong opposition for three days. It managed to force a crossing on the evening of October 18. Meanwhile, the British 7th Armoured Division bridged the Volturno on October 16 and advanced slowly across wet ground. The British 56th Infantry Division fought along the Triflisco Ridge to get to Route 6 and Teano. Some of the ridge crests were so narrow that only a single platoon could be moved out at a time. Supplies sometimes had to be carried by the men. It was slow going, but by October 22, the division was ready to make an attack down into the Teano Valley. But, first, General McCreery shifted divisions, putting the 7th into territory more suitable for armored operations.

On October 30, McCreery launched his attack, hoping to catch the Germans off guard. The 46th moved through Cascano Pass and took the Sessa Aurunca area; the 7th cleared the region as far as the Lower Garigliano River. But they did not catch the Germans off balance. The action had consisted only of eliminating machine-gun positions because it was apparent that the 14th Panzer Corps had abandoned the Barbara Line.

The 10th Corps then turned to the hills to the north: Monte Camino, Monte de la Difensa, and Monte Maggiore. This mountain barrier extended eight miles between Cascano Pass and the Mignano Gap and was the way to Cassino, which was 12 miles beyond. To make a drive possible to Cassino, 10th Corps would first have to take possession of those three high peaks on the left of Route 6, while 6th Corps took the high ground on the right. So it would be more mountain warfare.

During the last ten days of October, the Fifteenth Army Group staff carried out a review of the military situation. Eleven Allied divisions were attacking nine German divisions in country that gave every advantage to the defense. In northern Italy, there were another eight German divisions.

The Allies were limited in the forces they could use in Italy. There was not enough shipping, and it had to be shared among several tasks, including the establishment of air bases in the Foggia area, particularly for establishment of the U.S. Army 15th Air Force, which would be a strategic bombing force.

So what was the mission in Italy? It was to draw German divisions away from Russia and northwest Europe. The only way to do this, said General Alexander, was to attack. As General Eisenhower put it in a message to the Combined Chiefs of Staff: "If we can keep him [Hitler] on his heels until early spring, then the more divisions he uses in a counter offensive against us the better it will be for Overlord and then it makes little difference what happens to us."[11]

So the Allied leaders set about planning a series of offensives to bring Rome into Allied hands by Christmas. In fact the leaders in the Mediterranean were taking on unrealistic goals, given their resources.

Eisenhower sent a request to the Combined Chiefs of Staff for a delay in the return of shipping that was supposed to be returned to England in November. When that request was received, the balloon went up suddenly. When General Marshall saw that message, it aroused all the fears he had been nursing since the Mediterranean adventure began: that Churchill would somehow manage to foul up the plans for Operation Overlord and divert the Allied effort to the Mediterranean. In Washington it was apparent that the plan to reach Rome in eight weeks was totally unrealistic because it meant that the forces would have to advance twice the distance they had advanced in seven weeks from Salerno to the crossing of the Volturno, and there was a major German defense line that had to be reached before they could go for Rome. But the Combined Chiefs gave the Mediterranean theater an extension of shipping until December 15, much to Marshall's dismay. He could see the Mediterranean tail beginning to wag the Atlantic dog. The autumn rains had broken and the Germans now proposed to withdraw their mobile divisions and replace them with infantry. General von Senger, in command of the 15th Panzer Corps, put his 94th Infantry Division along the high ground overlooking the Garigliano River. Four German divisions in the line and the five in reserve were now opposed by only six American and British divisions, which gave the Germans a definite edge in strength.

The first attempt of the Allies to breach the Bernhardt Line was a failure. The American 3rd Infantry Division and the British 56th Infantry Division attacked Monte Camino on November 5. After ten days they had gotten nowhere; the 15th Panzer Grenadier Division had beaten them solidly. The U.S. 45th and 34th Infantry Divisions did better above Venafro, until the Germans reinforced the area. Then it became apparent that the Germans had fought the Allies to a standstill in this area. Only a combined Eighth Army and Fifth Army offensive, well planned and executed, could dislodge the Germans. So General Alexander told General Clark to stop his offensive and regroup.

The Eighth Army opened its offensive across the Trigno River on the night of November 2. They were supported by the naval forces off the coast and the Desert Air Force. They made progress to Isertia, but then were stopped. The 78th Infantry Division reached Sangro on November 8, but could not get much farther.

It was time for the combined offensive of the Eighth and Fifth Armies. The offensive would be a one–two punch. Montgomery would attack the Germans at Sangro, and when they moved their reserves to meet the threat, then General Clark would strike the Bernhardt Line, in a major attempt to break through.

On the German side, Kesselring had won Hitler's support for his plan of holding south of Rome. It was now necessary to organize a new command for Italy to bring the effort of defense into one headquarters. Rommel's headquarters was to be dissolved and a new Fourteenth Army headquarters was to be established under General Oberst Eberhard von Mackensen. Both this organization and von Vietinghoff's Tenth Army would come under Army Group C, which was the title of Kesselring's new command. For a time it seemed that the command would be given to Rommel, but Hitler changed his mind at the last moment and sent Rommel to France to organize the forces for defense from the Allied attack across the channel. Thus, Hitler showed his understanding of the basic Allied strategy: to fight in Italy and then to switch the major effort to France. But what this meant in Italy for the Allies was a unified command, with Kesselring now free to move troops anywhere in the theater that he wished.

So the stage was now set for the Battle for Rome, with the Germans unified in their defense, and the Allies becoming unified in their assault.

15

The Advance Is Stopped

General Montgomery was building up for a great assault in the tradition he knew—the set battle—with plenty of reserves and plenty of fire-power. For weeks he had been planning this triumph to reach the Avezzano area, from which he could then march on Rome. There were four approaches, but the obvious one—along the coast road—was the best by far because it could handle all the traffic necessary. The other three roads were limited in traffic capability but would also be used, albeit by fewer troops, to keep the Germans from lumping all their reserves on the coast road.

The Sangro River, which runs on a wide gravel bed, is normally only a few feet deep. The Germans decided not to defend the riverbank; instead, they put their main line of resistance on high ground, three miles north of the river.

The main feature of the defense line was the Li Colli Ridge, which runs parallel to the river, from the village of Fossacesia (near the beach) through Mozzagrogna and Santa Maria to Casoli. The line then swung away from the river to follow Route 84 to Castel di Sangro and Alfre-dena. In the hills were the infantry, on the flat was the 16th Panzer Division in reserve. In the mountains were the men of the 1st Parachute Corps, in country so rugged they used pack animals for supply. In all, four German divisions held a 40-mile front against five Allied divisions. The Allies had the advantage of air, artillery, and tank superiority, but the Germans had the advantage of terrain, which obviated much of the Allied advantage.

The 13th Corps was to carry out a deception program, at which the British were masters. A pretense was made that Montgomery was moving his headquarters to 13th Corps. Ammunition dumps and supply dumps were shown openly, while those on the coast were concealed. The British 1st Airborne Division, which was awaiting transportation to England, would stage elaborate preparations for an amphibious landing at Pescara, and the Royal Navy would bombard Pescara.

But the real assault was to be by the British 5th Corps with the 78th Infantry and 8th Indian Divisions breaking through the German line. Fifth Corps would attack Mozzagrogna and then Fossacesia, supported by tanks and airpower. This was decided when it was learned that the Germans had left the steep slopes up to the Li Colli Ridge uncovered by antitank guns in the belief that the terrain was too steep for tanks. General Alfrey, who commanded the British 5th Corps, thought the tanks could make a successful surprise attack here. Of course they depended on the river remaining fordable and the approaches firm, which meant "keep the rain away."

The New Zealand Division was to make a silent attack along the demolished bridge site near Casoli on Route 81, while the 13th Corps would make noisy preparations that were intended to confuse the enemy. The New Zealanders would move into position behind the 19th Indian Brigade.

Preliminary operations were to begin on the night of November 19 and the main attack was to be made on November 20. However, the weather took a hand. It began to rain on November 15 and kept raining. By November 16, the river was too high for wading, and the riverbanks were too soft for tanks. It seemed that the attack would have to be postponed; but on November 19, the river began to fall, the rain stopped, and so the preliminary operations were continued, although the river was still too high for the New Zealanders to move across. On November 20, however, it rained and rained, and every effort had to be made to ferry troops to the forward units of 78th Infantry Division, which was stranded on the far bank without support. For several days, all effort was directed to securing the bridgehead. The hope of a tank attack on Li Colli Ridge waned when, on November 23, the river submerged three bridges, which had been built by the engineers. So a new plan had to be laid, one that did not depend on tanks.

The New Zealand attack started, but stealth had to be discarded because of the weather, and full air and artillery support was called for. The 19th Indian Brigade was sent to take some high ground overlooking the New Zealand fording places. They took the ground but were then cut off by rising floodwaters behind them. The bad weather affected everything: patrolling was cut down and the British commanders suffered from lack of up-to-date intelligence about the enemy.

On November 21, Hitler appointed Field Marshal Kesselring as commander in chief of the southwest. Kesselring visited the front and ordered the defense at Mozzagrogna to be strengthened, so the 16th Panzer Division moved a regiment to the sector opposite the New Zealanders. The reinforcing unit—the 90th Panzer Grenadier Division—was starting to arrive and the 26th Panzer Division was coming up to relieve the 16th Panzer Division. Thus, the weather had played into the German's hands, because if the Allied attack had taken place as planned, the Germans would have had relatively inexperienced troops in the line but now they would have elements of three experienced mobile divisions as well.

After the flood of November 23, the river varied from day to day. In the air, the Desert Air Force flew 400 sorties a day against the enemy defenses. All the British divisions fought the mud to try to build up bridgeheads on the far side of the river, so they would be ready to hit when the ground dried. On November 27, 100 tanks paved the way, and that evening, the 8th Indian Division took Mozzagrogna, but the 26th Panzer Division later drove them out. On the night of November 28, Alfrey thought it would still be possible to run tanks along the Li Colli Ridge. And so a plan was made for the Indians to take Mozzagrogna again during the night and then for British 78th Infantry Division to mount a combined tank and infantry attack on November 29. The British had some luck with the weather; it remained fine and the air force and artillery were able to give full support. They put on a show that had the Germans complaining that they never saw such bombardment, even in Russia.

The Indians captured Mozzagrogna, and the tanks climbed the ridge and turned left and took Santa Maria. The next day the attack was renewed and went north along the ridge to capture Fossacesia and by nightfall the 78th had cleared the ridge all the way to the Adriatic coast.

The New Zealand attack, started on November 28, began slowly because it was hampered by accurate Luftwaffe attacks on the tanks and vehicles. But on November 29, the Germans began to withdraw northward, and on November 30, the New Zealanders were approaching Castel Frentano, having given the German 65th Panzer Division a severe drubbing, knocking out of action the division commander and one regimental commander and taking 1,000 prisoners. Other German elements came to the rescue and established a new line of defense on high ground overlooking the Moro River. The New Zealanders pressed on from Castel Frentano and attacked Orsogna, the next dominating place blocking the road to Chieti. They reached the center of the town, but were then driven out by the 26th Panzer Division, and had to fall back. That flurry of attack marked the high point of the Allied attacks on the German line.

German historians have said that after defeating the 65th Panzer Division the New Zealanders were in a position to break through to Pescara, but they were stopped by Montgomery's timidity. British historians say that conditions were such that the Germans had the advantage of being able to bring in fresh troops. The British superiority lay in its armor, artillery, and airpower, all of which were hampered by the weather. They could expect the weather to worsen and the difficulties of the roads to slow the supply of ammunition. Besides, said the British historians, Montgomery would have been unwise to concentrate troops ahead of the Sangro River until he had an all-weather supply line across the river. It took his engineers until December 6 to build a flood-proof bridge.

All this, of course, is begging the issue, which is that Montgomery failed to break through the German line because he would not move when opportunity presented itself. To him there was no gamble worth the effort in war. Here, as in North Africa, he insisted on having superiority in every way before he would attack. One might even say that the conditions under which he would attack almost obviated the need for a commander. Certainly a Rommel or a Patton would have exploited the opportunity that faced Montgomery that day. But not Montgomery.

After being stopped at Orsogno, Montgomery reorganized his force, putting the 1st Canadian Infantry Division forward as his striking force and the 78th Infantry Division into a less-demanding position on the left flank in the Appenines. The Canadians attacked across the Moro on December 8, hoping then to turn east and capture the port of Ortona, but the 90th Panzer Grenadier Division stopped them for 12 days. They put patrols in Ortona on December 20, but that was the best they could do. Two more attacks on Ortona failed. The Germans did not pull back; they held their line. The struggle developed into an extended street fight, with the German 3rd Parachute Regiment defending against the 2nd Canadian Brigade. The Canadians fought their way from house to house. As soon as they took a building, it had to be occupied or the Germans would infiltrate it again and the whole process would have to be done over. The fighting in Ortona was so close that artillery support was impossible. In one house a whole Canadian platoon was destroyed by a time bomb, and in another a German patrol of paratroopers was wiped out by a Canadian booby trap. The Canadians fought like tigers, and on December 28 they fought their way through the town; but by that time, the Germans had (typically) withdrawn and the 3rd Parachute Regiment was waiting on the other side of the Riccio River to stop any further Allied advance.

During the last week of December, General Montgomery reviewed the military situation. He advised General Alexander that the offensive should be stopped on the Adriatic side of Italy because there was no hope, he said, of breaking through to Rome that winter. (In Washington, General Marshall had known this from the beginning.) His biggest concern was ammunition for the future. Alexander agreed that Montgomery should stop on the Adriatic side of Italy and told him to settle down to a holding action. On December 30, having missed the chance for breakthrough in Italy, Montgomery left for England to take over the Twenty-first Army Group scheduled for the Normandy invasion in the spring.

On the other side of the Italian peninsula, General Clark spent the last of November regrouping and prepared for the celebrated coordinated offensive. As happened with Montgomery, bad weather delayed the start of operations, and Montgomery's delay made further delays for Clark. He had lost the 82nd Airborne Division to the claims of Operation Overlord, but he acquired the II Corps from Sicily, that is, what was left of it. Two divisions had been removed to England: the U.S. 1st Armored Division and several polyglot organizations consisting of the 1st Special Service Corps (mixed American–Canadian Commando types), the French–North African 2nd Moroccan Division, and the 1st Italian Motorized Group.

Clark's plan was to grind up the Bernhardt Line from the south. First, they would take Monte Camino. Then they would take Monte Lungo and Monte Samoucro, and then they would exploit the Liri Valley.

The first action was called Operation Raincoat, and it involved the attack on Monte Camino. It was preceded by a number of deception measures to take the German attention away from what was really happening. Dummy tanks and guns were established near the Garigliano River. Landing craft were loaded with troops in Naples to bother the Germans on the seaward side and 6th Corps made a great show of movement on the other end of the Fifth Army front.

The attack itself was carried out by the British 46th and 56th Infantry Divisions and the Special Service Force and the U.S. 36th Infantry Division. In the bombardment of the 15th Panzer Grenadier Division positions on the mountain, some 4,000 tons of ammunition were fired, but with virtually no effect. The artillery bombardment was withstood by the stout German dugouts; and the aerial bombardment was totally inaccurate.

So the infantry had to virtually go it alone climbing the mountain. They fought for each position until the Germans fell back, and then went on. It was hard moving ammunition and supplies by hand against determined opposition, and so Monte Camino did not fall until December to the British 56th Infantry Division. It took four more days to clear up the western slope. British 10th Corps did most of the fighting and suffered heavily, with 1,000 casualties in the ten-day battle. The Germans resisted so stoutly that some of them got left behind and had to abandon their heavy equipment to the rising river and swim for it to get away.

The second phase of the Fifth Army battle was the attack on Monte Samoucro, which began on December 7 by the U.S. 36th Infantry Division. At first the going was easy, but then the 29th Panzer Grenadier Division, which had been suppressed in the beginning, counterattacked and stopped the American advance. That same day the Italian group attacked Monte Lungo and was driven back. A new attack by II Corps carried the mountain by December 17 and both mountains were in American hands, but the casualties had been very high; and the 36th was exhausted. They had reached the village of San Pietro, overlooking Route 6, but could not get to the road because they were stopped by German positions at San Vittore. These would have to be captured before Route 6 could be used for advance.

To the north, 6th Corps was stopped by an Austrian unit—the 44th Hoch and Deutsch Meister Infantry Division—which had been fighting in Stalingrad not so long before. To its north was the 5th Mountain Division, which had been fighting at Leningrad. Neither of these divisions was experienced in mountain fighting and neither were the Americans, but when the Moroccans came up, it was different. They were experts in mountain warfare and they forced the Germans back toward the Gustav Line. But it was too late.

For months, Generals Eisenhower and Clark had been thinking about an amphibious operation. Eisenhower had been stunned by a remark made by General Marshall at the time of the Sicily invasion that he showed very little resilience and imagination, and he had been fretting about it ever since. The operation that he and Clark wanted to carry out was an end run around the Axis lines of defense. Ultimately, that fall, it had settled on the Anzio area. The problem was shipping, because the Allies had to return to Britain 56 British LSTs and 12 American LSTs destined for Operation Overlord. They had managed to keep them until now, and Eisenhower asked to keep them until January 15, in anticipation of making the Anzio landing in December. The Combined Chiefs agreed because they hoped to continue the Mediterranean pressure on the Germans, but Stalin was objecting to this. Meeting at Cairo and then at Tehran, the British and Americans were reacting to Stalin's insistence that troops were being drained from southern Europe and sent to the Russian Front. He wanted this stopped by the invasion of France, north and south. Churchill was specifically upset by this threat to his Mediterranean hopes, and the Americans and British high commands hoped that perhaps Clark could bring off the landing at Anzio in time to use the shipping before it was taken away, and solve a lot of their political problems with Stalin. But first the Fifth Army had to advance some 50 miles from Mignano to Frosinone. On December 18, Clark decided his progress had not been rapid enough for him to reach the entrance to the Liri Valley in time to do any good. He had wanted to make an assault on Anzio before that time, but now he said it could not be done in the next few months.

And so the Allies were stopped in southern Italy. The Germans had done a masterful job of rear guarding, delaying the Allied drive at almost every crossing, and stabilizing the front for the winter. The Allied armies were exhausted by the mud and the rain, their losses were growing, and their gains were too small. The war in Italy threatened to bog down into the type of trench warfare that had characterized the earlier European struggle during the period 1914–1918. So the Allied offensive stopped, and the two armies settled down. The American 36th Infantry Division was exhausted, and the 34th Infantry Division replaced it in the Fifth Army line at the end of December. Other changes were made as well. The French sent in a second division, and the 45th Infantry Division, which was also exhausted, was moved out for a rest. At the same time the Germans were making a change: pulling out the tired 29th Panzer Grenadier Division and replacing it with the 44th Panzer Grenadier Division.

General Lucas's 6th Corps was pulled out, and he settled down to prepare for a new move: the amphibious operation that was to carry the Fifth Army all the way to Rome.

So Monte Lungo, San Pietro, and Monte Samoucro had been captured at heavy cost in material and casualties. The absence of reserves had prevented the Americans from following up.

One thing had been proved in the recent months of fighting. The Germans had revised their opinion of the American soldier, although British General Alexander still had his reservations. A German military newspaper had this to say about their new opponents from North America: "The Americans use quasi Indian tactics. They search for the boundary lines between battalions or regiments, they look for gaps between our strong points, they look for the steepest mountain passages (guided by treacherous civilians), they infiltrate through these passages with a patrol, a platoon at first, mostly at dusk. At night they reinforce the infiltrated units, and in the morning they are often in the rear of the German unit which is being attacked from behind, or also from the flanks simultaneously."

And so the year 1943 came to an end. The plan for the Allied amphibious landing, which had almost, but not quite, come off in 1943, was delayed until 1944. But it would not be carried out by General Eisenhower. He was being detached from command in the Mediterranean and moved to England to take command of the Allied Forces that would be fighting in France in the spring. He was replaced by General Henry M. Wilson as supreme commander in the Mediterranean.

The campaign in Italy would go on, and General Marshall urged General Clark to get to Rome in the spring, before the Cross Channel Attack was launched. In fact, the plans called for Rome to be captured by February 1944.

All these changes were surmounted by one other. The control of the armies in the Mediterranean would now pass to the British Chiefs of Staff. The policy planning would move across the Atlantic into the hands of Prime Minister Churchill. The Mediterranean was now becoming, once again, a British show.

The first example of the change was the restored Anzio Operation. Yes, having been laid aside by Eisenhower and Clark as impossible to complete in time to meet the shipping requirements, when the British took over, the Anzio plan was brushed off and reconsidered. The deciding factor was Churchill's active involvement after the conferences of Cairo and Tehran. He arrived in Tunis with pneumonia, spent a week recovering, and then began putting his hand on operations in the Italian campaign. "The stagnation of the whole campaign on the Italian front is becoming scandalous," he informed the British Chiefs of Staff, and demanded action.

As the year ended, Churchill reluctantly gave up one of his favorite plans: luring Turkey into the war on the Allied side. He also gave up hope that the Americans could be persuaded into broadening operations in the Mediterranean and, thus, concentrated his efforts on capturing Rome. To do this the Mediterranean command would have to keep the LSTs for an additional month.

Churchill spent Christmas Eve talking with his leading British officers—General Wilson, General Alexander, and Chief Air Marshal Tedder—about the Anzio Operation. They told him two divisions would be needed in the landing. They had to keep those LSTs for another three weeks.

On Christmas morning, they brought Admiral Cunningham into the discussion as well as General Eisenhower, although General Eisenhower kept his mouth shut. At the end of it, Churchill sent Roosevelt a message asking to keep the LSTs until after the Anzio Operation could be launched.

And so Anzio became a fact, with everyone's knowledge that it faced many troubles: with shipping, with distances between the landing and the Fifth Army front, and with the very great German strength in Italy. It was, as everyone agreed, a very hazardous venture, but Churchill would have his way, or most of his way. He made one last stab at trying to scuttle the scheduled landings in the south of France the next year, and failed. But at least he had Rome almost in his grasp.

16

The Rapido River Fiasco

During the last two months of 1943, the Allies assaulting the Bernhardt Line in Italy had suffered high casualties and had been pinned down much of the time. Field Marshal Kesselring's defense had been superb, and the Allies had been sucked into a fight that sapped their resources and their military strength. Even Hitler, who had not believed it possible to defend southern Italy, had been impressed by Kesselring's success in reducing the Allied drive to a snail's pace.

With the passing of control of the Italian campaign into British hands in December 1943, it was evident that some strong Allied action would be taken soon, because Prime Minister Churchill was adamant: "We must have the big Rome amphibious operation. In no case can we sacrifice Rome for the Riviera."[12]

But when the Fifth Army's Chief of Staff Major General Alfred M. Gruenther went to Algiers at the end of the year, there was serious consideration of scrapping the Anzio Operation and the race for Rome because it might interfere with the invasion of the south of France. The strongest argument against Anzio was that the Mediterranean command would lose those LSTs held back from England, and that there would be no shipping available after that to resupply the Anzio beachhead once it was established. Thus, the success or failure of the Anzio landings would depend on the main body of the Fifth Army and its ability to advance in time to link up with the Anzio contingent and then continue a general advance. The risks of the Anzio Operation were so great that many officers questioned its feasibility. Even General Clark, who had at first been enthusiastic, lost his feeling that the Anzio Operation was possible and wrote in his diary that he believed it would be cancelled. But he did not want to cancel it, and so he began a process of justification that would make Anzio—the Shingle Operation—seem reasonable. He intended to attack with the greatest possible strength in the Liri Valley several days in advance of Operation Shingle. His objective was to draw the maximum number of enemy reserves to that front and take care of them there.

The Anzio scheme had appeared to be very attractive earlier, when everyone in the Mediterranean believed that the shipping would be available to support the operation. It had captured Clark's imagination and also General Alexander's. The news that the shipping absolutely must be returned to England early in February came as a shock, but by this time the commanders were so set on Anzio that they began justifying all sorts of shortcuts.

Churchill hoped to see a thrust toward the Alban Hills, which would cut the German lines of communication and put Rome in Allied hands. Alexander saw the operation in terms of a one–two punch, with the main body of the Fifth Army being his right hand, which would hit the Gustav Line and draw Kesselring's reserves south. As soon as these reserves were committed to defense of the Liri Valley, the Shingle Operation would begin at Anzio, and the loss of strength and fear of being cut off should unsettle the German divisions in front of the Fifth Army and lead to breakthrough.

Clark remembered what had happened at Salerno very clearly and so his orders to General Lucas were to seize the beachhead and hold it—no talk here about rapid exploitation. Lucas was worried about the inevitable counterattacks because of what had happened at Salerno. He planned a buildup at Anzio and then a thrust toward the Alban Hills when he was strong enough. The British would hold the left side of the beachhead, and they would direct their effort along the Anzio–Albano Road toward Campoleone. The Americans would hold the right and would thrust at Cisterna on Route 7. But before any breakout could happen, the perimeter must be secure, based on the Moletta River and the Mussolini Canal. The gap between would be strewn with minefields.

Field Marshal Alexander knew that the attempts to draw the German reserves out could not prevent the Germans from building up its forces around the beachhead quicker than the Allies could land troops from the sea, owing to their limited shipping. So he had to rely on the air forces to attack Kesselring's communications and destroy any German columns on the road. It was obvious that the whole operation could be endangered by bad weather, but supplies for 37 days were to be landed immediately. And to speed the operation along, fully loaded lorries were to be embarked in the LSTs. They would land, unload their supplies at the dumps, and return empty by the same ships to Naples where the process would be repeated. This rescued handling time, and time was the essential factor here. Obviously, with shipping so complicated that Alexander could not expect to have adequate reinforcement by sea, this was going to be very much a gamble, the sort that General Montgomery, for example, would have never entertained. The success of Anzio would depend on the other troops of the Fifth Army fighting their way 75 miles up the coast. Success in this struggle would depend on the Fifth Army's ability to enter the Liri Valley and hasten across its broad flat plain. But access to the valley was blocked to the Rapido River and so an attack across the Rapido became absolutely essential to the success of the new Anzio landings. All this was decided on January 8, with the operation to be carried out a scant two weeks later.

The risk was so great that Alexander insisted on a mixed British–American operation so that the dangers would be equally shared and there would be no question of a British commander putting an American force at hazard.

What was planned was an attack that would pin down German forces and prevent them from moving against the Anzio beachhead. It would be more useful if it attracted additional German forces, which would keep them away from Anzio. It would be completely successful if the troops were able to break through to the Liri Valley and drive beyond Frosinone to link up with the Anzio beachhead. Before the troops could advance over 80 miles of broken ground to the Bernhardt Line to get to the Rapido, they must take San Vittore, La Chiaia, Monte Majo, Cervaro, Cedro Hill, Monte Pochia, and Monte Trocchio. And they had to do this and cross the Rapido before the amphibious troops landed at Anzio.

After several hard months of fighting, the Allied troops were very tired; but by making a determined effort, they managed to move forward during the first two weeks of January, albeit with very heavy losses. The divisions were not only tired but they had lost about 26,000 men, since the crossing of the Volturno, 16,000 of them while breaking through the Bernhardt Line. Now they were facing the Gustav Line. One reason was that the Germans, having completed work on the Gustav Line, had moved back to that line. By January 11, Kesselring had begun the reorganization of the German front. Seven German divisions were settling in at their fixed defensive positions.

On January 9, the 6th Corps left the line and retired to Salerno for a practice landing before sailing for Anzio. The British 1st Infantry Division's practice went all right, but the American 3rd Infantry Division got into trouble. The weather was rough. Many of their DUKWs were sunk, and very few troops landed in the right places. It was a very bad start, but there was no more time for rehearsal. Combat loading had to begin for Anzio.

Kesselring was fully aware of the possibility of an Allied amphibious landing, but his troops could not be everywhere at once. Thus, he had to draw up a master plan, setting up procedures to define this area and that (whichever were under attack), the troops who would move, and the routes they would take. The code word for the Anzio area was "Richard," and the commander responsible for defense was General Schlemmer, commander of the 1st Paratroop Corps. The only German unit actually in the area was a single battalion of the 29th Panzer Grenadier Division, which had been sent there to rest, refit, and practice demolition work by blowing up Anzio Harbor.

The Allied deception efforts had been successful, and Admiral Wilhelm F. Canaris, the head of OKW intelligence, had visited Kesselring and announced that a major amphibious landing was not likely.

Beginning on January 12, the Fifth Army was to pin down the Germans on the Gustav Line—so they would not move to Anzio and attract additional troops to the Gustav Line—break through that line and rush across the Liri Valley to attack with the Anzio force, and bring the supply train up quickly enough to supply both their own attacks and the Anzio force attacks. A conservative military man looking at the plan would have said they were crazy, and several did; but the romance of capturing Rome had seized all those fighting in the Italian campaign. Urged on by Churchill and the British, the Anzio plan forged ahead.

On January 12, the French Expeditionary Force, which was on the right, was to cross the Upper Rapido River and move through the high ground immediately behind Monte Cassino, which dominated the Liri Valley from the northeast. Five days later the British 10th Corps on the left was to cross the Garigliano River at two places and set up two bridgeheads: one near the coast at Minturno and the other near Sant'Ambrogio. From there the British would move east to take the high ground overlooking the Liri Valley from the west. Three days later, on January 20, the 6th Corps was to deliver the coup de grace to the Germans by staging a massive crossing of the Rapido River near Sant'Angelo d'Alife, and enter the Liri Valley, then scud across it to Anzio to join up with the amphibious landing forces that would arrive on January 22.

Very heavy rains during the last few weeks and melting snow from the mountains had turned the Rapido and the other waterways that lay ahead of the Fifth Army into torrents. All of the rivers and streams had overflowed their banks and flooded much of the lowland. The German defenders had taken advantage of this and improved on nature by diverting the Rapido to create an artificial marsh that would last until the dry season, with a bog too soft for vehicular travel for any distance. Back of the river and the bog lay the main German line—their final line of defense south of Rome. The Todt Organization in the last three months had built concrete bunkers, weapons pits, steel turrets for machine guns, and barbed-wire entanglements on the slopes and had placed mines in the area, particularly box mines that contained almost no metal and thus passed examination by metal detectors. These fortifications on the high ground and the barren steep slopes of Monte Cassino and in the hills around Sant'Ambrogio were manned by the highly trained and highly motivated German defenders.

On the lower ground behind the Rapido, where the Liri Valley begins, the Germans had also erected stout defenses centered on the village of Sant'Angelo d'Alife, the town of Cassino, and the village of Sant'Ambrogio. On the hills around and the top of Monte Cassino, they had observation points to keep the Allied movements under watch.

For four months, Kesselring and his staff had been supervising the perfection of the defenses. He was now confident that they could stop the Allies. General von Vietinghoff's Tenth Army had 90,000 troops under the direction of Generals von Senger and Etterlin in the Gustav Line. Besides these troops on the western side of Italy, Kesselring had another 25,000 men in two divisions under the 1st Parachute Division, which would be available to counter any Allied amphibious operation. He also had two more divisions at rest in the Rome area that could be brought into action very swiftly.

General Keyes, the commander of the U.S. II Corps, who replaced Brigadier General Bradley, had noted to General Clark that the high ground at Cassino was very important, and provided the enemy with a close observation point covering Sant'Angelo. At a conference of generals early in January, Keyes had recommended that 10th Corps and II Corps together attack across the Garigliano River and then move into the Liri Valley from the west. But General McCreery had objected because his troops were not equipped or trained for mountain warfare, and that is what would be required. Thus, the plan was dropped.

Clark's eye was on Anzio and getting there as quickly as possible. The direct route was across the Rapido and into the Liri Valley. Once into the valley, Clark planned to send the U.S. 1st Armored Division racing to the beachhead. But Major General Fred Walker, commander of the U.S. 36th Infantry Division, which would make the crossing, was full of forebodings. A frontal attack across the Rapido, he was sure, would be disastrous. He wanted to cross along the Upper Rapido were the river was narrow, get into the mountains, and move into the Liri Valley from the east, which would then be behind the Gustav Line. But the French, who were operating in the east, lacked the strength to take the mountain wall behind Cassino.

Walker voiced his objections to Clark and Keyes, and they listened, but it always came back to the same point: the river had to be crossed near Sant'Angelo and the 36th had to do it. What Clark never explained to Walker was that it did not really make much difference if the 36th failed to cross as long as it tied down the Germans on the Gustav Line and made them bring reinforcements. In plain words, the 36th was expendable.

On January 15, the British were ready to begin the part they would play in the Fifth Army surge. The German positions on the Garigliano were held by the 94th Infantry Division. It had the hard task of defending the river and the coast around the Gulf of Gaeta. General Pfeiffer, the German commander, put the bulk of his division on the high ground back of the river with an outpost line to the river.

One regiment held the Minturno Ridge from the sea to the Ausente Valley. Another held the Castelforte Ridge from the Ausente north to the southern edge of the Liri Valley where it met the 15th Panzer Grenadier Division positions. The third regiment was in the coastal sector. The 94th had been on the Garigliano for some time and had been able to prepare its positions. All the obvious crossing points were heavily mined and held by outposts in fortified positions on both banks.

General McCreery planned 10th Corps' attack against the 94th using two divisions. The British 5th Infantry Division from the Eighth Army was to attack in the coast sector along Route 7 with the Minturno Ridge as its objective. The British 56th Infantry Division was to attack the Castelforte positions to secure the high ground overlooking the road that ran up the Ausente Valley to Ausonia and the rear of the Gustav Line positions in the Liri Valley. The British 46th Infantry Division was to wait and support the flank of the American II Corps when it attacked across the Rapido River.

The British decided to use some 14 rafts, including two strong enough for tanks, in the early crossings. The engineer had plenty of equipment for bridge building, but they would not try until the direct artillery observation points had been cleared off the bridge sites. They had to use the existing road approaches to the river because the flooding had made the fields on both sides too soft to carry a large number of military vehicles in wet weather, and these roads were certainly registered by German guns.

All the early parts of the operation went well. Assembly of the artillery, and the vast quantity of ammunition needed, and elimination of the enemy outposts without alarming the Germans, all were accomplished, using the one good road, Route 7.

On January 16–17, Allied planes swooped down and dropped bombs and strafed troops of the German 94th Infantry Division in their line, and two cruisers and five destroyers fired shells on German positions from close inshore. Kesslring called General von Vietinghoff to ask whether he thought something was going to happen. But von Vietinghoff, on the evening of January 17, saw nothing amiss. The moonless nights they had been having obviously were keeping the Allies from moving.

The British attack started at 9:00 p.m. on January 17. General Pfeiffer's 94th was taken by surprise. By dawn the next morning, the 10th Corps had ten battalions over the river, with rafts bringing antitank guns and other heavy weapons. During January 18, the two divisions expanded their bridgeheads. The British 4th Indian Infantry Division had some difficulty on the seaward flank, and poor navigation by some of the landing craft did not help. However, by evening, the 5th Infantry Division was firmly established on the Minturno Ridge, and the 56th Infantry Division was on the high ground on either side of Castelforte, although it had not taken the town. Bridging went slowly because of accurate German artillery fire. The first 30-ton bridge was opened in the early hours of January 20. Even then the bridges could only be used at night because the approach roads were under German artillery observation and were shelled whenever a vehicle attempted to move down to the river in daylight. This situation was to exist for three months, because the German observation posts were not cleared off the river line until the whole Gustav Line collapsed in May.

The British 10th Corps buildup, however was fast enough to allow the troops in the bridgeheads to defeat the 94th Infantry Division's first counterattacks. General von Senger visited the 94th area on the morning of January 18. He could see that the Allies were trying to turn both flanks of his 14th Panzer Corps. He had stopped the French in the north with his own reserves. He asked Kesselring to release the 29th and 30th Panzer Grenadier Divisions, which were south of Rome in reserve to counterattack the threat posed by 10th Corps. This posed a big dilemma for Kesserling. The purpose of those divisions south of Rome was to fend off any amphibious assault that might develop; and Kesselring fully expected one. However, German intelligence had found no indications of any such activity. Admiral Canaris had been sure and most persuasive. On January 15, he said to the German commanders in Italy: "I consider an allied landing operation as being out of the question for the next four to six weeks."[13]

Since there was no apparent prospect of an Allied invasion on the east coast, and because the British might expand their bridgehead and damage the Gustav Line irreparably, and because the ability of the Tenth Army to hold in the Gustav Line was hanging "by a slender thread," against his own better judgment, Kesselring ordered General Schlemmer, commander of the 1st Paratroop Corps near Rome, to move south with those two divisions and part of the Hermann Goering Panzer Division to fend off the British in the 94th Infantry Division sector.

"I am convinced that we are facing the greatest crisis yet encountered,"[14] said Kesselring. What bothered him most was the failure of the

German minefields to stop the British movement. Depending on those mines, the Germans had placed 13 of the 15 battalions in corps and army reserve on the east side of the Liri River to block the crossing of the Rapido.

Schlemmer's counterattack on 10th Corps started on January 20, and soon the British were engaged in hard fighting. Any idea of moving up the Ausente Valley was now fading. The second crossing in the British 10th Corps area was turned back. Near the junction of the Liri and Gari Rivers, assault troops of the British 46th Infantry Division made three attempts to get across on the night of January 19 but failed each time. The swift current broke their raft and ferry cables and the German resistance was too strong. So on the early morning of January 20, only a handful of British troops were on the far side of the river near Sant'Ambrogio. When daylight brought an increase in German pressure with the arrival of more troops, McCreery ordered those British troops brought back and further efforts to cross abandoned.

A major reason for the British failure here went back to the Anzio rehearsal in which the American 3rd Infantry Division had lost 40 DUKWs, which had to be replaced for the Anzio landing. Because of the shortage in all sorts of seagoing vessels, the only place General Clark could get replacements from was 10th Corps, which had planned to use them to take the 46th Infantry Division across the Garigliano, but had to give up the amphibious craft.

Despite this failure, at the Fifteenth Army Group level, General Alexander was delighted, because if all went well, there would be no German reserves left near Rome to oppose the Anzio landing. The future looked very bright at that moment from Army Group headquarters.

When the Americans learned of McCreery's plans for the assault on the Garigliano, they were very unhappy. General Keyes had understood that the British 46th Infantry Division was to cross at Sant'Ambrogio on January 18, which would have given the division 48 hours to secure a bridgehead, which would protect the left flank of the 36th Infantry Division when it attacked on January 20. At the last moment, he learned that McCreery had delayed the crossing for a day. This would give the 46th only 24 hours to complete the operation of safeguarding the 36th's flank. Keyes wanted to delay the American crossing of the Rapido by 24 hours then. But General Clark refused because the river crossings were linked up with the timing of the Anzio beach landings.

Keyes had very little confidence in McCreery. He criticized his unwillingness to launch attacks in force. To be of help to the 36th, the British would have to make a strong crossing with most of its strength committed. Unless the 46th gave real assistance that the 36th needed, Keyes told Clark, the effort of the 36th would probably get nowhere.

Now, the 46th had failed to give that punch, and when the 36th attacked across the Rapido that evening, its left flank would be exposed. This was quite a shock to Generals Clark, Keyes, and Walker. Their concern about the Rapido River crossing mounted. McCreery of 10th Corps suggested that the crossing be abandoned because it had very little chance of success because of the heavy defensive position of the Germans west of the Rapido.

But Clark felt that it was essential that the attacks be made even though there would be heavy losses. In other words, he reiterated the expendability of the 36th. What he wanted was the clearing of the way for the Anzio landing that had been planned on such a shoestring that unless the Germans were drawn off, it was bound to fail. So the 36th was to be sacrificed to the "God of War" with every indication before the crossing was made that it would fail.

In fact, the announced purpose of the crossing had already been achieved by the British success in crossing the Garigliano, and drawing those two German divisions down from the Rome area. But the announced purpose was not the real purpose of the need to get into the Liri Valley. So weak was the whole Anzio operation that unless the Allies got into the Liri Valley and could link up with the beachhead, the whole one–two punch planned by General Alexander was likely to fail.

In the American sector of the line, at a meeting of division commanders of the II Corps on January 18, two days before the crossing, Walker outlined his plans. He described the German positions near Sant'Angelo. He warned that the job was going to be tough for his division. But he bravely said something he did not believe: His division would accomplish its mission and be in Sant'Angelo on the morning following the attack. Three days earlier, the French had bogged down completely after fighting their way four miles to the Upper Rapido, where they had run into the main line of German defense, and had paused, exhausted. Walker was aware of this. He was also well aware on January 20 of the failure of the 46th Infantry Division to give him the left flank protection he had expected.

Keyes, who had heard Walker's earlier protest about the Rapido crossing, was cheered by the general's confidence. Keyes was confident because he had brought up a very strong contingent of artillery to support the crossing.

So, as the 36th Infantry Division prepared for its task, its leaders expressed confidence that the junior officers and men did not feel. Their lack of enthusiasm brought a lethargy to the division that was to be its undoing.

17

Crossing

If the 36th Infantry Division could establish a bridgehead two-and-a-half miles deep at Sant'Angelo, it could open the Liri Valley, and this was the objective. It was to have as much help as General Clark could give it. The 34th Infantry Division would make a fake attack on the division's right to fool the Germans, but it was to be ready to move in several different directions as opportunity arose. The crossing would be supported by the artillery and attached tank battalions of the 34th as well as its own, plus the artillery and tanks of Combat Command B of the 1st Armored Division, and 12 battalions of corps artillery. Besides, the 12th Air Support Command would bomb and strafe the enemy.

But the stream was high (9–12 feet deep) and would be difficult to cross in this season because it was 25–50 feet wide. On the west bank, the Germans held the battered village of Sant'Angelo on a 40-foot bluff, just high enough to allow them to see much of the river and the flats on the American side. And Sant'Angelo was only the high point of a strong defense system all along the line, with dugouts, machine-gun nests, slit trenches, and concrete bunkers, protected by double-apron wire fences and mines and booby traps. The Germans had had time, too, to mine the American bank and the flats that were concealed by the manmade marsh. The defenders were the 15th Panzer Grenadier Division, one of the most experienced in Italy.

As General Walker considered the problem of the attack, he was concerned about several matters. One was Monte Cassino, which dominated the whole area. The abbey might be manned by German observers, but that really made no difference. There were so many high points on the German side of the river, that Walker could see that the only way to escape constant observation was to make a night attack.

So the 36th Infantry Division would keep one regiment in reserve and attack with two. One regiment would cross the river north of Sant'Angelo, the other would cross south of the village. The plan called for the 36th's Cavalry Reconnaissance Troop to cross on the south and make contact with the British 46th Infantry Division. But the 46th delayed and was not across the Garagliano to protect the 36th's left flank by January 20, the day of the 36th's crossing.

Before the crossing, Walker expressed confidence that the 36th would manage the operation, but he really felt no such confidence. He felt that the chances for success were virtually nil. But he never indicated this feeling to his superiors, and General Keyes, his immediate superior, as commander of II Corps, thought Walker really was confident. But his regimental commanders knew different, and they soon began to share Walker's pessimism about the undertaking. That pessimism walked straight down the line to battalions and companies. So, on the eve of the crossing, the soldiers who were going to go across felt that they were facing a suicide mission, and many of them behaved accordingly. The feelings of doom were not helped when the 36th learned of the failure of the British 46th, which made it tough for Walker's men who now would not have any of the advantages that the 46th's crossing would have provided.

The key to the 36th's successful crossing of the Rapido had to be complete cooperation between the engineers and the infantry. In January, Walker had told his division engineer to plan for the crossing. The engineer quickly discovered that basic engineer supplies were very short in the area. Standard footbridges could not be found. The division engineer told the corps engineer that an attack through a muddy valley without suitable approaches and exits—a valley blocked by organized defenses behind a river that could not be forded—would create an impossible situation and end in failure and great loss of life. The corps engineer agreed. And that was the position from which the engineers began.

The engineers were scheduled to do all that was possible to assist in the enterprise. The 111th Engineer Combat Battalion, reinforced by two other companies, would have all crossing sites cleared of mines by the day of crossing. They would build bridge approaches and exits, clear mines in the bridgehead, and build two Bailey bridges. The 19th Engineer Combat Regiment was to send a battalion to each infantry regiment. These engineers would provide 30 rubber boats, 20 assault boats, and four improvised footbridges, which would be put in place the night before the crossing, in a convenient place for the infantry. They would also build bridges after the capture of Sant'Angelo. As it turned out, almost none of these conditions was met.

These engineers found 100 wooden assault boats and 100 rubber boats. They planned to improvise footbridges with 50 sections of catwalk. They also found pneumatic floats, each of which would carry 24 men, 14 of them paddling, with four men on shore to guide the craft across by rope. The plan was that all this would be brought to the water's edge, but when the engineers got down to the river, they found there were no roads to the stream that could support the weight of two-and-a-half-ton trucks even after they spread gravel. After the rains, the ground was so wet that it was impassable to wheeled vehicles. So the engineers put the crossing materials into two dumps near the base of Mount Trocchio, several miles from the river. The boats and bridge materials would have to be carried by hand to the riverbank.

Again, the accidents at the Anzio practice landing in Naples had their effect. The division was to have a dozen amphibious tractors, but these had to be given up for the actual Anzio landings when so many were lost in the rehearsal.

In the training, the 142nd and 143rd Infantry Regiments were taught how to cross the river. After the training, Walker substituted the 141st Infantry Regiment for the 142nd, which meant that one of his regiments would make the crossing with no training at all. And in the practice, the infantry did not make any attempt to learn from the engineers and, in fact, rebuffed the engineers when they offered advice.

So the 141st and the 143rd prepared to cross the Rapido. The men were combat-weary; they had fought at Monte Maggiore, Monte Samoucro, Monte Lungo, and San Pietro in December, and each regiment was short almost 1,000 men. Early in January, replacements started coming in, but only about half the number needed. So the regiments would go into the operation under strength, with so many new men involved that they hardly knew the names of their leaders, and the officers did not know the men and their capabilities. After January 17, extensive patrolling discovered that the enemy was very strong on the opposite bank, both banks were heavily mined, and although the engineers had taped lanes through the minefields, they were not at all sure the Germans would not get in and redo the fields.

On the night of January 19, the regiments moved up to assembly areas at the base of Mount Trocchio, flat marshland where it was hard to find cover. On January 20, the air force P-40s and A-20 bombers bombed the Germans around Cassino.

As night approached, Walker succumbed to gloom, feeling that the mission should never have been assigned to any troops with flanks exposed. He felt that General Clark was now feeling that he had made an unwise decision. But he closed his diary that night with the words: "If we get some breaks, we may succeed."[15]

With darkness that night of January 20 came a heavy fog. The men of the 141st Infantry Regiment set out, each with an extra bandolier of ammunition and bayonets were fixed to their rifles. At 6 o'clock, they moved to the dump to pick up their boats, only to find that several of them had been wrecked by German shell fire. Just after 7 o'clock, they started out with the serviceable boats.

The artillery began a rolling barrage, which was to move inland against the enemy as the men crossed. But as the men crossed the flats and neared the stream, the German artillery replied and shells began to come into the line. Thirty men were lost to Company B, including the company commander and the executive officer. The troops scattered for cover, dropping their boats and sometimes their weapons. Some of them moved into the minefields, and there were more casualties. Enemy fire had destroyed many of the markers the engineers had put up.

By H Hour, the men were still struggling to get to the crossing site. One-quarter of the engineering equipment had already been lost. As quickly as they were brought up, the boats and bridges were damaged or destroyed by the enemy shelling. Some were simply abandoned by infantrymen who then headed for cover. By the time the material got to the stream, half of it was useless.

Everything seemed to be going wrong. Men got lost in the fog. Bodies of men killed blocked the boat lanes. Boats were put in the water, sank promptly from holes put into them by the enemy artillery, and sometimes carried down whole squads. Some good boats were deserted because of the shell fire. And the infantrymen resented being given orders by engineers, and sometimes would not follow them.

By 9 o'clock that night, a handful of men from Companies A, B, and C had made their way across the river. There were fewer than 100 in all; they dug in and waited for more men to come. They were to have a long wait.

Behind them the engineers were trying to put up bridges, only to see them destroyed by enemy shell fire. Using parts of the destroyed bridges, the engineers put together one footbridge, at 4 o'clock in the morning, but an hour later the bridge was damaged by shellfire. Using this damaged bridge and the handful of boats that worked, most of the 1st Battalion of the 141st Infantry Regiment crossed the river by 6:30 in the morning. But shortly before daybreak, enemy fire knocked out the telephone wires. All radios had been lost or damaged, so communications ceased. The only way the Americans on the near bank knew that the men on the enemy side were still alive was from the sound of American rifle fire. At this point, General Wilbur, the assistant division commander, decided to order the men on the American bank to retire to the assembly area and take cover before daylight brought heavy German fire on them. He instructed the men on the far bank to dig in and hold. A few minutes later Colonel Aaron Wyatt, the regimental commander, ordered the men on the far side to come back. Most of them could not make it because of heavy German fire. They were pinned down in foxholes about 200 yards from the bank.

At 7:15 A.M. on January 21, Wyatt was planning a second attack to back up the men who were across the river. But there was no way to do it. The Germans had perfect view of the river, and the Americans did not have any smoke equipment to help. So the Americans on the far side fought hopelessly, and one by one were lost.

Below Sant'Angelo, the 143rd Infantry Regiment had much better organization and much better luck. The cooperation between engineers and infantry was better, and a platoon of Company C launched on the river at H Hour—10:00 P.M. on January 20—got across the river without difficulty. However, as the boats came back to the American side, the German artillery and machine guns worked them over, and they were all destroyed, and many casualties were inflicted on Company B and Company C on both sides of the river. A footbridge completed 20 minutes after H Hour was knocked out a few minutes after being put into use, and heavy shell fire prevented anyone from repairing it.

By 9:30 P.M., still only the 1st Platoon of Company C was across the river, but in the next hour enough boats were put into operation to get the rest of Company C across. At 10:45 P.M., the regimental commander, Colonel Martin, went to the riverbank. He found Major David Frazier, the 1st Battalion commander, trying to get more boats forward, but since there were no engineers around he was not doing very well. They went back to the boat dump and found a platoon of engineers sitting in foxholes. They put the engineers to work. In a short time, the 1st Battalion of the 143rd Infantry Regiment had crossed the river.

But on the far bank, all efforts to make progress failed. The German position were too strong, and by 7:00 A.M. the next morning, the American infantrymen had been forced into a pocket with the river at their backs. Frazier asked permission to withdraw, but General Walker had the request denied, and told the battalion to stay and wait for reinforcements. But by 10:00 A.M., Frazier saw that his position was completely untenable and he was taking heavy casualties, so he brought all the men who could move back to the near bank.

The 3rd Battalion of the 143rd got into serious trouble when the engineer guides, by mistake, led them into a minefield, and the casualties totally disorganized both engineers and infantry. They never got organized again, although eventually that night the regimental commander relieved the 3rd Battalion commander. One reason for the relief was the feeling that the battalion commander did not have the confidence to get on with the job. And after the fight, it was discovered that most of the men of the battalion did not have any faith in their ability to cross and defeat the enemy.

So the crossing of the Rapido River failed. It was so great a failure, caused primarily by the German artillery and American incompetence, that the German infantry was not aware that a major effort was being made. General Von Vietinghoff, commander of the Tenth Army, did not even call on any reserves to stop it.

Early on January 21, General Walker ordered another crossing of the Rapido, primarily to rescue the men stuck on the far side. Again it was agreed that the crossing would have to be a night maneuver because of the enemy shell fire. But morale was extremely low, and engineers and infantry still were not really cooperating. When General Keyes announced that the crossing would have to be made that day, because General Clark was in a hurry to get tanks into the Liri Valley to support the Anzio operation that was going on, Walker again predicted failure of the 36th Infantry Division's efforts, just as the one the previous night had been.

In fact the crossing was delayed again by the 141st Infantry Regiment until after nightfall because the boats promised by the engineers did not come up. The 143rd started crossing below Sant'Angelo at 4 o'clock in the afternoon using smoke to conceal the movement. By 6:30 P.M. all the rifle companies were across the river, and soon heavy weapons began to come across. The 3rd Battalion was entirely across, and Colonel Martin ordered the 2nd Battalion across. On the far bank the troops advanced 1,500 yards, but they were pinned down there.

What the American troops needed was close support from tanks and tank destroyers, but the vehicles could not cross because there were no bridges. That night, changes were made in orders so that Bailey bridges would be built instead of pontoon bridges which usually were built in a river crossing at the second stage. The engineers were confused by the request. They tried hard to comply, but they did not get a bridge up that second night, and so the tanks were not able to cross.

At 10:00 A.M. on January 22, the 141st held a shallow bridgehead with parts of the three companies ashore, but all the work on Bailey bridges had been brought to a halt by enemy shelling.

At around noon, with no hope of getting any tanks across because no bridges had been built, Martin ordered his units to withdraw from the far bank. By early afternoon, all three battalions were back, with only a few isolated groups in enemy territory.

North of Sant'Angelo, the 141st got going again around 9 o'clock on the night of January 21. Company F crossed, and its members eliminated German riflemen and machine gunners who were firing on the crossing point. Engineers put up two footbridges, and two hours later the 2nd

Battalion crossed the river. The riflemen of the 3rd Battalion also crossed over. They found no survivors of the first crossing the night before, but the two battalions advanced 1,000 yards beyond the river, before severe casualties caused them to stop and dig in. Only one footbridge survived the German artillery. The coming of morning brought mist and fog that helped the assault by limiting visibility. When the haze began to dissipate smoke pots were set, but German artillery fire was very heavy. Between 4:00 and 5:00 A.M., 300 round of artillery fire fell in the division command post area, causing many casualties. In the bridgehead, the continuing artillery fire made it impossible for the units to organize and resume the attack.

Early in the afternoon of the 22nd, the three battalions of the 143rd were withdrawing from the German side of the river down by Sant'Angelo. The position of the 141st began to deteriorate, first with the knockout of communications. Then, by 4:00 P.M., every officer on the far side of the river had been killed or wounded. Then a shell landed squarely on the footbridge and knocked it out. With all boats destroyed and no bridge, and no officer, the infantrymen on the far side were in bad shape. Between 6:00 and 7:00 P.M., some 40 men got back by swimming the river and reported the situation was hopeless. Then a few more men straggled in, and soon the sound of American weapons on the far bank ceased. All the others were killed or captured.

And that was the end of the attack. When it came time to count the losses, it was found that the 36th Infantry Division had lost 1,681 men—either killed, wounded, and missing—during the 48 hours of the operation. The Germans had negligible losses, and reported the capture of 500 Americans. So efficient had been the defenders of the Rapido that they saw nothing unusual in their victory, and it was some time before they even knew they had won.

As for the defeat, General Clark came to the Rapido and called for strong pressure against the enemy to keep them from sending troops to Anzio. The 36th was in no shape to give anyone strong resistance. The debacle for the division was so noteworthy that after the war it was the subject of a Congressional investigation, which turned out to be a farce because no reliable witnesses would testify.

As for General Clark, who received the brunt of criticism for the crossing of the Rapido, he admitted cheerfully that he had given the orders. He knew that it would be bloody and costly, but felt that it was imperative to draw as many Germans to the front so the way could be cleared for Anzio.

So that is how the battle ended and why General Clark decided that some blood had to be spilled, and that the American 36th Infantry Division would be the one to spill it.

18

Anzio

The force destined to land at Anzio consisted of 6th Corps—more than 110,000 men, both British and American. The British units were the 1st Infantry Division and two Commando battalions. The American force consisted of the 3rd Infantry Division, the 504th Parachute Infantry Battalion, the 509th Parachute Infantry Battalion, and three Ranger Battalions. In addition, General Clark added part of the U.S. 1st Armored Division and one regiment of the 45th Infantry Division in followup roles.

As General Alexander saw the operation, its purpose was to cut the enemy's main communications in the Alban Hills area southeast of Rome and threaten the German rear. The landing should compel the Germans to weaken their Gustav Line defenses and this would let Clark break through the line and make contact with the beachhead.

He believed the Germans had two divisions in reserve near Rome but that Allied air attacks could hinder the move of the Germans. Clark's estimate was not quite so optimistic. He believed that the landing would constitute such a serious threat to the Germans that they would react violently and employ all the resources available to the German High Command in Italy to combat it. They could bring in a division from the Axiatic front in three days, and bring in two more divisions in northern Italy in the first two weeks. So Clark's orders establishing the landing were deliberately vague. He directed 6th Corps to secure a beachhead in the Anzio area and to advance on the Alban Hills. He did not say advance to the Alban Hills. He expected the Anzio force to meet powerful resistance, and therefore, it could make immediate defense preparations and dig in. A strong reserve would be kept to resist counterattack. Whether or not General Lucas, 6th Corps commander, went on the attack immediately would depend on his judgment of the situation at Anzio.

As noted, the Anzio forces held a rehearsal on the beach near Naples on January 18. In the 3rd Infantry Division area, it was a disaster, causing the loss of 43 amphibious landing craft and 19 105-mm Howitzers. These losses had to be made up from the Fifth Army's forces ashore. Clark blamed navy mishandling of the exercise for the losses.

Lucas was very apprehensive about the whole operation because of the shortage of shipping and men. To him the whole Anzio adventure had "a strong odor of Gallipoli, and apparently the same amateur was on the coach's bench." The rehearsal at Naples seemed to bear out his pessimism: "They will end up putting me ashore with inadequate forces and get me in a serious jam. Then who will take the blame?"[16]

However, by the time of the landings, his natural optimism had returned and he felt they had a good chance of success, but he still wished the higher headquarters were not so optimistic. He was particularly concerned about a last-minute message from Clark that changed the nature of the mission. At first the plan had been to capture the port of Anzio to handle supplies, and the Alban Hills because of their commanding position over the whole area. However, because of the number of troops at hand and the shipping situation, Clark had become worried lest they were taking on too much, and so he threw the monkey onto Lucas's back. He was to interpret his orders as he saw fit. If he had the chance, he was to capture the port of Anzio. But if it seemed that he might lose the beachhead by spreading the forces too thin, he was to immediately go on the defensive. The high command was having it both ways: ordering an offensive operation, but telling the commander to be careful and not overstep. Lucas's position was not a comfortable one; being given responsibility without backup.

On January 21, 1944, the ships of the Allied assault convoy left Naples for Anzio carrying 40,000 men and 5,000 vehicles under the command of Rear Admiral Frank J. Lowry of the U.S. Navy and Rear Admiral Thomas H. Troubridge, of the British Royal Navy. Their two task forces were made up of American, British, Dutch, Greek, Polish, and French vessels. They included two command ships, five cruisers, 24 destroyers, two antiaircraft ships, two gunboats, 23 minesweepers, ten subchasers, six repair ships, eight LSIs, 84 LSTs, 96 LCIs, and 50 LCTs. British and American air forces would give air cover to the landings.

The convoy moved south around Capri to deceive the Germans, but after nightfall the ships turned north toward Anzio. At five minutes after midnight, they dropped anchor off the Anzio shore. Shortly before 2:00 A.M. on January 22, the boats of the first assault waves were heading toward the beach. At 1:50 A.M. two British landing craft launched a five-minute rocket barrage on the beaches.

The commanders had expected fierce resistance from the shore. Instead, there was complete silence. As the troops swarmed onto the beaches, there was no opposition. There were no Germans at Anzio. General Lucas wrote in his diary: "We achieved what is certainly one of the most complete surprises in history."[17]

Allied planes flew 1,200 sorties on the beaches that day, but the only fire came from a few small coast artillery and antiaircraft units in the area. The most danger was from small minefields in the port of Anzio. Two battalions that had been recently removed from the Gustav Line offered some resistance, but they were undermanned and quickly overrun. By midmorning, the U.S. 3rd Infantry Division was ashore with all its artillery and tanks. They destroyed four bridges along the Mussolini Canal to protect their flank and dug in to repel a German counterattack. No attack came.

It was a warm, sunny day. Three battalions of Rangers occupied Anzio and the 509th Parachute Infantry Battalion went down the coast road and occupied Nettuno, two miles away. Behind came the 504th Parachute Infantry Battalion. It was just like a hike on maneuvers.

The British 1st Infantry Division landed on beaches north of Anzio, where some mines caused delay. By midday, the troops were two miles inland, and the Commandos had swung over to cut the road to Albano with a roadblock just north of Anzio.

By midday, the engineers were hard at work clearing minefields, bulldozing exits across the dunes, and moving streams of men and supplies ashore. During the day, the Luftwaffe made three brief raids and some guns of the Germans shelled from long range, but the beachhead was fully organized. Casualties were a minesweeper damaged by a mine and and an LCI sunk by a German bomb. By afternoon, the port of Anzio was opened. By midnight, 6th Corps and 36,000 men and most of the supplies were ashore. Casualties were 13 killed, 97 wounded, and 44 missing. The 6th Corps had to look hard to find 227 prisoners.

The attacks along the Garagliano and Rapido Rivers had succeeded splendidly in drawing German attention to the Gustav Line and away from Anzio. When the Germans heard of the landings, they had virtually no troops in the Rome area. Field Marshal Kesselring's two reserve divisions had gone to the Gustav Line. If Allied troops could reach Valmontane at the end of the Liri Valley, could cut the lines of communication to the Tenth German Army, if they turned to directly threaten the Tenth Army rear, or if they established a base for a later offensive, they would force the Germans to desert the Gustav Line.

When Kesselring learned of the landings, he estimated that it was a full-scale operation and that it could jeopardize his whole strategy in

Italy. Five hours after the landing began Kesselring ordered the 4th Parachute Division and several replacement units of the Hermann Goering Panzer Division to block the roads from Anzio to the Alban Hills, and he asked the OKW for reinforcements. That day, the OKW ordered the 715th Infantry Division to move down from southern France, and the 114th Jaeger Division to move from the Balkans and what amounted to another division from Germany. The OKW also authorized the formation of a new division—the 92nd Infantry—from replacement units in Italy.

By 7 o'clock in the morning, the Germans ordered units of the Fourteenth Army from northern Italy to Anzio, and by evening of the first day, they were moving. Kesselring also asked General von Vietinghoff to transfer all the troops from the Gustav Line that he could spare. That day, about two-and-a-half divisions began to march toward Anzio. Later that day, von Vietinghoff would also send about a division and a half from the Adriatic front to Anzio.

By 5 o'clock in the evening, the first German units arrived and took over defenses; and by nightfall, a thin line of Germans forces had encircled the Allied bridgehead. Kesselring was becoming more optimistic because the Allies had missed their chance to move northward to seize the Alban Hills (as had been the original plan, which had been decimated by shortfalls). Kesselring quite properly assessed the Allied plan as very conservative, involving the establishment of a small beachhead and then a wait for more troops. This would give him time to bring troops to prevent an Allied breakthrough, and he was losing no time.

The Allied move had done everything it was supposed to do, if it had been powerful enough and had been followed by strong and immediate Allied movement out of the beachhead. That evening von Vietinghoff telephoned Kesselring and suggested that he pull out of the Gustav Line because he could not hold it with the troops now at hand. Kesselring told him to stand fast—so one German crisis was prevented. Hitler was adamant that the Germans hold along the Gustav line. "The Gustav line must be held at all costs for the sake of the political consequences which would follow a completely successful defense. The Fuehrer expects the bitterest struggle for every yard."[18]

Kesselring fully expected an Allied attack on the Alban Hills, and he suspected that it should succeed. He could not move enough troops up fast enough to stop it. On the other side, Rome lay undefended, and it was very possible that the Allies would reach Rome.

But to Kesselring's surprise the Allies did nothing, except increase the size of the beachhead slightly. By the second evening, Kesselring decided that the Allied beachhead's large-scale expansion was not going to happen. The next day, January 24, the British 1st Infantry Division moved a few miles forward to the Moletta River and the American 3rd Infantry Division took several more bridges across the Mussolini Canal, thus securing the Allied left and right flanks. The beachhead was seven miles deep and 16 miles long, but the Allies were making no preparations for a full-scale attack, Kesselring saw.

By this time Kesselring was truly relieved. The Allies had given him time to bring up enough reinforcements that he was no longer concerned about the possibility of Allied breakthrough at Anzio. As General Westphal, Kesselring's chief of staff, later wrote: "On January 22 and even the following day, an audacious and enterprising formation of enemy troops could have penetrated into the city of Rome itself without having to overcome any serious opposition, but the landed enemy forces lost time and hesitated."[19]

So the chance for a quick capture of Rome had been lost by a combination of events that went back to before the Trident Conference, to that day that General Marshall had insisted that the Cross Channel Attack was everything and the Mediterranean could be no more than a diversionary action. Since that time, everything that had happened had eroded the volition of the Allied commanders and their confidence in audacious action.

The reinforcements came rushing in to Anzio at a speed that astounded the Allies, from all over Italy, from France, from southern Germany, and Yugoslavia. Here was proof of Prime Minister Churchill's contention that Allied activity in the Mediterranean would draw the Germans as quickly as the Cross Channel Attack, if not proof that operations in the south could prove as decisive and as swift as in the north.

Kesselring was given plenty of time to organize his defense. On January 24, he brought the Fourteenth Army headquarters from Verona to take over command. When General Oberst von Mackensen assumed command of the defense the following day, he had parts of eight divisions deployed around the Allied beachhead and elements of five more divisions on the way. Kesselring ordered von Mackensen to launch a counterattack without delay and destroy the Allied beachhead. He had only been lent all these troops for a short time, and they must be returned, the Balkan troops to keep order in the Balkans, and the troops from France and Germany back where they came from to be prepared for the Cross Channel Attack that was expected in the spring.

Von Mackensen scheduled his attack for February 2; but it never happened. Belatedly, the Allies launched their attack on Anzio, now that they sacrificed the initiative. And the cause? It had to be placed at the feet of the Mediterranean high command and particularly Generals Alexander and Clark, who had given General Lucas conflicting signals that would make him damned if he moved and damned if he did not. The high brass in Washington and London was growing restive about his failure to move, not knowing that Clark had so intimated Lucas about the possibility of loss of the beachhead that this had become his overriding concern. For once, without General Montgomery in the picture, the British were on the side of action, and the Americans were dragging their feet.

As for the Germans, they reorganized their defenses for the coming battle. The Tenth Army controlled the Gustav Line, with seven divisions. Three German divisions faced the British Eighth Army on the Adriatic coast, eight divisions surrounded the Anzio beachhead, and six divisions were holding northern Italy and the Lubljana Gap. All this was done with great speed.

On January 25, Alexander and Clark visited the Anzio beachhead and took an entirely different attitude from the one exhibited to Lucas just before the landings. Before, they had been concerned about the German counterattack, and there had been no counterattack. They had not been concerned about Lucas's advancement to the Alban Hills and to Rome; now this was their major concern. It was quite natural that all this had changed because the Allies had miscalculated the German defenses and now they were miscalculating again. They had seen strength where there had been weakness. Now they saw weakness where there was strength. Why didn't Lucas attack? Clark demanded.

So on January 25, Lucas ordered an attack: the American 3rd Infantry Division toward Cisterna and the the British 1st Infantry Division toward Campoleone. The 3rd was stopped by the Hermann Goering Panzer Division, and the 1st was stopped by the 3rd Panzer Grenadier Division. The Allies had missed their chance for a quick capture of Rome.

Some British historians have indicated that the chance was really nonexistent, that if Lucas had rushed to Rome he would have been cut off and hopelessly extended and the bridgehead would have been destroyed. But that argument fails to take into consideration Clark's promise of the 45th Infantry Division and Alexander's promise of other troops.

What had happened up until the Anzio landings had all been part of an audacious plan. The crossing of the Garigliano and the failed crossing of the Rapido had achieved their objectives of pinning down the troops of the Gustav Line and draining off the reinforcements in the Rome area, leaving Rome bare for attack. The failure to exploit that promptly from the Anzio beachhead had converted an audacious plan of attack to a mundane military operation. And for the next few months, the Allies were to pay a high price for that failure as the Germans reacted in the manner that Churchill had expected and changed the whole nature of the Italian campaign.

This fact began to become apparent the following week. Alexander had visited the beachhead on January 25 and he urged Clark to open a coordinated offensive to capture Cisterna and Campoleone before the Germans could build them up. He did not know that the building had already begun on these two points that blocked the roads that led to the

Alban Hills. The U.S. 1st Armored Division was assembling at the beach-head along with the 45th, and they should be able to support the attack. So a week after the initial landing, the first coordinated attack took off just after midnight on January 30. The Rangers went first, and then the 3rd attacked. Two of the three Ranger battalions fell into a German ambush, were surrounded, and had to surrender; the third battalion suffered very heavy casualties; and the 3rd was stopped without taking Cisterna.

The British 1st Infantry Division, supported by the American 1st Armored Division, got going very well toward Campoleone, and reached the railroad south of the town, but could go no farther; nor could the American tanks. The Germans were there in strength and they repelled the advance. The 1st Infantry Division was then stuck out on a salient on the Anzio–Campoleone Road.

At the beginning of February, it was apparent that something had gone wrong. The Allied troops were penned in a shallow beachhead—all of it under German artillery fire. No airfield had been captured, so all air support for the beachhead had to come from Naples. The Luftwaffe raided constantly, and effectively, sinking warships and supply ships.

The way to change the situation, Clark believed, was to get the main element of the Fifth Army moving, break through the Gustav Line into the Liri Valley, and join up with the bridgehead and then drive on Rome. So the scene of action shifted from Anzio, which was now a besieged fortress, to the Fifth Army on the Garigliano and Rapido River fronts.

19

The Attack on Cassino

General Clark wanted the 10th Corps to attack and expand its bridgeheads over the Garigliano River; and if General Alphonse-Pierre Juin could turn his French troops to the southwest in a wide envelopment move, they could outflank the Germans. Meanwhile the II Corps commander, General Keyes, would try again on the Rapido, in a much less ambitious attack that would envelop the defenses just north of the town of Cassino.

In the south, General McCreery's 10th Corps was too close to exhaustion to do very much, so there was little action on that front. Juin prepared to attack on January 25 against Monte Belvedere, about five miles north of Cassino.

Since the U.S. 36th Infantry Division was virtually wrecked and needed reorganization, the U.S. 34th Infantry Division was chosen by Keyes to make the attack in the center. The attack would be two-pronged. One arm would strike for Cassino on the river, the other arm would strike across the Monte Cassino Massif, a collection of mountain peaks that stands over the valleys of the Rapido and the Liri. Once across the high ground, the 34th would be in the Liri Valley, three miles behind the Rapido River and Monte Cassino. To support the 34th, Keyes ordered the 36th to make a feint to cross the Rapido—in the area where it had failed before. Also the 142nd Infantry Regiment, which had not been involved in the first effort, was to be used to make a crossing north of Sant'Angelo. Once the crossing was made, the 1st Armored Division's

Combat Command B, which had been held back from the force that went to Anzio, would exploit the advance and head for Anzio.

The first objective of the 34th was an Italian military barracks just north of Cassino. Here stood a group of some 20 one-story buildings that had been destroyed by artillery fire but now were fortified by the Germans with pillboxes and other refined defenses. South of them to Cassino, the bank of the Rapido was a narrow shelf about 300 yards wide. Beneath the shadow of Monte Cassino on this shelf, the troops would have protection from the German artillery: north of the barracks the high ground was farther from the Rapido. And two miles away at the village of Cairo, a flat plain stretched for a mile between two hills called "Hill 56" and "Hill 213."

Starting the drive from the far side of the Rapido, Major General Charles W. Ryder, commander of the 34th Infantry Division, planned to send one force south of Cassino and the other west. With its first objective being Monte Castellone, three miles north of the barracks area. There the troops were to turn out and advance to the slope overlooking the Liri Valley.

First the 34th would have to take the barracks area, a hard job because the Germans had thoroughly mined the approaches and had artillery trained on the area. The Americans would have to cross open ground that had been flooded, rendering armor and heavy vehicles useless.

Ryder ordered the 133rd Infantry Regiment to take the barracks area. The 1st and 3rd Battalions would cross the Rapido to the north and south of Monte Villa, and then the 100th Infantry Battalion* would cross and turn south of the road leading into Cassino.

Once the 100th got across the river, the 756th Tank Battalion would follow with 71 tanks and give supporting fire, while the 753rd and 760th Tank Battalions were to add support fire, and make ready to cross.

To avoid German observation the 133rd started its attack at 10:00 P.M. on January 24. Almost at once the attack was stopped. Mud disorganized the units—it grasped and held the tanks—and strong fire from the barracks area made the advance seemingly impossible. At 4:30 in the morning, Ryder decided to move to the right where the ground seemed firm. The 3rd Battalion sloped to the right of the 1st Battalion, and the 100th Battalion moved still farther north. An artillery barrage helped the 100th get a few men across the river, but there they were stopped by barbed-wire entanglements covered by machine-gun fire. They cleared a lane through the wire, and four-and-a-half hours later, the 100th had several squads across the Rapido. Four hours after that, the 3rd Battalion had

---

*The 100th Infantry Battalion, which was now the 2nd Battalion of the 133rd Infantry Regiment, was allowed to keep its distinctive name because it was made up almost entirely of Nisei—second-generation Japanese–Americans—and was the first Nisei unit organized by the U.S. Army from the Hawaii National Guard.

consolidated a small bridgehead. By midnight, the 133rd consolidated that small bridgehead.

On January 25, the regiment was told to hold and that night to expand its bridgehead so that tanks could be moved across. But the German fire was such that the troops were unable to get practically anywhere that day. By nightfall on January 26, they were still close to the river.

The problem, as Ryder saw it, was fire coming from Hill 213, northeast of the barracks area, so he committed the 135th Infantry Regiment to cross the Rapido and strike toward Hill 213 from the south. Seizure of the hill would open the way for the assault west to Monte Castellone and to the Liri Valley.

During the night of January 26, the 135th got a company across the river, but it was almost immediately entangled in barbed wire, flooded ditches, minefields, and soggy ground. The tanks could not ford the stream—six tanks tried and got stuck.

So parts of two regiments held small bridgeheads across the Rapido, but that was not enough. Keyes wanted his armor across, and he pressed Ryder to get going. So Ryder ordered the 168th Infantry Regiment to pass through the 133rd on the morning of January 27 and renew the attack.

Ryder was going to send two battalions to attack abreast, each preceded by a platoon of tanks. The tanks would break down the wire, overrun antipersonnel mines, and destroy the enemy blockhouses. They would have artillery operation for an hour, and then a rolling barrage. The Americans were learning something about the terrain and their enemy. If the tanks could make a go for the river and then get across, Ryder thought he had a chance to succeed where the previous efforts had failed.

The barrage began just before dawn on January 27. Tanks started to move. Some of them slipped off the narrow paths and hung up in the mud, or under water. But two tanks got across the river and then two more, but they had so churned up the soft ground that the others could not follow. The engineers began to build corduroy roads to the river, but this would take hours, and so the infantrymen began to go ahead. The two assault battalions, despite strong enemy fire, each got a company across the river. What a change, and what it largely represented was morale from divisional top to bottom. The 34th Infantry Division thought it could be done, whereas the 36th Infantry Division had been sure they would fail, and so they had.

By three o'clock in the afternoon, those four tanks were all out of action. But they had given the infantry a start and the riflemen worked their way across the level ground. By nightfall, they reached the base of Hill 213. They had incurred heavy losses, but they had arrived at their jumping-off point. A fifth company crossed the river after dark and climbed to the top of Hill 213, undetected by the Germans.

But there the company commander made a dreadful mistake. He decided that his position was too far forward and that he had to go back. His men thought he was retreating in the face of the enemy and the movement became a rout, with the troops fleeing across the river. Their panic was infectious and the other two companies also panicked and ran, not stopping until they were back on the American side. This meant the other two companies that were left on the German shore were in a critical position so they had to be brought back, and two days of hard work were totally undone, with many men killed, wounded, and missing—all because of one officer's panic.

But all was not lost. These two companies were still organized, and they were led to another crossing 500 yards north. They went across again and moved about a mile toward the village of Cairo, between the Rapido and the village. Two platoons occupied defensive positions in the shadow of Monte Cairo. The rest of the companies tried to protect the route from the enemy. If a trail could be forged by the engineers for the tanks, the division would be able to recover and complete its Rapido crossing.

Meanwhile, the French were also moving. General Juin attacked on the morning of January 25 to capture Monte Belvedere. The fight took two days. But at the end of the second day, the 3rd Algerian Division had the mountain, which meant they had made a real threat to the Gustav Line. The problem was that the French troop's power stretched thin, and they were near the point of exhaustion after their Herculean feat. They could not move on to the next point and take Mount Abate.

What was needed now, said General Juin in a letter to General Clark, was for the 34th Infantry Division to take the heights to the southeast of Monte Cairo and Monte Castellone. The French had done an astounding job, but now they needed help, and fast.

So the situation had again changed. The French had saved the day, although at heavy expense. General Keyes was ordered to help them with the dispatch of a unit into the area between the 3rd Algerian and 34th Infantry Divisions to drive west to Monte Castellone. Keyes put together a rump force, using the 36th Infantry Division's 142nd Infantry Regiment. With tanks and tank destroyers, that regiment was to lead the tanks force in an attack to help the French and capitalize on their success.

General Ryder was continuing the attack of the 34th. The 168th Infantry Regiment committed all its battalions across the Rapido to advance on the Cairo plain against Hill 213 and Hill 56. The attack started early on the morning of January 29, and by 7:00 A.M., seven tanks had crossed the river. Although four of them were either hit or used up all their ammunition very quickly, the presence of the tanks helped the morale of the infantry immeasurably, and they made steady progress in the struggle to cross the plain.

That afternoon, the 756th Tank Battalion found a new approach to the Rapido and was able to ford it. Twenty-three tanks crossed the river and began firing at the German machine guns at the base of the massif. This produced excellent results for the infantry. The tanks fired their 75-mm guns, and the rifle companies advanced across the plain until by 6:45 A.M. they had all reached the base of the hills. The tank shells had ripped up the barbed wire and so the troops had no trouble getting through. By dawn on January 30, the infantry held the hills.

But the next morning the Germans counterattacked, and did so again the following day. The American communications failed—their radios had been soaked in the river crossing—and on January 30, they were out of communication with the command across the river. The tanks brought up ammunition, but while the French and American assaults had made an indentation in the Gustav Line, they had not broken through it. The Germans held on to the key military barracks area and they intended to hold the Cassino area, even if it meant moving troops from other areas.

At the beginning of February, the Allies faced the problem of getting troops to join up with the Anzio beachhead. The Germans faced the problem of eliminating the beachhead and holding the Gustav Line. But they could not move troops from the Gustav Line to wipe out the Anzio beachhead. It was quite the other way. Kesselring was having to take troops out of Anzio to bolster the defense of the Gustav Line. In early February, the line held about six divisions, or about half as many again as had been there at the time of the first Rapido River crossing attempt in January.

The Allied attack on the Cassino area continued in February. On February 2, the 133rd Infantry Regiment took the barracks area and tried to move on the town of Cassino but were promptly stopped by German machine-gun and artillery fire. On February 3, they reached the outskirts and then began a new tactic: street fighting. This entailed clearing each house individually. Five or six men would work together against a single building. Three men would creep close to the house under cover of fire from the others, throw one or two hand grenades into the lower rooms, and then rush the doors and windows as soon as the grenade exploded. They would also fire rifle grenades through the upper windows to drive the Germans downstairs, where they were killed or captured.

On the mountain side, the rocky ground made it impossible to dig foxholes, so the men piled rocks around themselves for protection. The weather stayed wet, and cold. Snow and ice made the trails treacherous. Trench foot was a common ailment. But so close did the 34th Infantry Division seem to a breakthrough that the assault continued on February 4 without a let up. One attack came within several hundred yards of the Monte Cassino abbey.

But by the end of February 4, the 34th was exhausted and so General Ryder called a halt. For three days, infantrymen rested while the artillery carried the battle.

Ryder planned a new assault as part of the Fifth Army assault. Tenth Corps attacked on the night of February 7; II Corps at daybreak on February 8; and the 133rd with tank support managed to get a foothold in Cassino. But at the end of February 14, they would still be fighting to hold that small bit of ground, and it was the same with the 36th Infantry Division—all the attempts to break into the Liri Valley failed.

At the beginning of February, General Alexander had created a new unit—the New Zealand Corps—which consisted of the 2nd New Zealand Division and the 4th Indian Infantry Division. He was now considering putting that unit into the line because the 34th and 36th Infantry Divisions were virtually exhausted and the 36th was estimated to be down to 25 percent effectiveness. A breakthrough was in reach: the fighting had brought II Corps to within a mile of Route 6 in the Liri Valley. But II Corps could do no more. It was now up to the New Zealand Corps.

20

The Bombing of Monte Cassino

Since the beginning of the Italian campaign, the Allied forces in the field had been aware of a special problem in the fighting on Italian soil: the preservation of the works of art of ancient and medieval societies. This matter had first been brought to the attention of General Eisenhower before the invasion of Sicily. It was not forgotten. Soon after the Fifth Army crossed the Volturno River, General Clark reminded his troops that every precaution must be taken to protect church properties, and, therefore would be carefully avoided, with the caveat that if a situation warranted military action, it would be taken.

The old Benedictine Abbey atop Monte Cassino was a case in point. This was the original home of the Benedictines. Early in the campaign, Italian museum authorities in southern Italy had explained its historic significance, and Clark's staff had stressed the necessity of avoiding the bombardment of the abbey. It seemed unlikely that any damage would be done by the Allied forces.

But in the fighting around the base of the mountain in January, some artillery got out of control and hits were made on the abbey. A report came from the Vatican that the abbey had been seriously damaged by artillery fire. When the Fifth Army artillery officer investigated, he had to concede that it might be true, although he claimed that if so it had been accidental because they had been firing on the town of Cassino at the base of the mountain. In any case, new instructions were given to the artillery to avoid any hits on the abbey.

At the time, General Alexander's headquarters added a proviso: "Consideration for the safety of such areas will not be allowed to interfere with military necessity."[20]

In fact, the monastery and the 70 monks who lived there had already been bothered more than a little by the war. In October, several hundred civilian refugees, fleeing from the fighting zones, had taken refuge there, creating problems for the monks. Worse, a German pilot had inadvertently crashed his plane into the wires that controlled the funicular railroad that ran from the base of the mountain to the top, destroying it. As the war raged around the abbey, there was no hope of repair, so the single six-mile road up the mountain from the town to the abbey became the only method of communication. That month of October, the Allies, too, added to the damage to the abbey when they were bombing the town of Cassino and several bombs went astray. But these were all regarded as accidents of war, and the monks remained confident that both the Allies and the Germans would respect the sanctity of the monastery. As far as the Germans were concerned, they had every assurance. General von Vietinghoff was himself a Roman Catholic, and he had promised that no harm would come to the abbey from his troops, nor would they use the abbey for military purposes, thus giving the Allies an excuse to destroy it.

After the Allied bombing in October, the Germans came to the abbot—Archbishop Don Gregorio Diamare—and offered to evacuate all the art treasures of the abbey, just in case. But the abbot was feeling secure in the promises of the Germans and the promises of the Allies, so he refused the offer. Still, the Germans came back a few days later, and this time the abbot decided they might be right, that somehow in the fighting the abbey would get hurt. So he acquiesced in the removal of the artwork. In the next few days German military trucks hauled several loads of art treasures out of the abbey and took them to the Vatican.

Convinced now that the defense line all around the abbey made it a danger zone, most of the monks left the abbey for Rome, and so did the nuns, orphans, and schoolchildren normally housed there. Most of the civilian refugees left as well, but more kept arriving, so there were always some in residence. Also remaining at the abbey were the abbot, five monks, five lay brothers, and about 150 civilian refugees.

The Germans were seriously concerned about the abbey knowing that the fighting around it would endanger it. It became a matter of the highest concern to the command and was discussed by von Vietinghoff and Kesselring. The field marshal assured the Vatican representatives that the Germans would not enter the abbey or use it for military purposes, and General von Senger was informed that no German troops were to occupy the abbey, so von Senger put if off limits. A line was drawn two yards from the abbey all around it and the army stationed military policemen around the abbey to keep all the Germans out.

But Kesselring did not expect the Allies to honor any agreements about the sacred land, so he stipulated that the protected zone included only the monastery and not the hill itself. So all the outlying buildings were demolished and the Germans set up fields of fire, observation posts, and guns. They also built an ammunition dump close to the monastery.

Early in January the Germans asked the abbot to vacate the monastery but he refused. They evacuated all the refugees except a few who were too sick to leave. Stray American and British artillery rounds kept falling on the hilltop, and on February 5, one round killed a civilian. A violent bombardment of the neighboring farmhouses caused about 40 women to seek sanctuary in the monastery, even though shells kept falling inside. By February 8, the monastery had been hit about 100 times by "accidental" Allied shelling.

The German attack at Anzio caused the Allies to double their effort in February to break through to the Liri Valley. In this effort, II Corps became exhausted, and the task was turned over to the New Zealand Corps under General Freyberg, the officer who had commanded the British troops on Crete with so little success. The New Zealand Corps consisted of the 2nd New Zealand Division which occupied the area on the flats east of Cassino and directly in front of the entrance to the Liri Valley— and the 4th Indian Infantry Division—which was to clear the high ground behind the town of Cassino and then move into the Liri Valley from the north. In support, the American 36th Infantry Division was on Monte Castellone, and the 34th Infantry Division's 133rd Infantry Regiment was in the northeast corner of Cassino. The British 78th Infantry Division was ordered up from the Adriatic to bolster the left flank of the New Zealand Corps, which had its own artillery and the support of the II Corps artillery as well.

Freyberg was a difficult officer even for the British. They treated him with kid gloves because they needed the New Zealand troops, and referred often to his reputation as a hero of the 1914–1918 War. General Clark met with him on February 4 and was not very impressed. Freyberg intimated that single-handedly he could win the war. Clark wondered if he would litter up the Liri Valley with his oversupply of vehicles. Clark had a sense then that Freyberg meant trouble to the command.

They met again on February 9, and Freyberg complained that the Monte Cassino monastery might interfere with his operations. Clark then adopted the indeterminate stance used by all the Allied high command: He gave Freyberg a written directive authorizing him to fire on the monastery if, in his judgment, it was necessary.

At about this time the commander of the 4th Indian Infantry Division, Major General F.S. Tuker, took a look at the Americans of the II Corps. They had suffered enormous casualties in their efforts to get into the Liri

Valley. Tuker immediately decided that the monastery must be destroyed so his troops could carry out their mission. He asked Freyberg to arrange for an aerial bombardment to destroy the monastery.

Freyberg, who had shown at Crete that he did not know the first thing about aerial operations, called the Fifth Army and asked for three missions of 12 planes each, the planes to be British Kitty bombers, carrying 1,000-pound bombs. General Gruenther, the chief of staff, who took the call, noted that this was a very slight bombardment, but he did not question Freyberg. He promised that Clark would try to divert air support from Anzio for the purpose. When Gruenther told Freyberg that the abbey was not on the list of approved targets, Freyberg insisted that it must be attacked. As he put it, if no other targets were attacked, he wanted the monastery destroyed.

Gruenther could not get in touch with Clark so he called General Alexander's superior command and laid it out for him. Freyberg insisted on the monastery being bombed. Clark had told him repeatedly that in his opinion there was no military necessity to bomb the monastery, but Freyberg still insisted.

While they waited for Alexander to act, Clark called in to his headquarters and again said that the monastery was not a necessary target. "General Clark also stated that this was a matter which caused him some embarrassment, in view of the extremely strong views of General Freyberg. General Clark felt that unless General Freyberg receded from this position it would place General Clark in a very difficult position in the event that the attack should fail."

Gruenther then asked General Keyes, the commander of II Corps, what he thought. Keyes said it was unnecessary to bomb the monastery, and that if it was destroyed, the rubble would enhance its value as a military obstacle because then the Germans would feel free to use it as a barricade. They then called on the artillerymen, who said 2,000 refugees had taken shelter in the monastery and that they knew it was not being used as a firing point.

So the Americans were united. The destruction of the monastery was not necessary nor was it advisable. But then Alexander's headquarters called back and said that the field marshal had said that if Freyberg wanted the monastery destroyed, it should be destroyed. Alexander said he had faith in Freyberg's judgment.

Gruenther made it quite clear that Clark was against bombing the monastery and that if the request came from an American commander he would refuse it. It was only because the request was British, and furthermore came from one of the touchy Commonwealth commanders, that he was even considering it. But Alexander now joined in the insistence, and so it was decided that the British should have their way and the monastery would be destroyed. However, they still tried to talk Freyberg out of his decision, but he threatened Clark that if he did not authorize the bombing, and the attack failed, he would be held responsible.

The bombardment was postponed. Alexander consulted Clark again, and Clark told him the bombardment was only being authorized because the British insisted on it. Alexander then went to General Wilson, the theater commander, who supported the Freyberg position. So the question had developed into a British–American confrontation, and within it were all the frustrations and irritations of both sides. Freyberg's position had now become that the monastery must be totally destroyed before the Indians could take the hill.

The bombardment was scheduled for February 16 and leaflets were dropped in the area. But the leaflets were very carelessly dropped and none of them fell inside the monastery. The only way the abbot learned of the coming bombing was because a civilian had picked up a leaflet on the hill and had brought it to him. The abbot then sent word to the Germans that he needed help to evacuate the civilians. Agreement was reached that the civilians would leave the abbey at five o'clock in the morning on February 16. But the American force—a squadron of A-36 bombers carrying 500-pound bombs—began the bombing 19 hours beforehand, hitting the abbey with bombs from 250 bombers until the abbey was reduced to a mass of rubble. About 600 tons of high explosives fell on the abbey. How many civilians were killed has never been revealed, but there were an estimated 2,500 inside when the bombing began as a complete surprise.

The bombing had several effects, all of them anticipated by the Americans. After the planes had left, the Germans emerged from their shelters and occupied the area, using the rubble for defense. Two days later, after the abbot had left the ruins, other Germans took over the whole system, and found the ruins excellent for defensive purposes. Within five days the paratroopers had constructed a virtually impregnable strong point. The Indians pulled back just before the bombardment—but not fast enough as it turned out because they suffered 24 casualties—which allowed the Germans to take over their old positions, which the Americans had fought bitterly to win.

The propaganda damage to the Allied cause was enormous. The Germans played this Allied error for all it was worth. On the morning of February 18, General von Senger and the abbot appeared before movie cameras that recorded the destruction of the ancient abbey for the Nazi Ministry of Propaganda.

"The Abbey Montecassino is completely destroyed," said the officer who introduced the interview. "A senseless act of force of the Anglo–American air force has robbed civilized mankind of one of its most valuable cultural monuments. Abbot Bishop Gregorio Diamare has been brought out of the ruins of his abbey under the protection of the German Armed Forces. He voluntarily placed himself in their protection and by them was brought through a ring of fire of Allied artillery which has been laid around the monastery without interruption since the aerial bombardment, and into the Command Post of the Commanding General.

"The old abbot, who today is 80 years old, found here a place of refuge and recovery after four days of horror which he, his monks, and numerous refugees, women, children, old men, crippled, sick, and wounded civilians had to undergo because of the order of the Allied Supreme Commander. We find the general and the abbot in a voluntary discussion into which we now cut in."

General von Senger: Everything was done on the part of the German Armed Forces, definitely everything, in order to give the opponent no military ground for attacking the monastery.

Abbot: General, I can only confirm this. You declared the Abbey Montecassino a protected zone. You forbade German soldiers to step within the area of the abbey. You ordered that within a specified perimeter around the abbey there be neither weapons, no observation posts, or billeting of troops. You have tirelessly taken care that these orders were most strictly observed. Until the moment of destruction of the Montecassino Abbey there was within the area of the abbey no German soldier, nor any German weapon, nor any German military installation.

General von Senger: It came to my attention much too late that leaflets which announced the bombing of the area were dropped over the monastery. I first learned this after the bombing. No leaflets were dropped over our German positions.

Abbot: I have the feeling that the leaflets were intentionally dropped so late in order to give us no possibility to notify the German commander or on the other hand to bring some 800 guests of the monastery out of the danger zone. We simply did not believe the English and the Americans would attack the abbey. And when they came with their bombs, we laid out white cloths in order to say to them, do nothing to us, we are no military objective, here it is a holy place. It did not help. They have destroyed the monastery and killed hundreds of innocent people.

General von Senger: Can I do anything more?

Abbot: No, general. You have done everything—even today the German Armed Forces provide for us and for the refugees in model fashion. But I have something still to do, namely to thank you and the German Armed Forces for all the consideration given to the original abode of the Benedictine Order both before and after the bombardment. I thank you.[21]

The Vatican protested the bombing, and President Roosevelt answered that it was an unfortunate necessity of war. But the world never believed it. The blame was fixed on General Clark, and he was castigated for the bombing for many years thereafter. The damage in neutral countries, particularly Roman Catholic countries, was irreparable, although the Germans played the scene for so much that the Vatican finally protested.

The irony is that the affair turned out just as General Clark had feared it would. The bombing did absolutely no good militarily; instead, it strengthened the German positions on the mountain. The Indians were not told when the air attack was going to happen, so they were not ready to take advantage of the shock to the enemy in the area. Instead, they attacked at midnight on February 17 with a Rajputani Rifle Battalion and two Gurkha Battalions. The Rajputanis took their objective, losing all but two of their officers in the process and found that their way to the monastery was still blocked by the Germans in depth. The first Gurkha Battalion mistook a belt of brush shown on aerial photos for the sort of brush they would find on an Indian hillside, and ran into five-foot-high thornbushes laced with wire and antipersonnel mines, and covered by strong German positions they had not noticed before the advance.

The Gurkhas fought hard but could not break through and had to withdraw. The second Gurkha Battalion was directed to clear the ridge in front of the Rajputani Rifle position, and they did; but as dawn came up, they found that they were in the open and exposed to fire from the Germans who had now taken over the ruins of the monastery. So the attack was withdrawn before full daylight arrived. Down below the mount, on the railway, the Maoris of the New Zealand division took the station but soon were driven off by a counterattack.

What the British call "the Third Battle of Cassino" was fought from March 15 to March 23, with the New Zealanders again attacking Cassino and the 5th Indian Brigade going through the New Zealanders at dark and up Castle Hill to move against the monastery.

At 8:30 on the morning of March 15, General Alexander and his staff, with a party of journalists, watched from a farmhouse five miles away as 500 bombers plastered Cassino. Then the artillery barrage started after three-and-a-half hours, and the New Zealanders moved forward. They met heavy fire from the Germans. They reached Route 6 but could not go forward. The Castle Hill force reached the lower hairpin bends of the road as darkness came. Rain fell that night in torrents, the moon was drowned out and the sappers, who were clearing tank routes, got mixed up with the advancing Indians, who were coming up to fight, and the Indians were stopped when they tried to take the upper hairpin bend on the Castle Road. One battalion was almost completely wiped out by German artillery fire. One Gurkha Battalion went on alone and got separated and confused and ended up holding the Castle and lower hairpin, with an isolated company on Hangman's Hill.

The Germans were reinforced during the night, and the next day they started the fight all over again: positions changed hands almost by the hour. For two days and two nights this went on. On March 18, General Freyberg decided to make a coordinated attack the next morning. The Indians were to take Hangman's Hill and then the monastery; but the Germans attacked first, and so dislocated the Allied plan that it was ultimately called off. The Allied position grew worse on the night of March 19. For three more days General Alexander pursued the attack and failed. The Indians were evacuated and the battle was over on March 25, having cost the New Zealand Corps 4,000 men and accomplished nothing. It seems to have been a problem of inept leadership. Alexander must have thought so as well because the New Zealand Corps was disbanded and its battered units were posted to other corps. Instead of winning the war, General Freyberg was relegated to obscurity.

So March ended, and the Germans still held firmly to the Gustav Line.

21

The Germans at Anzio

In the early days of February 1944, German General van Mackensen prepared the offensive with which he proposed to push the Allied beachhead off the Anzio shore. Three new divisions arrived plus a special regiment: the Berlin–Spandau Infantry Lehr Regiment, which was to teach the recruits how to conduct an assault. This regiment was one of Hitler's dream schemes. The other new units were the 29th Panzer Grenadier Division, which came from the Tenth Army front; the 114th Jaeger Division, which had been rushed from Yugoslavia; and the 362nd Infantry Division, which came from northern Italy.

General van Mackensen set his attack for February 16. The Lehr Regiment would lead the attack as Hitler had ordered. The other units in the main attack would be the 3rd Panzer Grenadier, 114th Jaeger, and 715th Infantry Divisions. In the second wave would come the 29th Panzer Grenadier and 26th Panzer Divisions to exploit the breakthrough and drive to the coast. Meanwhile, a diversionary attack would be made by the 1st Paratroop Corps, with the 4th Parachute and 65th Infantry Divisions. To mask the entire enterprise, van Mackensen ordered small-scale attacks all along the front.

At this point the German Fourteenth Army consisted of 125,000 men against the Allied troops of 100,000. The situation had indeed changed. Instead of being in a position to make a dash on Rome, the Allies now had to be concerned about their ability to hold on at Anzio.

On the morning of February 16, the Hermann Goering Panzer Division launched a feint attack on the American 3rd Infantry Division but met little success. The 4th Parachute Division did better, and broke the 56th Infantry Division line and moved two miles before it was stopped by British reserves. The main attack on both sides of the Anzio–Albano Road struck the American 45th Infantry Division whose three regiments were along a six-mile front in the center of the beachhead perimeter. Fierce fighting went on all day, but the Germans did not get very far. They had counted on tank support to carry the battle for them. The tanks started out on ground that had frozen during the night, but by mid-morning, it had turned to slush and tank maneuvers off the roads became impossible.

The Infantry Lehr Regiment proved to be a big disappointment like so many of Hitler's favorite schemes. The inexperienced troops lost many officers and suffered heavy casualties, and they panicked and ran. Thus, the attack was not a success and had failed in van Mackensen's prime purpose, which was to force the Americans to commit to battle their reserves: the 1st Armored Division. That was van Mackensen's goal for the second day of the attack.

The Germans kept up the pressure on the American 157th Infantry Regiment all night. In the fighting, Company E was all but wiped out. By dawn, when they were permitted to withdraw from their position, it was found that there were only 14 riflemen were left. This left a gap between two of the 45th Infantry Division's regiments.

The morning brought attack on the 45th's area by 35 German planes that bombed and strafed. Then came 60 tanks to hit the 2nd Battalion of the 179th Infantry Regiment. They destroyed one company and forced the rest of the battalion back almost to General Lucas's final beachhead line. By noon, the Germans had driven a wedge into the center of the 45th's line. The 179th drew back, and the Germans tore them to shreds as they did so. Small groups of men scattered and made their way back to the final beachhead line. The line was saved when Lucas made tanks and artillery available to the 179th and called fire from the ships offshore, while Allied planes came in to attack the Germans. The British 1st Infantry Division was brought up to back up the 179th, and a tank battalion of the American 1st Armored Division also was called into the battle.

In the afternoon, van Mackensen sent 14 battalions of infantry and tanks to try to force the issue, but the Allied line did not break because they were supported by very heavy artillery fire.

On the night of the second day, van Mackensen considered breaking off the battle because his assault divisions had taken so many casualties. The average battalion was down to between 120 and 150 men. His chief of staff thought they were winning and convinced van Mackensen that it would be a crime to break off at this point; so on the third day, February 18, the Germans renewed that assault. The 29th Panzer Grenadier and 26th Panzer Divisions virtually destroyed a battalion of the 179th

Infantry Regiment before noon and made deep penetration and were on the point of pushing forward to the final Allied line. The commander of the 179th asked to withdraw from the line to a place of safety in the concealment of the woods, but the commander of the 45th Infantry Division said there would be no withdrawal. The line held that afternoon, and the German attack failed. The British and the Americans fought very effectively and made the best use of their artillery. By evening, van Mackensen knew that his attack had failed. The Germans made a further attack the next day to try to consolidate their lines, but the Allies counterattacked and took 400 prisoners. One more German thrust was made on the 20th, but it failed as well, and the struggle ended.

The Allies had taken serious casualties in this struggle. The 45th alone suffered 400 killed, 2,000 wounded, and 1,000 missing, plus another 2,500 men suffering from frostbite, trench foot, and exhaustion.

General Alexander had visited the front and did not like Lucas's leadership. He told General Clark about it, and Clark agreed to make a change after the battle. So the shooting had scarcely stopped when Lucas was fired. Why? He was seen as too tired, for one thing. But actually he was fired for not taking the Alban Hills, when if he had taken them, and rushed on and been cut off by the enemy and lost the beachhead, he would have been fired for doing it that way. All the way through, Lucas's orders had been fuzzy, representing the confusion of the higher command, which could not decide what it wanted to do. From the beginning Lucas had expected to be the goat, and he was not disappointed.

Now Alexander spoke of needing a man like General Patton, who could be counted on to make any thrust offered, and he told Clark that. He got Major General Truscott, the commander of the 3rd Infantry Division.

Pressed by Hitler, the Germans planned another attack at Anzio on February 22 to drive on the other side of the beachhead, and reach Nettuno. He would use the Hermann Goering Panzer Division, the 26th Panzer Division, and the 362nd Infantry Division, with the 29th Panzer Division in reserve. He would make spectacular displays to fool the Allies.

The attack was set for daylight on February 28, but 24 hours before the attack, he requested a postponement because of the bad weather. Kesselring agreed to the postponement and was glad he had because on the 28th a torrential rain fell on the battle zone. The Germans thought it would lull the Allies; and during the rainy afternoon, the Germans shifted their troops around and got ready. Around midnight, the Germans began a barrage against the 3rd Infantry Division. The men of the 3rd were exhausted from six weeks of fighting. General O'Daniel expected an attack. He had only been in command of the division since February 17, but he had a sense of the dramatic, and he ordered artillery fire on the routes the Germans would have to use. But the artillery did not disrupt the German attack, and they overran a company of the 509th Parachute Battalion on the left of the 3rd. Only one officer and 22 men escaped to reach the main line of resistance, where a company of 96 men stopped the Germans.

On the main front, the Germans struck the front of the 3rd with tanks and infantry; the division line gave, but did not break. On the east the Germans did break through the 504th Parachute Infantry, but the break was quickly sealed off. Against the Special Service Force along the Mussolini Canal, the Germans did not make any progress at all.

Heavy fighting continued all day, with clouds and squalls making visibility difficult. Allied planes were grounded in the morning, but in the afternoon 17 fighter bombers and 24 light bombers made close support attacks on the Germans. At the end of the day, the 3rd made a counterattack and regained all the ground that had been lost during the day.

Van Mackensen continued the attack on March 1, but he had suffered so many losses that the effort was weak and made no progress. At the end of the day, he had to admit to Kesselring that he had failed to dislodge the beachhead, and Kesselring told him to go on the defensive.

March 2 dawned bright and clear. Allied planes came over in strength: 341 heavy bombers and 175 fighters dropped tons of bombs behind the German lines, hitting German tanks and guns. Light bombers and medium bombers came in to work over the Germans some more. All this, plus the offensive, had cost the Germans a great deal: 3,000 casualties and about 40 tanks. It was the last offensive the Germans would make against the beachhead. It was, of course, Hitler's idea to raise morale at home, and it had failed miserably and cost the Germans in Italy a great deal.

Kesselring now expected a respite because he knew the Allies had also sustained heavy casualties in the recent battles. He sent his chief of staff to see Hitler and explain. General Westphal went with considerable nervousness, but he was eloquent in his explanations of the German position and got Hitler to agree that any more attacks at Anzio would be foolhardy and wasteful at the present time. Kesselring had to build up his forces once again before he could manage any moves.

So Kesselring established a new line of defense, from the mouth of the Tiber River through Cisterna, Valmontone, and Avezzano to Pescara, which was called the Caesar Line. So the situation at Anzio quieted down in March as it did along the Gustav Line where the Allies had exhausted themselves. Both sides settled down to wait for spring.

22

Spring Offensive

As spring came to Italy in 1944, the German armies had stopped the Allied advance between the Adriatic and the Mediterranean below Rome at the Gustav Line. They also surrounded an 30-mile-long Allied beachhead south of Rome at Anzio, extending 15 miles from Anzio northwestward toward the German stronghold of Cisterna.

The main Allied front stretched for 100 miles from the Gulf of Gaeta on the Tyrrhenian Sea across the Appenine Mountains to the Adriatic Sea. On May 11, 1944, the Allies launched a new attack along the Gustav Line, called "Operation Diadem." One cannot say it was unexpected by the Germans, they were always expecting attack in Italy, but it came at a time when most of the senior German officers involved in the defense were away from the Gustav Line. General von Vietinghoff, commander of the Tenth Army, was in Germany getting an award from Hitler. General Westphal was in Germany on convalescent leave. General von Senger, the 14th Panzer Corps commander, was home on 30-day leave.

In this extraordinary situation, at 11:00 P.M., the massed artillery of two Allied armies—1,600 field guns—opened fire along the front from Cassino to the Tyrrhenian Sea. Troops of the U.S. II Corps and the French Expeditionary Force began moving up the slopes of the hills on the lower reaches of the Garigliano River. At 11:45 P.M., the British Eighth Army opened its attack with their 13th Corps on the Rapido River. At 1:00 A.M., the Polish II Corps attacked Monte Cassino, and within two hours captured two high points of ground—the Phantom Ridge and Point 593—but the German resistance and counterattack was so severe that the next day the Poles were forced to withdraw to their line of departure northeast of Monte Cassino. They had lost half their number and had accomplished nothing.

The main British attack was in the valley below, where the 13th Corps established a bridgehead across the Rapido with the British 4th Indian Infantry Division on the right and the 8th Indian Infantry Division on the left. The British bridgehead was shallow and insecure but the Indians did better, and by afternoon, they were two miles south of Cassino. For the first time, the Allies had put two vehicular bridges across the Rapido.

On the Fifth Army front, there was no river to cross. The American 88th and 85th Infantry Divisions attacked at the break point between the German 71st Light Infantry Division and the 94th Infantry Division under an artillery barrage that had begun hours before.

The main advance here would be made by the 351st Infantry Regiment to the village of Santa Maria Infante, and then across the Ausonia Road to the Petrella escarpment. The 349th and the 350th Infantry Regiments would support this attack to the northeast and northwest. The 350th did a magnificent job, largely because of Staff Sergeant Charles W. Shea of Company F, who single-handedly attacked three sepearate German machine-gun positions and captured them all, which allowed the 2nd Battalion to reach the summit of Mount Damiano. Within 13 hours, the 350th had captured its first objective, but this victory was the only one for the whole corps during the first day of the offensive. The 351st ran into veteran Germans of the 94th Infantry Division. The battalion and company organizations broke down in the violence of the fighting and the advance of the division was stalled. Colonel Raymond Kendall, commander of the 2nd Battalion of the 351st, led his men in gallant fighting, until he was mortally wounded. His executive officer took over, but the 351st attack failed to make significant headway against determined and intelligent German opposition.

At nightfall on May 12, the Germans still held Santa Maria Infante. On the left the 339th Infantry Regiment encountered the same sort of opposition. Everywhere the Germans had held, and although they had been hurt, the Americans did not know it. The artillery had caused the Germans a great deal of loss; and when daylight came on May 12, the Allied fighters and bombers took over and added to the damage.

The French captured Mount Majo after Moroccan infantrymen first took Monte Feucci and thus forced the Germans to withdraw. So the French had really breached the Gustav Line. This attack had unhinged the whole German defense and had brought the French into position to put pressure on the German defense of the right flank in the Liri Valley. Seeing this, Kesselring on May 13, sent the 90th Panzer Grenadier Division from the mouth of the Tiber River southeast to the southern front. Early on the morning of the 14th, the Germans began to move. The 200th

Panzer Grenadier Regiment was the first to reach the front, 75 miles away. It was committed to trying to stop the French advance from Monte Majo to the town of San Giorgio on the southern edge of the Liri Valley.

So everything had changed. The key to the Gustav Line did not seem to be Monte Cassino but Monte Majo. But, then, the fording of the Germans to move troops to prevent the French advance had enabled the British 13th Corps to widen its bridgehead beyond the Rapido. On the 13th, the British 4th Indian Infantry Division succeeded in bridging the Rapido with three pontoon bridges, and soon had a bridgehead of 2,500 yards in depth. So the Eighth Army had done what the Fifth Army had failed to do the year before: conquer the defenses of the Rapido. Although Monte Cassino remained in German hands, the British now had bridges that enabled them to reinforce their units, and they did so. The 78th Infantry Division assembled east of the Rapido, ready to cross through the 4th Indian Infantry Division. A strong air attack that day turned out to be ineffective and reminded the Allies how strong and well constructed the German positions were along the Gustav Line. That was not the only problem. Traffic congestion on the handful of roads and German artillery fire combined to slow down the 78th, and it could not get into position to attack. The highways could not be reached by the morning of the 15th as had been hoped. So the Polish attack on Monte Cassino was scrubbed. The Eighth Army had made a hole through the Gustav Line, but they had not penetrated it in strength enough to destroy the defenses. The Germans still controlled the Liri Valley.

On the Fifth Army front, the German command ordered a counterattack by the 94th Infantry Division to pinch off the penetrations by the U.S. II Corps. All along the line, the German line troops called for reinforcements, but they did not get them. General Keyes, the corps commander, called on the 88th and 85th Infantry Divisions to strike and break through what he saw as weakened German resistance. General Clark arrived on the field and called on the corps to carry the attack through the night, with the 88th driving through Santa Maria Infante and capturing the village of Spigno and then thrusting across the mountains.

The 351st Infantry Regiment was slow in getting going, and it was six hours before its 1st Battalion began to move, so the regimental attack was delayed. But the 2nd Battalion did not get the word and moved out into the face of heavy German fire that stalled them at their first objective. On the left, a tank infantry team also did not get the word of postponement and attacked. The tanks stalled in the valley, but the infantry charged up the hill and took the objective. They lost half their men. The Germans counterattacked, and the Americans had to retreat to their line of departure with such heavy losses that by evening the unit consisted only of 13 men.

After two hours of waiting for his first battalion, Colonel Champeny of the 351st Infantry Regiment moved to envelop Santa Maria Infante, but its positioning was wrong now, and the Germans put forth such heavy fire that the lead companies fell back in disorder. Finally, the 1st Battalion moved in an attack on Hill 109, with one company making a frontal assault after which another company was to move through. They did not know that the Germans, not Americans, held the next hill: Hill 131. Colonel Champeny sent a company to take it. They managed to claim the hill because the Germans were falling back. So Hills 109 and 131 were in Allied hands.

During the night, the Germans withdrew across the Ausonia Corridor, leaving only a rear guard behind to reestablish itself in the Gustav Line's rearmost positions along high ground from Monte Scauri to the crest of the hills overlooking the Ausonia Corridor from the west. There they linked up with the German 71st Light Infantry Division.

The French continued to advance toward San Giorgio on the southern end of the Liri Valley. The Germans were now finding control of their front line difficult to maintain and again called for reinforcement. General Steinmetz said that without them his 94th Infantry Division would have to withdraw to the Hitler Line, the second line of defense.

Before dawn on May 14, the 349th Infantry Regiment occupied Monte Bracchi with ease; and the 351st Infantry Regiment closed in on Santa Maria Infante. That day, the village was cleared. On the 88th Infantry Division's right flank, the 350th Infantry Regiment had moved to Monte Cerri. This was after a problem with morale had thrown one company into panic and confusion, but its officers succeeded in getting the men to move, and they captured Monte Cerri after a brisk fight, and with morale restored, they were ready to go on.

So the 88th had been fighting for three days, and had lost 2,000 men, but the Germans had been hurt sorely. On the night of May 14, General Steinmetz reported that his 94th had lost 40 percent of its combat strength. Now he was afraid that the Americans would move against Monte Civita, and he was right. That afternoon, the 350th moved against Spigno and the 349th against Monte Civita. The mountain fell easily on that night and the Americans surprised a German artillery unit that was still firing on the American troops in the valley below. The 350th advanced on Spigno, but General Clark grew impatient, and the 351st was sent to move through the 350th and take the town. They did this without trouble.

Clark now ordered the 88th to move across the mountains to Itri, the road junction on the enemy's lateral communications routes. He was looking for a breakout from the Anzio beachhead, and he planned to move the 36th Infantry Division up and the 85th Infantry Division to Anzio. He hoped to break through the Gustav Line at Castellonorato, which sat beneath a steep hill atop which was perched an ancient castle. This was the stronghold of the Gustav Line in that sector. But it was dominated by German positions on Hill 108, which had to be removed first. The task of taking Hill 108 was given to the 85th's 337th Infantry Regiment which would then go on and capture Castellonorato.

The attack did not go smoothly. It was stalled when engineers came under heavy fire as they tried to prepare a fording site for tanks to cross a small stream a mile-and-a-half from the hill. But eventually the tanks and infantry got going and took Hill 108, while the Germans fled toward Castellonorato. The reserve battalion of the regiment then made the final attack on the town but was held up by the setbacks that had delayed the capture of Hill 108. The next morning the infantry attacked under cover of an air bombardment and cleared the village of the enemy.

So the 85th Infantry Division and II Corps were through the Gustav Line on the seaward slope of the mountains, and the Germans were outflanked. Now they would have to withdraw from the Gustav Line.

23

The End of the Gustav Line

When the U.S. 85th Infantry Division plunged through the Gustav Line near the coast, General Hartmann, the commander of the German 14th Panzer Corps, recognized that his defense line was finished unless this breakthrough could be contained. He ordered General Steinmetz to drive the Americans out of the area. At the same time he reported to Tenth Army headquarters that either the 94th Infantry Division had to be reinforced to do the job, or the corps would have to fall back toward the next prepared defenses. But General von Vietinghoff, who had just returned from leave and knew nothing about what had developed since May 11, would not act except to authorize the withdrawal of the 94th's artillery.

To support his collapsing front, Steinmetz assembled three infantry companies and a platoon of heavy antitank guns that he rushed into position southwest of Castellonorato. The worry now was that the Americans might overrun the Dora Line before the Germans could occupy it. Then Hartmann got another company that had fought its way out of encirclement south of San Martino Hill.

General Keyes also recognized the importance of the breakthrough at Castellonorato, and on the night of May 15, he moved artillery and armor to the 85th Infantry Division, changing the focus of attack to the left to make that the main attack. From that point on, the attack was directed along the Castellonorato–Maranola Road. Keyes hoped to outflank the German communications. He did this without consulting General Clark because events were moving so fast.

On the morning of May 16, the French and II Corps had both broken through the Gustav Line between the Liri Valley and Thesea. The French had advanced into the heart of the Aurunci Mountains, and II Corps had outflanked the strongest part of the Gustav Line. But it had not been without cost. The casualties for the first 48 hours of the operation were 1,100, and total casualties were 3,000—more than in the Battle of Monte Cassino in the winter campaign. The difference was a new system of replacement by the 85th and 88th Infantry Divisions. The replacements were brought along with the unit, and trained with them, but were left behind in operations. Because of the training, they could easily be brought up when needed and slipped into the organization where they were prepared to function immediately. This was a great improvement in operations, preventing the sort of paralysis that had seized the 36th Infantry Division after its failure to cross the Rapido River.

The Eighth Army had now begun to move as well. Lieutenant General Sir Oliver Leese had assembled the 1st Canadian Infantry Division behind 13th Corps. The Canadians would cross the Rapido and help in the movement toward the Hitler Line. The British broke through the Gustav Line, and that night, the Canadians began crossing the Rapido. The next day the 78th Infantry Division attacked to cut Route 6, southwest of Cassino. The next morning, the Polish Corps resumed its attack on Monte Cassino, and on the 17th, the 13th Corps and the Poles launched a pincer attack on the Monte Cassino area. By afternoon, they had moved into the area southwest of Monte Cassino and seized the ridge north of the abbey, leaving the Germans only two escape routes: one along the Monte Cassino–Massa Albeneta Ridge, and the other along the flanks of the hills overlooking the highway. The Germans withdrew the 1st Parachute Division from the Cassino position, and a significant moment in the history of the campaign had arrived. Monte Cassino had fallen at last! So much attention had the world paid to this bit of ground, and so effective had the Nazi propaganda campaign been at its height, that all the world was aware of the Benedictine Abbey and its fate in the furious struggle between the Germans and the Allies here, and the word was radioed to Prime Minister Churchill and to President Roosevelt.

That night, the Germans counterattacked from the Villa Santa Lucia, a village two miles northwest of the abbey. It enabled the Germans to withdraw over the escape routes, and that was its only purpose. On the morning of May 18, a Polish patrol reached the ruins of the abbey, but all they found were 30 wounded German soldiers and several medical orderlies awaiting capture. That morning the Poles raised their flag over the ruins, thus ending the fourth battle for this eminence that had for so long controlled the Italian campaign. Thus, the Gustav Line was completely wiped out, and the Eighth Army could now move against the towns of Pontecorvo, Aquino, and Piedimonte San Germano, the strong points of the Hitler Line along the Liri Valley.

Field Marshal Kesselring was furious with his generals because he did not know what was going on. German field intelligence had broken down. "It is intolerable, that a division is engaged in combat for one and a half days without knowing what is going on in its sector."[23] But the fighting had been so fast and so fierce that the Tenth Army had been unable to keep abreast of events, and it had lost 2,000 men as prisoners, while taking only a handful of Allied troops from whom it could get information.

It was May 14 before General von Vietinghoff had learned that 11 Allied divisions were trying to break through the line. Shortly after the fight began the Germans had identified a number of Allied divisions that they had thought were in the rear. But two days later, they still thought that the Canadians and the South African 6th Armored Division were in Naples, possibly preparing for another amphibious landing. The British had been busily launching deception moves, and they had completely taken in the German agents in the Naples area. Thus, Kesselring had completely faulty information about Allied plans and movements for this period. He worried about a new possible amphibious landing on the Adriatic coast that was never planned, and so he was begrudging in his movement of reserves to meet the demands for reinforcement along the line. It had been a big factor in the Allied success.

On May 15, Kesselring ordered the 26th Panzer Division from the Rome area south into the Tenth Army sector, although he continued to hold it in reserve and did not commit it to von Vietinghoff. In the next few days, German Army Group C added several other units, including two regiments of the 3rd Panzer Grenadier Division to the Tenth Army sector. Von Vietinghoff moved two divisions from his Adriatic flank to the Liri Valley.

At supreme headquarters, Hitler ordered the 16th Panzer Grenadier Division from Germany to move to northern Italy. But he, too, was expecting another Allied amphibious landing, and so he refused to even think about committing more troops to the Liri Valley line.

It was now up to Alexander, who had become a field marshal, to close with the new German defenses on the Hitler Line. This line extended from the hill town of Piedimonte San Germano four miles west of Cassino to the west in the vicinity of Aquino and turned south to Pontecorvo, two-and-a-half miles away. Between Aquino and Pontecorvo, the depth of the defense was 500–1,000 yards. The Germans had built an antitank ditch and antitank minefields with belts of barbed wire at which they had set up fields of fire. Along the forward edge of the defenses were numerous prefabricated pillboxes, each of which could hold two men and a light machine gun. But the main defense was a system of reinforced concrete gun emplacements and weapons pits, all linked by tunnels and communications trenches. Nine Panther tank turrets had been mounted on concrete bases with underground bunkers for the crews. These turrets could revolve 360 degrees, and they had mobile antitank guns at their flanks. In all, 62 antitank guns—25 of them self-propelled—were on the line. The infantry was protected by deep shelters with concrete roofs five inches thick and covered with earth as much as 20 feet deep to protect against air and artillery bombardment.

But the defenses were far from perfect. The Germans were short-handed, and they had not had time to clear fields of fire through the lush vegetation that had sprung up since spring began. And they did not have enough troops to man the defenses as thoroughly as they should have and had planned earlier to have.

The troops defending the line were the 1st Parachute Division and the 90th Panzer Grenadier Division, both of which had suffered heavily in the defense of the Gustav Line. The 90th, for example, now included a number of panzer troops and engineers who were pressed into service as infantry in emergency situations. These troops were the defenders in the Piedimonte San Germano area and the Aquino–Pontecorvo area. Between Pontecorvo and Pico was the 26th Panzer Division, which had just been committed to the defense of the new line.

Field Marshal Alexander hoped that the Poles coming from the north and the French coming from the south might be able to turn the Hitler Line from the north and south and force the Germans to retreat again without a battle for the line itself. Lieutenant General Leese hoped to hit the Germans before they got set again and sent the 78th Infantry Division along Route 6 to capture Aquino. However, by the time they got there, the Germans had already set up their defenses in the Hitler Line. The attack was repulsed by fire so heavy that the British decided to stop and wait for the 1st Canadian Infantry Division to come up.

On the 19th, the assault began again under cover of a ground fog; but the fog dispersed, leaving the advancing troops in the open with very little cover. They faced well-directed fire from German antitank guns that drove the tanks from the field and left the infantry alone under mortar fire and antitank gun fire. The infantry fell back to the line of departure. The Canadians, who had attacked toward Pontecorvo, were stalled for lack of artillery support and traffic congestion. So Alexander's hope of a quick victory was dashed; and it seemed that a set piece battle against the strength of the Hitler Line was in the offing.

Meanwhile, the U.S. Fifth Army moved up to the Hitler Line through rugged territory. They encountered very few enemy troops in this terrain and so they were able to move fast. Their objectives were Itri and Pico: two key points in the German road system. On May 15, General Clark had directed the capture of Itri and now he called on the French to attack south of Pico. The Americans and the French both set off from Spigno, but that was a mistake. The steep tortuous road soon became jammed with American infantrymen, French colonial troops, mules, and motor vehicles of all sorts, and the road was choked with dust.

II Corps was to advance in two columns: the 88th Infantry Division through the Aurunci Mountains and the 85th Infantry Division to the left across the slopes of the mountains toward Maranola and Formia. The 351st Infantry Regiment led the 88th across the mountains, guided by two local farmers.

The two battalions in the lead started out early on May 16, from Monte Sant'Angelo. They moved fast, and soon outdistanced their telephone lines. By noon, they had reached Monte Sant'Angelo. They were just stopping for a rest when an urgent message sent them racing for Monte Ruazzo, their second objective.

As the two battalions had been marching, General von Senger strengthened his positions along the Itri–Pico Road, with self-propelled guns and motorized infantry, but his position was none too strong. On May 17, Kesselring finally decided to offer some help about the Tenth Army's right wing, although he was still worried about a new amphibious landing and also about a possible breakout from the Anzio beachhead. He authorized the shift of a battalion from the Liri Valley to the Aurunci Mountains where General Steinmetz needed the men desperately.

On that morning of May 17, Colonel Champeny's 351st Infantry Regiment reached the summit of Monte Ruazzo. They paused and then moved on toward Monte Grande, which overlooked Itri. Early the next morning, they reached the Itri–Pico Road and ran into a force of tanks and self-propelled guns. This stopped the Americans cold because they had left their artillery too far behind to be of any help. Only when the regiment's reserve battalion came up with its artillery could the 351st continue its advance.

Meanwhile, the 85th Infantry Division advanced on the left across the slopes of the Aurunci Mountains, one column along the coastal highway to Formia and the other on the seaward slopes of the mountains toward Maranola, three miles west of Castellonorato. On the afternoon of May 17, the 337th Infantry Regiment descended to take Maranola before dusk, cutting the only lateral road to Formia, two miles southwest.

And the French colonial troops closed in on Pico. They reached the outskirts of Esperia, where they overlooked the Liri Valley.

Early on the morning of May 19, the British Eighth Army began to race for the Hitler Line, and the Algerians rushed into Esperia, while the French Mountain Corps moved up on Pico. They were right up against the German Hitler Line.

24 ———————————

Breakthrough

As the Americans and the French closed in on the Hitler Line, German Tenth Army Chief of Staff Lieutenant General Fritz Wentzell told General Westphal, Field Marshal Kesselring's chief of staff, that the 71st Light Infantry Division had only 100 effective infantrymen left. Westphal promised reinforcements, but it was too late. As Kesselring now knew, the loss of the 14th Panzer Corps' southern sector was only a few hours away. This meant that General von Vietinghoff would have to withdraw the Tenth Army's right wing or face encirclement. To reinforce the Tenth Army's right flank, Kesselring had to call on his reserves. He chose the 29th Panzer Grenadier Division, one of his better units.

On the Tyhrrenian coast, the U.S. 337th Infantry Regiment captured Maranola, and the 338th Infantry Regiment moving up Route 7 caught up with that unit. The 338th then moved up to capture Formia. On the afternoon of May 18, they were to take the junction of the coast highway with the Itri–Pico Road.

General Keyes then formed a task force under Major General John E. Sloan, consisting of tanks and self-propelled guns and motorized infantry and engineers. The thought was to drive swiftly to link up with the Anzio beachhead. Meanwhile, the 91st Reconnaissance Squadron was sent southwest along the coast to the stronghold of Gaeta. The squadron entered the port almost unopposed on May 19, and then pushed north eight miles to Sperlonga. But then General Clark hesitated before sending the Sloan task force to Anzio. The British Eighth Army was having a lot of trouble at the other end of the Hitler Line, where the defense concentration was much stronger.

On May 7, Kesselring became aware of the disaster that had struck the southern sector of his Hitler Line. He feared encirclement by the French and the Americans coming up from the south, so he ordered the 26th Panzer Division to leave the Alban Hills where it was waiting to savage 6th Corps if it tried to break out of the Anzio beachhead and move to the Pontecorvo area. He also ordered the 305th and 334th Infantry Divisions from the Adriatic coast to stop the Americans and the French.

So when the battle for the Hitler Line began on 18 May, three of the five German mobile divisions had been committed. These key divisions were committed piecemeal and were being eaten up. The 15th Panzer Division had been wrecked first, trying to help the 71st Light Infantry and the 94th Infantry Divisions. The 90th Panzer Grenadier Division had gone next, sucked into the Liri cauldron, trying to stop the French. Now the 26th Panzer Division and the 305th were being drawn into the battle, while the 29th Panzer Grenadier Division and the Hermann Goering Panzer Division sat north of Rome, watching the coast and doing nothing. They were waiting for that second amphibious landing that never came.

After the Poles captured Monte Cassino, they moved along the southern spurs of Monte Cairo toward Piedmonte, the north bastion of the Hitler Line. From the south, the French attacked toward Pico; and in the middle, the Eighth Army's 13th Corps attacked Aquino and the 1st Canadian Infantry Division attacked Pontecorvo. Neither was successful in the flash attack, so it was apparent that a set battle would have to be fought. It would be the Canadians attacking Pontecorvo.

While the Canadians were getting ready in the middle of May, the French were closing in on Pico. They captured Monte Leucio but did not capture Pico until May 22. General Juin was then directed northwest toward Route 6. On the other flank, the Poles were in Piedmonte on May 20, but took five more days to clear the town of Germans.

The Eighth Army moved ponderously in the Liri Valley, largely because too many vehicles and too many soldiers were trying to use too few roads at the same time. The roads were remarkable for their old narrow bridges, which created monstrous traffic jams. They could have taken some lessons from the French, who used very few vehicles, mostly pack animals, and advanced quickly, while the British inched along like an army of bugs, all getting in the other's way. They were suffering from what might be called the "Montgomery Syndrome": assemble a vast force superior to the enemy in every way, and then attack him. As British historian General W.G.F. Jackson remarked, the British continued this ponderous error all through the war.

Luckily for the Allies the destruction of the Hitler Line by May 20 had lost its importance because the Americans had surged up through that line in the south. To try to contain them, Kesselring sent the 29th Panzer Grenadier Division to block the U.S. advance in the mountainous area along Route 7 between Fondi and Terracina. This was the last chance before the road emerged in the flat marsh area that led to the southern edge of the Anzio beachhead. Only if the 29th could stop the Allies here, could they be prevented from linking up with the beachhead.

General von Mackensen feared a breakout from the bridgehead and wanted to hold the division to meet that, but he was overruled by Kesselring. Still, von Mackensen stalled in making the move until Kesselring repeated the orders, and by the time the 29th arrived, it was too late to have any effect. The Americans already held the high ground by the time the division got there. It managed to hold the town of Terracina until May 24, when it had to pull back with the remains of the 94th Infantry Division and 71st Light Infantry Division through the Lepini Mountains. Kesselring was so furious with von Mackensen after this battle—the culmination of a series of disputes in which von Mackensen had delayed or refused orders—that he removed the general from command.

On May 18, Field Marshal Alexander authorized the release of the American 36th Infantry Division, which had been rebuilt since the dreadful failure at the Rapido. It had been held in reserve during these recent operations but now it was to go to the Anzio beachhead and participate in the Allied breakout through the German ring around the area. That would conform to attacks being made by the Eighth Army and the French on the Hitler Line and II Corps attack on Terracina. All was scheduled for May 23. The timing was agreed upon but what was not agreed was the point of the attacks. Alexander wanted to keep the focus on the Eighth Army and destruction of German divisions. General Clark had been infected with Prime Minister Churchill's belief in the importance of capturing Rome. The British put this down to Clark's ego and blamed him for interfering with their snug scheme of things to serve his personal ambition. Alexander felt that the capture of Rome by somebody would be an offshoot of his plan. That the somebody would turn out to be the British Eighth Army would not surprise anyone. So the inference is inescapable that the Allied high command broke down here in the disparate ambitions of the commanders.

Alexander wanted the breakout to be toward Valmonte, to cut Route 6. After some objections, Clark agreed to that course, but it was obvious that he had reservations about the plan.

The breakout started on May 23 with the U.S. 3rd Infantry Division's attack on the German strong point of Cisterna, in conjunction with the U.S. 1st Armored Division and the Special Service Force. It was then intended that the 36th Infantry Division would pass through the 3rd with the 1st Armored to Valmonte. The U.S. 45th Infantry Division would widen the gap toward the Alban Hills. The British 1st and 5th Infantry Divisions would hold the northern perimeter.

When the attack came, the 3rd and the 1st Armored surprised the Germans and opened a large hole in the defenses. One of the major reasons for this breakthrough was the destruction of the German minefields by a new weapon in the hands of the Allies. The American engineers had developed the "snake," a 400-foot-length of steel filled with high explosive, which could be pushed into position by tanks, and then detonated by machine-gun fire, producing wide gaps in the minefields.

On the morning of the attack—May 23—Major General E. N. Harmon's 1st Armored Division had a three-phase attack scheme with the two Combat Commands moving abreast. They would pass through the 34th Infantry Division and occupy the rail line three miles northeast of Cisterna, then allow the engineers time to prepare crossings and blast the minefields, and then proceed north and northeast of Cisterna, opening the gap. Meanwhile, the British on the left would carry out diversionary attacks.

Beginning at 4:30 A.M., the tanks began moving up. Two engineer guides led four tanks, each towing a 400-foot snake into two gaps through the minefield along the line of departure and into the enemy minefield beyond. The snakes were pushed into position. At H Hour, the tanks started to move forward, the leading tanks detonated the snakes, which blew up, blasting wide paths through the minefields, and other tanks brought other snakes into position. The smoke from the detonations filled the air as the tanks moved through the gaps into the German defenses, stunning the enemy.

The Americans had also learned in North Africa how to combat the German *panzerfaust* antitank weapon. They draped their tanks with sandbags, supported by welded steel rods, to protect the front and treads of the tanks. They moved forward in formation so that only the lead tank was exposed to enemy fire. When a *panzerfaust* was fired, all the tanks in the formation fired on the suspected point of origin. After a few such encounters, the *panzerfaust* fire stopped; the Germans found that to fire one round meant instant retaliation and probable death. And as for results, they were discouraging; when the *panzerfaust* rounds hit the tanks, they bounced off the sandbags.

Under the unsuspected fury of the American attack, the German 362nd Infantry Division position was penetrated to a depth of a mile. Two battalions of the 956th Infantry Division had been pushed back by Combat Command A, while Combat Command B had done the same to the 954th Infantry Division on the 362nd's left wing south of Cisterna. The 955th Infantry Division had better luck in holding off the 3rd Infantry

Division attack with help from the German paratroopers on the northern side of the beachhead.

General O'Daniel's 3rd Infantry Division was to send one regiment frontally against Cisterna, while the other two enveloped from right and left. Then, the center regiment was to penetrate the town. The 3rd faced the left regiment of the German 362nd Infantry Division and also the 715th Infantry Division. At H Hour (6:30 A.M.), the 15th Infantry Regiment, on the right, moved forward because there were no mines in its area. Company A seized a bridge over the Cisterna Canal but then was stopped by a hail of fire from a group of houses 600 yards away. When they brought up tanks, well-directed fire from German antitank guns knocked out two tanks and a tank destroyer. Major Michael Paulick took a special task force of tanks around to the right, and to the rear of the enemy-held houses. They opened fire on them, and Company A sent a platoon to attack. The Germans withdrew and the infantry closed in.

Two battalions of the 15th launched the main attack. One company moved across an open field to draw fire, while another company and a tank platoon made the main assault against a stand of trees. They made a bayonet charge (one of the few made by American troops during World War II) and swarmed over the enemy positions, killing 15 and capturing 80. Many more broke and ran.

On the left wing, the 3rd Battalion of the 5th Infantry Regiment employed another new device: a "battle sled." This consisted of an open-topped narrow steel tube mounted on flat runners, wide enough to carry one infantryman in a prone position. It protected him against small-arms fire and shell fragments. General O'Daniel, who invented it, called it a "portable foxhole." Teams of 60 men had been organized in each of the division's three regiments.

Five tanks towed battle sleds in the 3rd Battalion advance, but the tanks came upon a drainage ditch, which was too wide and deep to negotiate, so the soldiers came out of the sleds and continued the attack on foot. This was the sole test of this new superweapon; but the tanks that had been used to tow the sleds continued to be helpful to the infantry all that day.

In Cisterna, the Germans had constructed formidable defenses, controlled by a command post located in a wine cellar deep underneath a large building in the center of town. Other cellars and many tunnels honeycombed the ground beneath the town, sheltering the garrison from Allied artillery bombardment and air attacks. When the bombardment ended, the Germans came up and manned positions from which they contested every foot of ground. The American 7th Infantry Regiment faced these strong defenses. When the attack began at 6:30 A.M., the 7th's 3rd Battalion was immediately stopped, and for two-and-a-half hours could not move. The operations officer said they were pinned down.

Colonel Omohundrok, the regimental commander, said, "We have no such words in our vocabulary now. You're supposed to be at the railroad track at noon? You'll get a bonus if you do, something else if you don't."[23]

Urged by their colonel, the men moved forward one mile to within grenade-throwing distance. It took them three hours; but when they began hurling grenades, 16 Germans stood up and surrendered. They had penetrated the enemy by a mile, but in doing so they had suffered such high casualties that their attack was now blunted.

For two days the fighting was very fierce, and on the third day, elements of the Herman Goering Panzer Division began to appear. This meant Kesselring had been forced to commit his last free division to the fighting here. This division was moving south in the daytime and consequently suffered many losses to Allied air attacks. The 6th Corps claimed 600 German vehicles destroyed and 400 damaged. So many German vehicles were wrecked that the Americans advancing beyond Cisterna found the roads blocked by burnt-out German equipment.

By the evening of May 25, a wide break had been made in the German line and Cisterna, Cori, and the north edge of the Lepini Mountains were held by the Americans. The II Corps was advancing from Terracina, and this day a patrol of the 91st Reconnaissance Squadron moved across the Pontine marshes to the village of Borgo Grappo, where it met a patrol of engineers from 6th Corps from the Anzio beachhead. The Fifth Army was reunited after three months, and they had captured 2,500 German prisoners. The Anzio units had suffered heavy losses: the 1st Armored Division lost many tanks and the U.S. 3rd Infantry Division lost more than 1,000 men in the fighting, but both divisions were still effective.

25

The Fall of Rome

On the afternoon of May 24, General Clark decided to turn and change the direction of the Fifth Army assault. Instead of focusing on Valmontone and the chance to envelop thousands of Germans in conjunction with the British Eighth Army attack, he would head northwest, for the capital. He talked it over with General Truscott, commander of 6th Corps, and checked his intelligence reports and decided that General von Mackensen was moving so many troops into the Valmontone area that his forces would get bogged down there. Without consulting Field Marshal Alexander, he changed the focus of his attack. On May 25, he sent an emissary to tell Truscott that they were going for Rome.

Truscott was, as the official American history of the campaign relates, dumbfounded. There was no indication that the Germans had significantly weakened the defense of the Alban Hills, and this was the only condition that would justify altering the plan agreed upon with Alexander. Truscott said he wanted to talk to Clark before he made any change. Clark's emissary said that would be impossible because Clark had left for a battlefront tour and was out of reach by radio. Besides, there was no question about it, Clark had ordered the attack and he was the boss. Move northeast. It was an order.

Later in the day, to smooth ruffled feathers, Truscott telephoned Clark's headquarters and said he was enthusiastic about the new plan and was moving as fast as possible to meet it, but actually he believed Clark's decision to be wrong. That was not his problem. His problem was to carry out the order and persuade his division commanders to carry it out enthusiastically.

At about midnight that night, Truscott met with his 6th Corps commanders. They had already heard about the change and were very gloomy over the prospects before them. Generals Harmon and O'Daniel felt that they were throwing away a chance for victory. If they stuck to the original plan, they would soon be astride Route 6 and in possession of Valmontone and could make a rapid advance to Rome besides destroying the German Army. Many of them had the feeling that this was a contest between Clark and the British as to who would capture Rome.

Truscott presented the new plan as though he believed in it. Sixth Corps was to attack the next day on a three-mile front with the 34th and 45th Infantry Divisions abreast. The intelligence estimate said that they would attack between Campoleone and Lanuvio, facing the 1st Parachute Division and a few odd units. The 362nd and 715th Infantry Divisions, which they had already been fighting, were sorely hurt and not a big problem. That estimate was generally correct, although it did not take into account the fact that the 1st Parachute Division was a fresh unit and well entrenched in the only completed portion of the Caesar Line.

Only O'Daniel's 3rd Infantry Division and the 1st Special Service Force would continue on the road to Valmontone. They started out, but were almost immediately bombed and strafed by American planes, which killed 100 men and destroyed many vehicles. Later in the day, they met elements of the Hermann Goering Panzer Division who launched a suicidal attack through a mixup in orders. The Germans were greatly assisted by the American artillery that started firing on American troops in error, killing over half of a group of 160 replacements who had just come up, and killing the commander of the 1st Battalion of the 6th Armored Infantry. The Germans took advantage of the confusion and nearly broke through the American lines but were stopped by the infantry farther back.

It was all useless. On the 28th, Clark abandoned the drive on Valmontone altogether.

In London, Prime Minister Churchill was aghast. He saw the German Tenth Army escaping capture or destruction along Route 6 and at Valmontone because the Americans had quit the race. "The glory of this campaign," he announced to Field Marshal Alexander in his most sententious fashion, "will be measured, not by the capture of Rome, or the junction with the Anzio beachhead, but by the number of German divisions cut off."[24]

The German plan was to withdraw the Tenth Army into the Caesar Line alongside the Fourteenth Army. To do this, the Germans fought a delaying action against the Eighth Army, holding with rear guards, until the 51st Mountain Corps and the 14th Panzer Corps had escaped. The 29th Panzer Grenadier Division came back shepherding the remnants of the 71st Light Infantry and 94th Infantry Divisions. The 1st Parachute and 90th Panzer Grenadier Divisions served as rear guards, and held the Eighth Army.

On May 29, Clark ordered the continuation of the attack on Valmontone by the 3rd and 85th Infantry Divisions. The French had followed the 29th Panzer Grenadier Division through the mountains and were approaching the 3rd at Artena. Sixth Corps was now very tired, but Clark felt that one more effort might unnerve the Germans who, he believed, were also very tired. Then the U.S. 36th Infantry Division, which was patrolling on the night of May 30, found the high ground behind the town of Valmonte—Monte Artemisio—unoccupied. The 36th silently infiltrated two regiments to get onto this ground. The third regiment struck behind Vellitri, cutting off the German garrison's retreat. A dangerous gap then was cut into the strongest part of the Caesar Line. The Hermann Goering Panzer Division counterattacked but did not throw the Americans out. Clark ordered immediate attacks by both his corps for the next morning. II Corps, which included the 88th and 85th Infantry Divisions and the 3rd Infantry Division, was to attack around the northern side of the Alban Hills, cutting Route 6 and capturing Valmonte on the way.

Sixth Corps was to advance around the southwest side of the hills, while the 36th advanced through the center. American observers on Monte Artemesio could bring artillery fire on all the enemy positions.

During June 1 and June 2, Clark put every man and every weapon into a "typically American" power drive as the British, who did not like such maneuvers, called it. Eleven divisions, including the two British divisions on the coast, were ordered to smash forward against the tired Germans. The Hermann Goering Panzer and the 334th Infantry Divisions gave way first, letting II Corps through on Route 6. They retired on the night of June 2 east of Rome. The rest of the Fourteenth Army pulled back across the Tiber west of Rome, destroying the bridges and ferries behind them. Since Kesselring had declared Rome an open city, the bridges in Rome were left intact.

At 7:15 P.M. on June 4, the leading elements of the American 88th Infantry Division entered the Piazza Venezia in the center of Rome. Clark had won the race and his victory but he was never forgiven by the British for not letting them have a part of the glory.

The French Expeditionary Force came into the eastern outskirts of the city and then the Eighth Army cut across the hills, to continue its advance up the east bank of the Tiber, heading for Terni. But the advance was held up by the crowding on the roads by the two armies: the Fifth and the Eighth. There was just too much of the Allied force and the confusion was extreme. Now the task was to rout the Tenth and Fourteenth German Armies.

26

North from Rome

One day of glory, that was all the heroes of Rome were allowed. It was June 5, the day after the triumphal entry into the Holy City. They celebrated their victory and General Clark summoned his generals to the city hall atop Capitoline Hill for a conference. Starting from the Excelsior Hotel on the Via Veneto, a parade of jeeps wound its way up to the center of Roman glory of the past. The soldiers were greeted by jubilant throngs of Italians.

And then, on June 6, 1944, Rome and Italy were forgotten by the world as attention turned to the Allied invasion of Hitler's *Festung* Europe in Normandy. But there was still a job to be done in Italy, where the German presence was strong and resilient from Rome north to the Alps. The question was: how should it be done?

Three days after the entry into Rome, General Wilson informed London that he was prepared to mount a new amphibious operation on August 15. That would be the Anvil Operation—the invasion of southern France—so totally dreaded by the British. It would steal away resources and men from the Italian campaign, and if this could not be avoided, it would always be lamented.

A week later, Wilson directed Field Marshal Alexander to withdraw 6th Corps headquarters and the 45th, 36th, and 3rd Infantry Divisions in stages. The French would withdraw both of their divisions by early July. At the same time, Alexander gave conflicting orders, calling for the defeat of the Germans south of the Arno River. The conflict was between Allied forces facing the Tenth Army area at this time.

The German Tenth Army consisted of three army corps: the 14th Panzer and the 76th Panzer and the 51st Mountain Corps, and these included the 29th and 90th Panzer Grenadier Divisions; 1st Parachute, 5th Mountain, 44th, and 278th Infantry Divisions. On the Adriatic flank another provisional corps was operating—Group Hauck—in reserve were a panzer division, a Luftwaffe field division, an infantry division, and a Turkomen division of doubtful loyalty, since it consisted of former Russian prisoners of war with German officers and noncommissioned officers.

But this division and the Luftwaffe division, both doubtful quantities, would be sent to reinforce the Fourteenth Army. For the next few weeks the dominant German theme would be to establish a series of delaying positions south of the Arno River. Two sketchy defense lines were drawn—the Dora Line, running northwest–southeast above Rome, and the Frieda Line, running from Piombino, northwest of Grosseto to Lake Trasimeno and then to Porto Civitanova on the coast.

The Allied pursuit of the Germans actually began before Rome was settled down. On June 5, the 6th Corps seized the port of Citavecchia on Route 1. II Corps went up Route 2 to take Viterbo and its airfield complex, which would be useful to the Allied air forces. By June 9, both places were captured, and 6th Corps was relieved by the American 4th Corps, which had arrived in Italy in March, so that 6th Corps could get ready for an attack on southern France.

The British Eighth Army's 13th Corps and the South African 6th Armored Division advanced west of the Tiber on Route 3 and the British 6th Armoured Division advanced east of the river on Route 4. The South Africans made 35 miles that first day.

On June 7, Alexander directed the continuation of the pursuit, ordering the Eighth Army to advance to the Florence area and the Fifth Army to the Pisa area. The British 5th Corps was to come slowly up the Adriatic coast. Both the Fifth Army and the Eighth Army were told to take extreme risks if necessary to reach their assigned areas before the German armies could recover their balance.

For ten days the Allied armies moved fast, but then the Germans got hold of themselves and stiffened, increasing their blowing of bridges and other manmade assistances in the countryside and more thorough mining of the roads. By June 20, both Allied armies found themselves facing Field Marshal Kesselring's first delaying position from the Ombrone River to Chiusi and east of Lake Trasimeno. The pursuit phase was over, and the Germans had established a new line across the peninsula. From now on the Allies would have to fight for every yard, as Kesselring built his Gothic Line and delayed.

Just now as the troops in the field advanced to the first German line of defense, the greater fighting was being done between London and Washington, where the old quarrel about the importance of the southern theater was being fought all over again. The Americans were holding out for the invasion of southern France, and the British were trying to keep the southern show going, with a hope that they could then come up from underneath and strike Germany through Austria after having destroyed the German armies in Italy.

The strategic quarrel between the British and the Americans came to a head a few weeks after the Normandy invasion. A violent storm had destroyed the Mulberry artificial harbor in the American sector of Normandy, and the Americans were having great difficulty with supply. General Eisenhower looked forward with more than a little concern to the possibility of being stuck in Normandy by the fall rains and so he came out flatly in favor of the amphibious invasion of southern France, which the British disliked so much, because it would divert more resources from their Italian campaign. Eisenhower's endorsement was followed by that of the American Joint Chiefs of Staff, countered by Churchill and Field Marshal Jan Christian Smuts, and settled by President Roosevelt, who reminded all concerned that it had been agreed with Stalin that the Mediterranean was to play second fiddle all the way along. Roosevelt put the trump on it, by stating that he could not possibly survive, politically, in America if the invasion of France were to bog down, and it become known that he had countenanced the diversion of troops and material to the Balkans. So the American answer to the hopes of Churchill and Alexander was a resounding "No," and if Allied amity was to be maintained that had to be the end of the argument. The British, who seemed to have believed all along that in the end they would get their way, were extremely bitter about this turn of events. However, General Brooke gave them the wisest counsel: accept the inevitable and get on with the war. On July 2, the British Chiefs of Staff directed Field Marshal Wilson (he had been promoted) to launch the invasion of southern France with three divisions in assault about August 15. The Italian campaign was to continue, but with only about 18 divisions in the Fifteenth Army Group. The American Fifth Army was reduced to five divisions. The only reinforcements would be the American 32nd Infantry Division, a black organization, and a Brazilian division.

The Germans were ordered to hold the Gothic Line because as Hitler said, the breach of the line would have "incalculable military and political consequences."[25] Four new divisions had already been committed to the Italian theater, and now Kesselring was to receive three more divisions, which had been slated to go to the Russian front, and one division from the Russian front itself.

So the Fifth and the Eighth Armies pulled up to the line—now called the "Trasimeno Line"—and were brought to a halt by the regrouped German forces. The line covered the two important ports of Leghorn and Ancona, which would be extremely useful for the Allied armies in resupply as they moved north. The Eighth Army was now 200 miles beyond its railhead. The Trasimeno Line was really a temporary defense in depth, using a number of obstacles, rather than trying to establish a continuous obstacle. The country was a series of rolling hills, and the Germans blocked each of the north–south roads in depth.

So as the Allies attacked beginning on June 20 for ten days, the 14th Panzer Division arrived in time to slow down the American 4th Corps progress up Route 1. It was July 1 before they crossed the Cecina River, and they did so with heavy losses. The French entered Siena on July 3, but only because the Germans evacuated the place. French minds were on the coming invasion of southern France.

The hard fighting took place in the British sector in the center of the line, where the 13th Corps and 10th Corps tried to move up the two sides of Lake Trasimeno. The fighting was very brisk, until suddenly the Germans were gone. Kesselring had decided it was time to retire to his second temporary line of defense: the Arezzo Line which ran across the peninsula from Cecina to Ancona. Here the Germans stood, and when the Allies came up, they engaged them in a series of sharp conflicts, only to slip away again on the night of July 15. But now, the Germans fought a determined rear-guard action, blowing bridges and culverts and taking advantage of every favorable terrain position to launch a delaying fight that slowed the Allied advance. Sometimes when the Germans had an extremely favorable position, they would hold for two or three days, only then to slip away at night. In this way the Germans delayed and the summer days passed. It was August 4 before they had been forced back to the Arno Line, their last temporary position before the Gothic Line. They had abandoned Ancona on July 18 to the Polish Corps, which was coming slowly up the Adriatic side. On August 4, the Germans retired to the north bank of the Arno River, blowing up all the bridges including those in Florence. With the exception of the historic Ponte Vecchio—which the Germans blocked off by demolishing and mining the houses at both ends of it—all of the bridges were rendered impassible. Now the Gothic Line, the position Kesselring hoped to hold all winter, lay just 15 miles ahead of the Allies.

What was to be done about it? Alexander's chief of staff, General Harding, had figured out the situations of both sides, and he estimated that the German strength would rise to perhaps 21 divisions. To continue the assault, as Kesselring pulled back from the Gothic Line to the Po River, and from the Po to the Adige River, and from the Adige to the Ljubljana Gap, the allies would need 18 fighting divisions with half-a-dozen divisions in reserve, refitting and resting. But the Allied force was now down to 18 divisons and only two more coming from America and Brazil could be counted on.

What of Britain's resources? They were strained almost to the limit and nothing could be spared from home. Alexander might eye the 50 divisions piling up in Britain, waiting to enter the war in northwest Europe, but he had no chance of getting his hands on one of them. The Americans were quite complacent with the situation. Alexander, they saw, had enough forces to keep fighting and keep the Germans at bay in Italy but not enough to do what the Americans always feared the British would try: go off on excursions into the Balkans. The American Joint Chiefs of Staff were very comfortable with Alexander's situation.

As Alexander contemplated the future, it seemed grim indeed. He was told by London that if he wanted more troops he was at liberty to raise Italian divisions and equip them with British gear and stores. That was all London could do for him.

Then came a historic meeting with General Leese on the Orvieto airfield on August 4. Leese had not been very happy with Alexander's plans for the next few months as announced. The loss of the French troops to the southern France operation deprived the army of its mountain forces, and the American Fifth Army had been so reduced in force that the British Eighth Army was going to have bear the bulk of the responsibility. It had no mountain troops, but it did have a great powerful force of armor and artillery, neither of which was going to be of much use in the heights of the Appenines. So General Leese proposed that the plan be changed and that the Eighth Army move to the Adriatic coast where it should attack through the Polish Corps sector and break the Gothic Line where the hills were lowest, around Rimini. Then the armor and the artillery could scud across the Plain of Lombardy and fight the sort of battles in open land that they were used to in Africa. One additional advantage to the plan was that it had unwittingly been set up by the lethargic movement of the Polish Corps, which had been enjoined all summer to move slowly and not use up too much of the Allied resources in its followup of the major armies. So the Germans were unlikely to be looking for trouble coming along the Adriatic front.

27

Cracking the Gothic Line

One of the major reasons that General Leese wanted to change the basic approach to the Gothic Line was to get away from his American allies. He did not like working closely with General Clark's Fifth Army. Leese had experienced difficulties with American General Bradley in Sicily and Clark in the Liri Valley. American ways were not British ways, and despite general goodwill, there were many points of friction in actual operations that magnified the differences between the two English-speaking armies. Clark undoubtedly felt the same way, particularly after the bombing of the Monte Cassino Abbey.

Leese's proposal appealed enormously to Field Marshal Alexander because of his liking for the "one–two punch." He could see how this approach would let the Fifteenth Army Group strike first with the Eighth Army on the shore of the Adriatic, and then when the German reserves were drawn there, the Fifth Army could move against the weakened center. Field Marshal Kesselring would then move his reserves back to the center, and the Eighth Army would then make the decisive breakthrough in the Rimini sector.

The change meant an enormous amount of work for the staff of the Fifteenth Army Group and the Eighth Army because the stage was set for the army to break the line in the center, and seven fresh divisions were concentrating around Lake Trasimeno, waiting. The logistics were already set, with the railhead moving to Arezzo. The movement to the Adriatic meant supplies would have to be pushed across only two roads in Allied hands, from the town of Foligno and across the Appenines to the Polish Corps. This would create a major bottleneck. In addition the two roads—Routes 76 and 77—had not been rebuilt because no one knew they would be needed so rapidly, and blown bridges and culverts would create a major problem for the engineers. Besides this, the cover plan to mask the reality of the coming operation was already in the works: It indicated that the major Allied effort would be against Rimini!

Nevertheless, Alexander accepted the plan on the spot. Leese was delighted; it would give him the chance to fight the battle in his own way. He would have few mountains to worry about with his heavy weapons. He would be able to use his armor and guns for set piece attacks, which were what the army had been practicing ever since it had been in the hands of General Montgomery. But most important, now Leese would not have to worry about rivalry with the Americans, and rivalry for world headlines.

The new plan was christened Olive. When the Eighth Army staff got wind of it, there was general agreement that the "Old Man" had made a bad mistake, but there was nothing to be done about it. Previous operations had taught the staff that facing a succession of river lines was hard going, and this is what they were now going to do. The Germans would have beautiful defensive positions along the coast where the spurs of the Appenines run down to the sea; and as the Germans fell back, their line would grow shorter and the British line longer. Also Route 9 would give the Germans excellent lateral communication between the Fifth and the Eighth Army sectors. And, there was something else about which they were soon to learn. When they spoke approvingly of the Plain of Lombardy as good tank country, they did not know what they were talking about. The trap was the area of the Romanga, north of Route 9, which makes the triangle from Rimini to Bologna to Lake Comacchio. With any rain, this would become swamp.

But in three weeks, observing the utmost secrecy, the staff swung the army around and pointed it in a new direction. The deception plan was now changed, to confuse everybody. The Fifth Army buildup was clearly indicated, drawing attention to the central sector of the line, while the guns, ammunition, and supplies for the Adriatic were funneled in secretly, and all that could wait for the last possible moment were made to wait.

The Polish Corps and the Canadian Corps were to set up the Eighth Army attack by pressing on with their advance north of Ancona to the Metauro River, 15 miles south of the Gothic Line. They were to put bridgeheads across the river through which the Eighth Army attack would pass the 5th Corps and the Canadians so that the Germans could be moved back without realizing at first that a major offensive was in progress. With luck enough to maintain secrecy of the movement across the Appenines, the Eighth Army would face only the 278th Infantry Division and the rebuilt 71st Light Infantry Division. Neither was considered to be first-class, but a first-class unit—the 1st Parachute Division—stood behind these two. The rest of Kesselring's mobile divisions were off to the west and need cause no immediate worry.

The Eighth Army would stage a complex attack. The Poles would take Pesaro at the eastern end of the Gothic Line and then go into reserve. The Canadians would attack in the center to the coast road north of Pesaro and along it to Rimini. The main attack force, the 5th Corps of five divisions would attack in the hills west of the Canadians to reach Route 9 in the Po River Valley west of Rimini. Tenth Corps would hold the mountain sector between the Eighth and the Fifth Armies, and 13th Corps would pass under the command of the Fifth Army, holding the sector north and east of Florence.

D Day was August 25. By August 22, 60,000 tanks, guns, and vehicles of the Eighth Army had crossed the Appenines by night, moving without lights to their concentration point behind the Polish screen, and the army's logistic center was shifted to Ancona.

While the Eighth Army was moving into position, much attention was focused on the Allied landings on the Riviera beaches. The operation had been renamed Dragoon. It was very successful, and the troops began to move immediately. By September 11, the Seventh Army had linked up with the American armies from Normandy at Dijon.

By that time the Americans had trapped 50,000 Germans in southern France, which symbolized the success of the American plan. The Russians were driving hard from the east, Bulgaria had quit the war, and the Hungarians were making quitting noises. In London, Prime Minister Churchill was watching the successes of the Russians with a certain reserve, foreseeing Stalin's triumphs leading to Russian control of the Balkans, but he was no more able to interest the Americans in trying to shape the postwar Europe than he had been from the beginning. President Roosevelt, like General Marshall, refused to get involved in such political thinking about the postwar future. The American military had certainly come of age in the past three years, but the political leadership still had a lot to learn about *Weltpolitik*. Churchill was still desperately hoping to salvage the Balkans, break through the Gothic Line, move into the Po Valley, and advance through Trieste and the Ljubljana Gap to Vienna before the Russians could get there.

When the Eighth Army began to move on August 25, the Germans were fooled into thinking that it was just an extension of the Polish advance which had been going on for several weeks. The Germans in this sector were relieving the 278th Infantry Division. Kesselring's attention was in the center and the west.

For the first four days, the Eighth Army steamed ahead, its own traffic problems causing more trouble than the enemy. The 71st Light Infantry

Division put up little resistance to the 5th Corps and the mixture of troops from the 278th and 1st Parachute Divisions in their relief operation was also very ineffectual. The three Allied corps reached the Foglia River on August 29, and it was only then, at the foot of the Gothic Line, that the Germans realized what was happening. Reinforcements were ordered, and the Germans staged a stand-fast defense, but it was too late to save the Adriatic sector of the Gothic Line. On August 30, the forward positions were overrun before they could be manned. But the next day, the German resistance became stouter as elements of the 26th Panzer Division arrived from the Arno. The German front formed up and the 98th Infantry Division from Bologna came in. On September 2, the Gothic defenses in front of the Eighth Army crumbled, and the Germans were forced back, in near panic, to the Conca River Line. The Poles captured Pesaro and went into reserve. The Canadians took a bridgehead across the Conca on the night of September 3. It looked as though the line would break, so the armored divisions were moved up, although the 56th Infantry and the 4th Indian Infantry Divisions had fallen back behind the Canadian left wing.

The key to breakthrough was Coriano Ridge, which stands between the Conca River and the Marecchia River. After this the Plain of Romanga stretches out for miles. If the British could capture this, they could go as long as the weather held, they thought.

On September 2, the leading armored units began to move forward, but the tracks were so bad that most of the journey had to be made in low gear. Many tanks fell out with mechanical troubles, and others kept going although they were in no state for a battle. And when they crossed the Conca at 10:30 A.M. on September 4, they learned that the 46th Infantry Division had not reached its objective. The plan was fouled up. It was not until midafternoon that the British 1st Armoured Division started to attack. The Germans had the sun behind them and the British gunners were staring into it. During the British delay, the Germans had brought up tanks and self-propelled guns, and in the fight that followed, they outclassed the British. The British tanks broke down and some bogged down. The attack was stopped at dusk when it was seen that the British infantry was too far back to take over from the tanks. More German reinforcements funneled through, and it was obvious that the attack had failed.

By morning, the Germans had three mobile divisions and three infantry divisions blocking the path of the Eighth Army. The British had taken 4,000 prisoners, but they were tired, and the weather was beginning to turn. Heavy rain fell on September 5 and 7, and two days later, when things were going no better, General Leese decided he must prepare for a set-piece attack. It would take four days to mount the effort.

When the direction and extent of the attack became apparent to the

Germans, Kesselring ordered a general retreat to the Gothic Line, and this saved Clark's Fifth Army from having to make an opposed crossing of the Arno River. On September 6, the Americans occupied Lucca, and, on September 12, Pistoia. American II Corps was brought up through Florence, which was an open city, and Clark was ordered to be ready to launch a major attack along with Leese's set-piece attack on September 12 on Coriano Ridge.

On September 8, Clark was ready. He chose the Il Giogo Pass on the secondary road to Bologna for the attack rather than the Futa Pass on Route 65 because he thought the main road pass would be more heavily defended. But to mask his intentions, he started off as though he were doing the opposite.

II Corps' advance began on September 10. By September 12, two U.S. divisions had forced the German 4th Parachute Division back into the Gothic Line on either side of Route 65. On September 13, the 85th Infantry Division came up, and the main offensive started. At first the going was slow because the defenses were stout and the German parachute troops were strong and able. In four days, 2,000 medium and fighter bomber missions were flown in support of the American attack. On the flank, the British 13th Corps broke through the defenses and up onto the Appenine watershed. On September 17, the 85th and the British 1st Infantry Division broke through the boundary between the German 4th Parachute and 715th Infantry Divisions. The German defenses collapsed all along Il Giogo Pass. The Germans were slow to reinforce, and it was not until September 20 that two divisions began to arrive in the area to contest the Fifth Army's salient, and by then the Gothic Line was gone. Futa Pass and Firenzuola surrendered on September 21.

Now was the time for the Americans to hit hard with their reserves. The 88th Infantry Division moved toward Imola and moved very quickly. On September 27, its leading battalion, guided by Italian partisans, seized Monte Battaglia, only 12 miles from Imola. Desperate German counterattacks were launched for a week. The Germans failed to retake the mountain, but they did stop the 88th thrust. The Americans suffered very heavy losses, and the weather turned bad, so Clark halted his offensive and switched his point of attack back to Route 65.

Meanwhile, the Eighth Army had begun its set-piece battle after midnight on September 12. It was a typical Eighth Army affair, begun with an enormous air and naval bombardment to soften up the enemy during the preparations. Fifth Corps and the Canadian Corps were to attack side by side, capture the Coriano Ridge, seize bridgeheads over the Marano River, and clear the high ground overlooking that river and advance past Rimini into the Plain of Romanga. It sounded simple and straightforward—a power play—but something went wrong.

The battle started out according to plan. The two corps were led by their armor to clear the Coriano Ridge. There were signs of difficulty, however. It was apparent that the wet weather of September 6 and 7 had made the going difficult for tanks.

The second phase of the battle started on September 15. The German resistance had solidified, and both corps crossed the Marano and gained a foothold on the high ground beyond the stream. But the elusive break-through did not come. The Germans resisted and then were reinforced. A Luftwaffe division arrived from the west on September 17, followed by elements of the 90th Panzer Grenadier Division. Parts of ten German divisions were now in the line. By the end of September 18, the British and Canadians had achieved their Phase II objectives and were fighting their way across another stream, the Ausa River. The Germans were holding the last low ridge before the plains began. Staff members of the Eighth Army had cause to remember now what they had been saying about the difficulties of dealing with one river after another.

The third phase of battle began on September 19 when the Canadians moved around the outskirts of Rimini. British 5th Corps did not do so well. The British 1st Armoured Division was supposed to exploit a break-through, but there had been no breakthrough of the divisions brought to attack Ceriano with the 56th Infantry Division. The divisions became muddled in crossing a single ford they both had to use. The 56th man-aged to reach the Ceriano Ridge but was hit hard by the 90th Panzer Grenadier Division. On September 20, the 1st Armoured sent a brigade to help the 56th, but the brigade ran into a hail of fire on the reverse slope of the ridge. Although the tankers fought valiantly, taking heavy losses, they were forced to retreat. The situation was saved when the Canadian successes posed a danger to the Germans and so they pulled out and blew up their installations at Rimini to move back to the Uso River, which was the Rubicon River of the ancient Romans. As if the British did not have enough to worry about, the rain poured down to cover the German retreat. This week had been the most costly ever fought by the Eighth Army, with casualties averaging 1,000 per day. In the end it had been worth less than expected. The operation was over. The Eighth Army had reached the Po Valley, but at what cost! Two hundred and fifty tanks had been lost to the enemy and 230 had bogged down or suffered mechanical failures beyond the capability of the local forces to repair. Infantry casualties had been so severe that all the British reinforcements in the whole Italian theater had been used up, and the battalions had to be reduced from four to three companies for the next six months. The British 1st Armoured Division was actually disbanded. Its headquarters remained but its units were dispersed, and one brigade of the 56th was reduced to cadre and withdrawn from the fighting line.

Worst of all, as the leading patrols of Fifth Corps and the Canadian Corps moved onto the Plain of Romanga, they discovered themselves in a swamp created by the rain, interspersed with rivers, dykes, and meadows that were grand for cows but most inimical to tanks and trucks. The rain came down in torrents, concealing the escape of the German rear guards, who moved out, leaving behind them demolished bridges and minefields. The Plain of Romanga was one huge tank trap, lush agricultural land reclaimed from the marshes and across it ran 13 rivers. The land between rivers was flat and drained by a network of irrigation ditches. Most of the rivers were not fordable and they were really tank obstacles. The soil was clay, which became glutinous mud.

South of Route 9 lay the spurs of the Appenines, which ran down to the road. The rivers were fordable but the problem was to scale the steep spurs between them where the German defenders could cover the crossing. Flanking attacks were very difficult because of the steep terrain and the paucity of decent roads and tracks. So the situation of the armor was not anything like the tankers had been led to expect. They had exchanged mountains for mud.

28

The Center of the Line

In the summer of 1944, after Field Marshal Alexander had accepted General Leese's plan for the breakthrough of the Gothic Line on the Adriatic coast instead of the middle, General Clark had to be informed of the change. A conference was called for August 10 at Leese's headquarters, and it was held in the open air in a grove of trees. There Alexander expounded on the new plan, while Leese lay back on the grass with the air of a man who had not a care in the world.

Clark agreed with Alexander on the new plan, but said he worried about his right flank. What he was obviously looking for was reinforcement of his force, in the shape of the British 13th Corps. Leese offered to make General McCreery the 13th Corps commander, which would mean that he and Clark would deal on equal terms. In the discussion that followed, Leese's obvious anti-American feeling erupted, and he said he refused to put any elements of the British Eighth Army under American command. As the argument grew heated and personal Alexander intervened, and pointed out that Clark was arguing from military logic and Leese was arguing from emotion. Leese finally yielded and Clark got the attachment of the 13th Corps under his command.

It was the salvation of Allied unity in Italy that this occurred because there was a great deal of American pressure on Clark just then to abandon the Italian campaign entirely to the British and take his army to France. Ever since the capture of Rome, Clark had been criticized inside the American military establishment for his decision to remain in Italy, and every day that passed without a new drive north increased the pressure. Particularly General Jacob L. Devers at the Mediterranean Command was arguing with General Marshall that the Americans should abandon Italy and let the British play their own game alone.

So the strategy changed. Clark was to withhold action until after the Eighth Army offensive began. He did so despite criticism from Devers, who visited the Allied Forces Headquarters at Caserta and noted the mutual distrust of Americans and British. The American feeling that the British would not fight hard enough to make the new plan work and the British concern that the Americans were all going to be withdrawn from Italy, leaving the Eighth Army with a job it could not handle.

The Germans were also just then experiencing a crisis in confidence. General Wentzell, the Tenth Army chief of staff, complained to a member of Field Marshal Kesselring's staff that as the war drew to a close and the Germans were losing it, they should be clustering around Germany instead of wasting their resources in these far-flung places. But Kesselring refused to listen to such talk. He was determined to hold the Gothic Line as long as possible. In the rear lay the rich hinterland of industrial Italy, the last bastion of Mussolini's new Fascist Republic. The German armies were committed to stand and fight.

The Fifth Army was to make a two-phased attack against the Gothic Line north of Florence. At first the II Corps would attack on the left and the British 13th Corps on the right, just north of Florence. In the second phase, II Corps was to attack along Route 6521, while the American 4th Corps was to simulate an attack to cross the Arno River.

But all this was discarded when the British attacked in the east and the Germans in the center pulled back to the Gothic Line, making the first moves unnecessary. Clark then ordered the 4th Corps to cross the Arno and advance as far as the German withdrawal would let them.

On September 1, then, the 1st Armored Division and the 370th Regimental Combat Team crossed the river, and headed for the Monte Pisano Massif and the city of Lucca at the foot of the mountains, ten miles northeast of Pisa. The South African 6th Armored Division of 13th Corps attacked on the right, aiming at the Monte Albano Ridge and the city of Pistoia 16 miles north. The advance was easy until September 3 when the South Africans approached a minefield. The 1st Armored Division also began to encounter some scattered small-arms fire. But on September 4 came indications that there were Germans up ahead; the South Africans ran into a roadblock and the 1st Armored Division ran into a German rear guard eight miles east of Lucca. The 370th had a similar experience, but by late afternoon was moving again. By the afternoon of September 5, 4th Corps had occupied three of its four objectives. It rained heavily on September 6, and the Americans found, from patrolling, that the Germans had retreated as far as they intended to go and that more advance would mean real fighting, so they ordered a halt and regrouping of the 4th Corps, which would wait for the II Corps assault on the Gothic Line.

It was this that had brought Clark up to the mountain pass where he had to decide between Futa and Il Giogo Pass for his assault on the line. As noted, he had chosen Il Giogo and had made a breakthrough that had caused the Germans to abandon Futa Pass.

By September 24, the German Tenth Army had been pushed back to within 15 miles of the Po Valley, but there had been no break in the line. Kesselring sent two divisions of reinforcements, but they did not prevent the 88th Infantry Division from thrusting north of Firenzuola. That day Brigadier General Paul W. Kendall emphasized the importance of moving into the Po Valley before the Germans could bring up reinforcements and slow the advance. The Americans were greatly assisted by the Italian partisans who had taken possession of Monte Battaglia and turned it over to the 350th Infantry Regiment. But the 350th had no sooner dug in there, than the Germans began counterattacking. Yet by the night of the 27th, the Americans held all but one of the heights around the Castel Delrio Road junction and from Monte Battaglia north the ground descended as the Santerno River threaded its way to join the Po. Elsewhere the II Corps had good progress toward Imola. But the weather now took a hand. Just as the rain fell on the British Eighth Army on the east, so it fell on the American sector; and for several days operations were hampered. Allied aircraft were grounded by rain and fog. During the hiatus, the Germans reinforced their forward units. Monte Battaglia was the scene of many more German attacks and much shelling, but the Americans held this forward position until the 351st Infantry Regiment captured nearby Monte Capello and the British came up on the right flank and the Germans disappeared.

But despite the 88th Infantry Division's advance, the thrust into the German line meant only a narrow salient, achieved at high cost in casualties. General Clark saw that the Firenzuola–Imola Road was incapable of carrying the traffic needed to make a serious advance. What he did not know was that the Germans had run out of reserves and were incapable of holding much longer here. So he abandoned the drive and shifted attention to the left to concentrate on the capture of Bologna by General Keyes. Thus, troops were moved around and the 88th joined the other divisions of II Corps along Route 65. The Americans on Monte Battaglia were stuck there for days, under such heavy German fire that all officers of one company were killed or wounded and the company was cut down to 50 men. The other two companies of this battalion were about the same. When the British arrived to relieve them, the Americans expected to get off the mountain immediately, but German shelling so impeded the progress that they did not get off the mountain until October 5. Since September 21, the 88th's three regiments had suffered 2,100 casualties, almost as many as the entire II Corps had suffered in the six-day breakthrough against Il Giogo Pass.

Because the Germans saw that General Clark had abandoned the thrust toward Imola, they concluded that the Allied command had shifted the focus of its operations from the Eighth Army flank on the Adriatic to the central sector south of Bologna and, thus, pressure from the Eighth Army would cease. But Kesselring was not so sure. He saw that General Clark was strong enough to carry a major effort against Bologna without help from the Eighth Army.

The Germans had blocked the road to Imola. But at Radicosa Pass three tall peaks were potentially formidable defense positions because they were higher than the Gothic Line. But the three German divisions defending the pass had been shifted to shore up the defenses in the Imola area, and so when the three American divisions advancing on the pass converged, the Germans saw no option but withdrawal. Under cover of fog and rain, on September 28, the Germans withdrew. During the night, the American 91st Infantry Division occupied Radicosa Pass, and on September 29, the division pushed forward through thick fog. On the flanks, the 34th and 85th Infantry Divisions kept pace, trying to find the enemy's new line of resistance.

By the end of September, the Fifth Army was 24 miles south of Bologna, and on a clear day the British on top of Monte Battaglia could see the Po River Valley ten miles away. On the right the British 13th Corps held a 17-mile front, so extended that the corps' three divisions could make only limited advances. Lieutenant General Willis Crittenberger's 4th Corps also held a wide front of 50 miles. All units but the 45th Infantry Division on the coast had passed through the Gothic Line. However, with the approach of winter, the 4th Corps could hardly be expected to advance much.

That fall the Allies in France seemed to be driving toward an early end to the war with Germany and so even General Marshall relaxed his inflexible position regarding the Italian front, indicating that he would make no attempt to withdraw the Fifth Army from the Italian campaign until Kesselring had been defeated. The Americans would even sanction a new amphibious landing and would supply landing craft for it, if it could be done in the fall.

Immediately, Prime Minister Churchill began thinking about the Balkans again and considered either an assault on the Istrian Peninsula, including Trieste, or a landing south of Fiume followed by the capture of that city. All this would be dependent on the state of affairs in Yugoslavia. There the Germans had an army of 240,000 men, including 15 German divisions and the rest mixed Middle Europeans with one Cossack division. Opposing them were 180,000 guerillas, most of them under Marshal Tito.

As it worked out however, the amphibious invasion did not ever come to pass. General Eisenhower was cautious about his ability to bring the war in Europe to an end before the end of the year. So the Combined Chiefs of Staff suggested that the Italian campaign be pursued "relentlessly" until the major offensive in the northwest had been launched against Germany at the end of December. They recommended that no more troops be brought to Italy, and President Roosevelt capped that a few days later by rejecting a request from Churchill for two or three more divisions of American troops that were about to leave for Europe.

Then, on a stopover from a trip to Moscow in late October, Churchill conferred with his commanders at Naples. The successes of the Russians in Czechoslovakia and Hungary had renewed Churchill's appetite for Balkan adventures, if he had ever suppressed it. He desperately wanted to prevent the Balkans from "going red," and still thought he could do it. Tito had just agreed with the Russians to have his partisans become part of the Red Army, and that meant that supply for the partisans, which the British had undertaken for years, could now be stopped.

So, acting on Churchill's instructions, Field Marshal Wilson proposed that as soon as the Fifth Army captured Bologna, Alexander could withdraw six divisions to make a landing on the Dalmatian coast. The beachhead would be established at Zara and three or four divisions would advance on Fiume and Trieste. After they captured Fiume, the Allied force in Yugoslavia would be increased to six divisions, and they would move north to cut Kesselring's line of communications with Austria and the German Army Group E in the Balkans. At the same time the Allied air forces in Italy and the partisans would cut the German escape routes across the Alps, while the remaining Allied forces in Italy crossed the Po Valley.

When the Combined Chiefs of Staff heard the proposal the Americans said to themselves, "There goes Winnie again" and shot the plan down. Churchill then reluctantly supported a British proposal to limit themselves on the eastern side of the Adriatic to aid the Yugoslav partisans. They reminded Wilson that his immediate objective was Bologna. After that the Allies should tie down as many German divisions in northern Italy as possible.

All this discussion of high strategy went on above the heads of the fighting troops, who attacked and retreated in the foggy mountains of the Appenines and along the flooded Plain of Romanga that autumn. On the Fifth Army front, General Keyes proposed to close the 20 miles that separated his four divisions from Bologna and the Po Valley. British 13th Corps and American 4th Corps, on the right and left, continued to make limited gains in support, and kept Kesselring from shifting divisions to oppose II Corps.

But the Fifth and the Eighth Armies were a long way from destroying the German Tenth and Fourteenth Armies. On September 21, Field Marshal Alexander informed London that the Allies had suffered severe losses, as well as the Germans, but that to clean up the Germans they would need a three to one superiority in troops and they had nothing like that. Therefore, Alexander said, it would be impossible for the Allies to achieve decisive victory in Italy before the end of the year. As far as replacements were concerned, if Alexander wanted them he would have to create them from within his own organization. So the British 1st Armoured Division was dissolved; its infantry was transferred to the 56th Infantry Division. Two infantry brigades were recruited from among Polish refugees, adding 10,000 men to the pool for the Eighth Army. Clark managed to get 3,000 infantrymen from Washington, originally scheduled for Western Europe.

Still, the prospects in Italy were discouraging. Clark got a division from 13th Corps, but during the first week of October, the II Corps had been taking casualties at the rate of 550 per day over the returns of previous casualties from hospitals. At that rate the four divisions could maintain their table of organization strength only through October 10.

Nonetheless, Keyes resumed a full-scale assault on Bologna. At 6 o'clock on the morning of October 10, II Corps attacked on a ten-mile front. The Germans held for four days, and on the night of October 4, fell back to the next ridge line. The next day, Clark flew to the 91st Infantry Division headquarters at Monghidoro where he had his first sight of the Po Valley and the snow-covered Alps beyond. Here was his objective.

The II Corps offensive went into its second phase on October 5 against Livergnano, a fight that involved all the divisions and took a week. On October 15, the 34th Infantry Division came out of reserve and into the line with Combat Command A of the 1st Armoured Division, to lead the attack toward Bologna. Alexander wanted to make one more try to take Bologna and Ravenna before winter. The Fifth Army would join with the Eighth Army to encircle and destroy the German Tenth Army.

At the end of October, many things changed. Kesselring was hurt in an automobile accident and was replaced in command of the troops by General von Vietinghoff. General Herr of the 76th Panzer Corps became commander of the German Tenth Army. The Fifth Army stopped to wait for the Eighth Army to draw off some of the German divisions that had packed the Fifth Army front. General Leese's anti-Americanism earned him shipment to a new command in Burma where he would not have the problem. General McCreery took over the Eighth Army.

There were complications anew. The Germans withdrew from Greece, in mid-October, and the British sent in the 4th Indian Infantry Division, which promptly got caught in the complications of the Greek civil war between the communists and royalists.

29

Winter Doldrums

On the Adriatic coast, the British Eighth Army had been stopped by the Germans along the Ronca River, and in the Appenine Mountains, the Fifth Army was stalled south of Bologna. The situation was galling to Field Marshal Alexander and his generals, but as far as the Allied strategy was concerned, it was just what was wanted. In order to defend, the Germans had to commit all their armies in northern Italy, which meant the plan to keep a maximum number of German divisions at bay was working very well.

Alexander was still planning his Adriatic amphibious foray for the spring. He hoped by February to occupy the Yugoslav ports of Zadar, Split, and Sibenik and to put the Eighth Army ashore and advance on Fiume and the Lubljana Gap and then to lower Austria. So the Allied armies prepared to capture Bologna and Ravenna, which would be needed for Eighth Army operations in the east.

But before undertaking such heroic feats, Alexander wanted to capture Bologna and Ravenna. The Eighth Army made the first effort—against Forli—on November 6. The Germans moved back a few miles to the Montone River and tried to take Faenza, but failed. The Germans held there until November 23, and then moved back six miles to the Lamone River.

Now politics and attrition changed the picture in Italy. Alexander's plans were knocked apart by the Yugoslavs and Germans. Marshal Tito, being a good Communist, announced that the British and the Americans would not be welcome in Yugoslavia. The Germans then proceeded to take control of the western half of Yugoslavia. So the idea of an amphibious landing died. Then Sir John Dill, head of the British military mission in Washington, died, and General Wilson was chosen by the British to take his place. Alexander then became theater commander, and General Clark took Alexander's old job as Fifteenth Army Group commander, but not quite. The British made sure that McCreery, the new Eighth Army commander, would report directly to Alexander and not to Clark. General Truscott returned from France to take over the Fifth Army. A new directive from above set out the aims of the Allies in Italy, which were now reduced to capturing Bologna and Ravenna, and tying up as many German divisions as possible. This was much more nearly the American concept than the British of the war they had been fighting for two years.

Early in December, the Eighth Army resumed its offensive against Faenza but the going was slow. General von Vietinghoff intended to stand fast and he was strengthened in that resolve by Hitler who, on December 7, ordered the German forces to stand fast at Faenza. When the British gained some ground there, he modified that order only slightly.

The British were having division troubles just then, which hampered their drive. They had to send the 46th Infantry Division off to Greece, but General Keighley, the commander of 5th Corps, had plenty to work with. He had 400 pieces of artillery to support his advance and the 10th Indian and 2nd New Zealand Divisions (both new units) to carry the action while the tired 56th Infantry Division was moved to a quiet sector of the line. The 5th Corps attacked on the night of December 14, and the German garrison of Faenza pulled back, but only three miles.

On the Fifth Army front, Truscott expected a German counterattack. Recently the 92nd Infantry Division had joined the Fifth Army. This was the Negro division that had not performed very well so far. The American army at this point was very distrustful of black troops and that feeling created a situation in which the blacks were usually badly trained. Not being regarded as equals they behaved accordingly. The 92nd was made up of Negro infantrymen, commanded by both white and black officers. The division was not well regarded in the army as a fighting unit, and the Germans apparently had the same opinion because they planned an assault on the Fifth Army line, directly against the 92nd. Luckily, Truscott had expected something of the sort and had that division backed up by additional units of 4th Corps.

On December 26, the Germans launched Operation Wintergewitter (Winter Thunderstorm) against the 92nd. The purpose was to destroy the 92nd's capability for offensive operations. Behind a screen of artillery and mortar fire, the Germans attacked along the slopes of the Serchio River Valley against the 1st and 2nd Battalions of the 370th Infantry

Regiment; but this was only a feint. The main attack was made against the 92nd units east of the Serchio. The 366th Infantry Regiment began to fall back in disarray, and it appeared that the Germans would break through. Company G panicked and left a 500-yard gap through which the Germans rushed into the village of Barga, despite the stout resistance of a handful of the black soldiers. The Germans pushed beyond to Barga, mopped up, and did their job of destroying the effectiveness of the black units, and then withdrew.

During the night of the 26th, the disorganized 370th passed through the lines of the Indian 19th Brigade, which had been positioned to back them up. The American troops were on their way to the rear to seek safety from German gun fire. The division commander, General Edward Almond, had them rounded up and taken to a point west of Serchio where they were put in position on the Indians' left and behind their own 1st Battalion. In the next four days, the Indians then set about recovering all the ground lost by the 92nd in those hours of panic. But the incident so unnerved the senior officers of the Fifth Army that they postponed the assault on Bologna until spring.

The operations of the Eighth Army also came to a halt at the end of the year 1944, although the Germans had been driven from Ravenna on December 4 and from Faenza and from Bagnacavallo. As had been feared by Alexander's staff much earlier, the British advances were made in terms of one river to the next, and the Germans were now holed up behind the Lamone River and behind them were the Imola and Santerno Rivers, which would have to be crossed. The rains had brought more mud, and the ground had not yet frozen. But weather and tough Germans were not the only problems of the Eighth Army. It was going to lose a corps headquarters and three divisions to Greece, where the civil war was growing worse and the British were stuck in the middle of it. The Canadian troops were being sent to join the other Canadians fighting in Western Europe.

And so the Fifth and the Eighth Armies went on the defensive and would remain so until April. Except for two limited objective operations in the Eighth Army sector and one in the Fifth Army side, the armies would remain static all winter long.

That winter, the British were troubled by high rates of desertion from the Eighth Army. Part of the reason for this must be attributed to bad morale, engendered by the weather, lack of amenities, and general low standard of living of the troops, who when not in combat had plenty of time and reason to complain. But another part of it has to be attributed to the almost unceasing complaint of the British officers that the whole direction of the war effort was wrong, and that they should be engaged in the Balkans. British historian General W.G.F. Jackson alludes to this state of affairs: "They could sense the uselessness of throwing away their lives when the Russians and Eisenhower's armies where doing the job for them and much more successfully. The concept of crossing the Adriatic and arriving as a victorious army in Vienna would have fired their enthusiasm; slogging away through the Romanga or the hills south of Bologna had few attractions for the commanders or their soldiers."[26]

The Americans alleviated the physical problems of their soldiers by building rest centers in the Arno Valley, including Florence and Montecatni, famous for its hot springs, and by winterizing many winter quarters, and bringing pyramidal tents with stoves up to the front lines.

But it was a hard winter in every sense of the word, and even the American troops suffered. They sang a favorite song that represented their feelings.

> Dear Mr. Truman, let the boys come home,
> They have conquered Naples, they have conquered Rome.
> They have beat the master race
> And spit right in Herr Hitler's face.
> Oh, let the boys come home.
> Let the boys at home see Rome.[27]

In the winter months, the limited military operations were aimed at tidying up the fronts. The Eighth Army conducted operations to wipe out two troublesome salients: one held by the 114th Jaeger Division on a bridgehead five miles northwest of Ravenna, and another held by the 278th Infantry Division southwest of that near Faranola. In the first week of January, both of these salients were removed, and the Eighth Army was then drawn up along the Senio River from the mountains to the sea.

The Fifth Army conducted one operation to clear up troop dispositions in the area occupied by the 92nd Infantry Division in the Serchio Valley. This was also to be a test of the fighting capabilities of the 92nd—the black division—that had been suspect before it got to Italy and so far had given no indication of trustworthiness. The main test came in the coastal corridor to the west where General Almond planned to have the 370th Infantry Regiment capture the Strettoia Hills, three miles inland overlooking the coastal corridor. On the right flank, the 371st Infantry Regiment was to keep abreast as the 370th's three battalions leapfrogged one another from one hill to the next. On the coastal flatlands, the 366th Infantry Regiment's 3rd Battalion, with tank support, was to cross the Cinquale Canal between the coast highway and the sea four miles south of Massa.

The offensive began on February 8 as Generals Truscott and Crittenberger watched from an observation post. From the outset, the plan went astray. After covering only 800 yards, the 371st stumbled onto an enemy minefield and came to a dead halt, exposing the 370th's right flank. Aircraft support enabled the 370th to go ahead despite this, and by late afternoon, it had occupied its initial objective. But the men had just dug in when the Germans counterattacked starting with a hail of mortar shells. The Germans overran the forward company and forced the second company to withdraw down the slopes of the Strettoia Hills. Units of another battalion proceeding with the leapfrog plan ran into men falling back under enemy fire. In the resulting confusion, the attack broke down altogether. The regiment began to fall apart, with men taking shelter from the fighting by hiding in houses and anywhere they could conceal themselves. The order was put out to search everywhere for stragglers and try to get the regiment together again. It was the same story of failure in the 366th sector. After three days, the assault failed completely; so disorganized was the 92nd that further attempts to complete the operation were given up, and General Almond cancelled it on the third day. The disaster had cost the 92nd 47 officers and 659 enlisted men killed, wounded, and missing, among the two battalions. That price was paid for by 145 German prisoners and no ground gain. After that Truscott decided that the 92nd could not be used in further offensive action.

A week after the abortive 92nd affair, Crittenberger launched the second limited American operation of 4th Corps, which was designed to put the corps in a better position to undertake the spring offensive. He chose his newest division: the 10th Mountain Division. This was an unusual military unit, with a much higher educational level than most. It had been organized in an unusual way: through the recruitment of the American civilian National Ski Patrol System, which contained a high number of ski enthusiasts and winter sports fans. Militarily it was very special, having only three battalions of 75-mm-pack Howitzers as compared to the three battalions of 105-mm Howitzers and one of 155-mm Howitzers of the standard infantry division. Because of its light armament, the division was unacceptable to other theaters of war but completely adapted for the mountain warfare in which the Fifth Army was engaged. The division commander, General Hays, was one of the best American field commanders.

For the operation—called "Operation Encore"—General Truscott wanted to secure the high ground commanding a ten-mile section of Route 64. The area consisted of a series of peaks and ridges about five miles west of the highway. In American hands, the ridge would provide observation as far as the Po Valley.

Early in February, the 10th Mountain Division was positioned in the valley of the Silla River. Dominating the area were two peaks that the Americans knew as Riva Ridge and Monte Belvedere: Monte della Torraccio Ridge. The side of the Riva Ridge was a cliff rising 1,500 feet above the valley floor. The mountain troops would have to scale that cliff to reach the Germans and then move to Monte Belvedere. Then they would begin the second phase of the operation to continue northeast about four miles, taking a series of lower ridges that led down the roads that descended into the Po Valley.

General Hays had secretly assembled the troops three miles south and east of the two ridges. To the right the Brazilian Expeditionary Force would cover their right flank. Because the mountain division was so light on artillery, General Crittenberger lent them a field artillery battalion with a 105-mm Howitzer and a Chemical Mortar Battalion, two tank destroyer battalions, and a tank battalion.

Crossing the snow-covered ground would be hard because of limited concealment provided by scattered clumps of stunted trees. Since the roads were narrow and bad in the mountains, transport would mostly be by pack mules, full tracked "weasels," and jeeps. Tanks could be used in part of the terrain.

The first moves would be made by climbing teams from each of the three rifle companies of the 86th Mountain Infantry Regiment's 1st Battalion and one from the 2nd Battalion. With coils of rope slung over their shoulders, the climbers moved off in the darkness, driving steel pitons in the rock, hooking snap links into them, and then fastening ropes to the snap links to provide hand lines for the main body of the climbers, who would follow.

When the advance party had reached the rim of the ridge, the 1st Battalion of the 86th Infantry Division followed, each company taking a different route. Before dawn, the entire battalion was on top, and they had not been detected by the enemy.

When morning revealed the Americans to the Germans, the 232nd Fusilier Battalion launched three counterattacks, but they were all repelled by the Americans. By the end of the day, the ridge was secured. That night, the 85th and 87th Mountain Infantry Regiments assembled at the base of the Monte Belvedere Ridge. They decided against artillery preparation in the interest of surprise, and attacked, the 85th frontally and the 87th up the western slope toward three mountain villages. The gamble paid off, and the men of the 87th were atop the enemy before they met resistance. The Germans were in a line of bunkers and machine-gun positions, and they had installed a number of minefields; but the two battalions made steady progress and within a few hours had control of two of the three villages and the Valpiana Ridge. The 85th Mountain Infantry Regiment had almost the same experience, and three hours after meeting the enemy had fought their way to the top of the Monte Belvedere Ridge.

To attack the last peak—Monte della Torraccio—the Americans brought the artillery into action to neutralize the enemy guns, while British Spitfires and American P-47s flew support missions. Here the enemy was stronger and on February 21 launched a counterattack against the

3rd Battalion of the 85th Mountain Infantry Regiment on Monte Belvedere. The counterattack stopped the American advance but failed to gain any ground for the Germans. On the American right, the Brazilians made an attack, only to discover that the drive toward Monte della Torraccio had caused the Germans to withdraw, and they captured their objective on Monte Castello without trouble.

So the advance continued on the afternoon of February 21. The Germans woke up and began to put up stiff resistance to the 2nd Battalion of the 85th, using artillery very effectively and stopping the Americans 400 yards short of their objective. By late afternoon of the 22nd, the battalion of 1,000 men was down to some 400 effectives, and General Hays relieved the 85th and substituted the 86th Infantry Regiment in the line. Assisted by air attack and artillery fire, the 86th moved steadily ahead: and on the afternoon of the 24th, the whole high ground was in American hands. They had taken 900 casualties, 203 of them killed.

With the Brazilians then, the 10th Mountain Division moved forward and advanced 12 miles to another line of crests after which the terrain into the Po Valley was a gentle slope down. These peaks would be the jump-off point for the spring offensive of 4th Corps. In two days, March 3 and 4, against heavy opposition the troops secured their objectives. The Germans sent part of the fresh 29th Panzer Grenadier Division to counterattack. In very brisk fighting the Allies drove off the Germans and then stopped the offensive, concerned lest the Germans get the idea that this would be the jump-off point and fortify the area. But the 10th Mountain Division now held a six-mile front suitable for the opening of the spring offensive when the time came.

30

To the Bitter End

By the end of March 1945, the Allies were ready to begin a new offensive. The British 13th Corps had been returned to the Eighth Army. The U.S. Fifth Army still had a broad front: General Crittenberger's 4th Corps held 50 miles from the Rebo River to the sea. II Corps was poised to lead the attack against Bologna and the Po River Valley. General Truscott intended to concentrate his efforts west of Route 64 to outflank the German defenses south of Bologna. Contact with the Eighth Army would be made near Bondeno where the Panaro River joins the Po. Thus, the German forces in the bend of the Rebo River would be encircled.

The American effort was to be delayed until the Eighth Army had crossed the Santerno River. It all looked easy because the Allies had overwhelming air support and a two to one edge on the Germans in artillery, two to one in infantry, and three to one in armor. The Eighth Army, for example, had more than 1,200 artillery pieces to the 187 guns and 36 *Nebelwerfers* of the Germans; the ratio of the Fifth Army was about the same. Besides this overwhelming force, the Allies had another weapon, about 50,000 Italian partisans who were organized into companies, battalions, and brigades and were well armed by the Allies over the past two years.

The initial effort of the spring came on the Eighth Army front on the night of April 1 when a flotilla of LVTs (landing vessels, tank) carrying the British 2nd Commando Brigade crossed the Comaccio Lagoon to set up an amphibious attack on Argenta. There was some difficulty when the LVTs ran aground in the shallows, but the troops were transferred to lighter boats, and the operation was carried out. By April 1, the enemy troops were cleared from this spit of land. On April 6, the 56th Infantry Division had cleared the area around the north bank of the Rebo River.

At the same time 120 miles to the west, a reorganized 92nd Infantry Division began operations in the Apuan Alps and the Serchio Valley. The best of the black troops had been formed into the 370th Infantry Regiment. The 442nd Regimental Combat Team of Nisei had replaced one of the other black regiments, while a third regiment, made up of former antiaircraft artillerymen, was formed. Thus, the 92nd was deemed combat-worthy.

The 370th and 442nd Regiments attacked first, the 370th toward Massa, where once again the black troops did not do very well. But the Nisei more than made up for it, and in three days moved up to capture 3,000-foot Monte Belvedere two miles northeast of Massa. The 473rd Infantry Regiment replaced the 370th in the line, and occupied Massa on April 10.

The Eighth Army attacked on April 9 after an impressive aerial bombardment of the German defense line parallel to the Senio River. Sixteen hundred heavy bombers and 600 medium bombers plastered the area between the Senio and Santerno Rivers, and fighter bombers carried out tactical support missions in the next two days as well. The troops began to move at 9:30 in the evening. The flamethrowing Churchill tanks went first, followed by the troops to establish bridgeheads across the Senio. The 2nd New Zealand and the 8th Indian Divisions led the way. By the evening of April 10, the New Zealanders had pushed three miles beyond the Senio to reach the east bank of the Santerno.

The Germans fought doggedly, but by April 12, the British 5th Corps and the Polish 2nd Corps had established bridgeheads beyond the Santerno. That afternoon the New Zealanders captured the town of Massa Lombarda.

Hitler, as usual, inveighed against any major withdrawals by the German troops, no matter the odds they might face. However, General von Vietinghoff had a much more practical view which he stated to the OKW:

> If the Supreme Command of the Armed Forces continues to maintain its intention of keeping the Anglo–Americans as far and as long as possible from the borders of the Reich, its aim can only be achieved if we defeat the known intentions of our enemies, the annihilation of the German armies. This can be done only if we avoid decisive battles by retreating if necessary to our prepared Ticino–Po defense positions. This decision must be made soon in order to allow for the difficult and necessary moves from the western Alps and from the Ligurian coast. As these moves will require at least two weeks we must act quickly in order to prevent the

enemy from reaching the Po on our eastern flank. This means that the Tenth Army would have to hold its sector at least two weeks after the commencement of our withdrawal from the western and alpine sectors of the army group's front. This is considered the only way in which the north Italian areas, so important to our war industry, can be preserved for the German army until the day of our decisive battle.[28]

Having said this, without asking Hitler, von Vietinghoff then withdrew the 1st Parachute Division from the Imola salient and pulled back into the Genghis Khan Line, while reinforcing the Argenta Gap as well as he could.

By April 16, the British 78th Infantry Division struck the line of the Marina Canal and managed to secure a bridgehead and the next morning passed east of Argenta. Within hours, British troops cleared the last German troops from Argenta.

Hitler replied to von Vietinghoff's demand for strategic withdrawal in a message dictated to General Jodl:

All further propoosals for a change in the present war strategy will be discontinued. I wish to point out particularly that under no circumstances must troops or commanders be allowed to waver or to adopt a defeatist attitude as a result of such ideas, apparently held by your headquarters. Where such danger is likely, the sharpest countermeasures must be employed. The Führer expects now, as before, the utmost steadfastness in the fulfillment of your present mission, to defend every inch of the north Italian areas entrusted to your command. I desire to point out the serious consequences for all those higher commanders, unit commanders, or staff officers, who do not carry out the Führer's orders to the last word.[29]

But it would take more than harsh words from Hitler to stop the Allies. The British had now nearly reached the Po, and the Americans of the 10th Mountain Division had attacked very successfully over the mountains, while other American elements had moved on the right and the left. On April 20, the Americans broke out of the Appenines and onto the plain south of Bologna and were moving up Route 65. On the 21st, the Allied troops, Poles included, occupied Bologna.

April 20 marked the turning of the Allied spring offensive all along the front. The Allies were approaching the Po River, and the Germans were withdrawing as rapidly as they could. The 85th Mountain Division crossed the Po on April 23 and headed for Verona, along the Adige River. German troops were surrendering by the hundreds, and those that were fleeing toward the Alps were abandoning equipment all along the roads. The British Eighth Army crossed the Po on April 24 and began pushing toward the Adige, ten miles away. The 2nd New Zealand Division crossed on April 26. On the 27th, the 5th Corps and 13th Corps crossed the Adige. Along with groups of partisans, the British were now mopping up mostly disorganized German units.

East of Lake Garda, the Germans had only two routes of escape. One, opposite the Eighth Army, led northeast to southeastern Germany and Yugoslavia. The other route, opposite the Fifth Army, led north along the shore of Lake Garda toward the Brenner Pass and the Reschen Pass into Austria. What was left of General Herr's German Tenth Army would follow the first route, and the remnants of Lieutenant General Joachim Lemelsen's Fourteenth Army would take the Lake Garda route.

As the Allied forces chased the retreating Germans toward the Alps, Allied headquarters issued a call for a general uprising of the Italian partisans in northern Italy. In most towns the republic set up by the Germans with Mussolini as the head had passed out of existence, and most towns were under partisan control. One by one, the cities were falling. The 442nd Nisei Regiment captured Turin and on May 1 linked up with the French 27th Alpine Division from the southern France theater. As of April 29, the Po Valley's northern exits were closed, and the Germans west of Lake Garda had no place to go and had to surrender. But three fighting groups of the 14th Panzer Corps were still full of fight, and had established a line running from Route 46 in the east across Route 12 to the town of Riva at the northern end of Lake Garda. Troops of the 10th Mountain Division ran into them on April 27 and for five days fought the last battle of the Italian campaign, on the shores of Lake Garda. The end of the battle was marked by the strange death of Colonel William Darby, who had just recently returned to Italy from Washington to become assistant commander of the 10th Mountain Division. The fighting was over. The Germans had retreated, and the colonel was strolling on the broad promenade along the lake talking over plans for a next move with one of his regimental commanders when a single artillery shell—the last fired from somewhere north of Riva—exploded in the air above him. An enlisted man was killed and Darby was mortally wounded.

On the British Eighth Army front, the 56th Infantry Division that was heading for Venice and the 2nd New Zealand that was heading for Trieste encountered nothing but small groups of German soldiers who were eager to surrender. On the 29th, the 56th captured Venice and the New Zealanders took Padua.

Since spring, the two Allied armies in Italy had taken 145,000 prisoners. By May 1, only company-size patrols were moving, and there was no fighting. On the afternoon of May 2, British and American units picked up a report from the BBC announcing the unconditional surrender of all the German armies in Italy. The Backwater War was over.

As the war came to an end in Italy, Mussolini was in Milan, vainly trying to come up with a plan that would restore him to power throughout the country. Some of his advisers suggested that he escape to Switzerland or to Spain, but he categorically refused to leave the country.

On April 20, when he learned that Bologna had been cut off, he gave orders that most of the government offices of his Salo Republic should be closed down. There was one final possibility. He would establish a redoubt in the Valtelline and hold out there waiting for what he hoped and expected to come about: war between the victors, the western Allies, and Soviet Russia. For this, he needed a number of officials who now clustered around him.

On Saturday, April 21, Bologna was captured by the Allies and the anti-Fascists ran amok, killing many of the old Fascist leaders. On April 22, Mussolini said he would not negotiate with the Allies, but he might transfer power to the Socialist partisan forces, hand over the city of Milan to them, and disappear. But the Socialists of the National Liberation Committee rejected Mussolini's offer contemptuously. On April 23, Mussolini was still thinking about the Alpine redoubt where he would hole up. The next day the Allied air forces were over Milan, and fighter planes machine-gunned the streets. That day Il Duce received a crazed message from Hitler:

> The struggle for existence or nonexistence has reached its climax. Using huge forces and materials, Bolshevism and Judaism have engaged themselves up to the hilt to assemble their destructive forces on German territory, to precipitate our continent into chaos. Nevertheless, with their obstinate scorn of death, the German people and all the others who are animated by the same sentiments will fling themselves to the rescue, however hard the struggle, and with their incomparable heroism will change the course of the war at this historic moment which will decide the fate of Europe for centuries to come.[30]

Hitler was obviously beyond use. If Mussolini was to save anything, he must do it himself. Before he retired to the redoubt, he would make one more effort to reach some agreement at Milan.

On April 25, virtually none of his government officials showed up at their offices. A general strike was about to be called in Milan, which the government could not stop. Mussolini decided to go to the redoubt. He met that day with members of the National Committee for Liberation at the house of Cardinal Schuster where Mussolini learned for the first time of the imminence of a German surrender. The committee wanted his surrender too. He promised an answer within the hour, and left the meeting. Then he went to his office, and shortly afterward left Milan in a convoy of the faithful. They drove to Como where they stayed overnight, and then went on up the lake to Menaggio, then to Grandola to stay at the Hotel Miravalle, only ten miles from the Swiss border. They listened to the radio and the sentence of death given Mussolini and the members of his government by the National Committee for Liberation.

At 4 o'clock on the morning of April 27, Mussolini was awakened and told that the local Fascists in Como had signed an instrument of surrender and the partisans controlled the city. After that it was a question of escape. Mussolini was still surrounded by the German personal guards given him by Hitler and they tried to smuggle him across the Swiss border, disguised as a German soldier. But the column was stopped at Dongo, Mussolini was discovered and put under guard, and the Germans went on.

Mussolini was kept in the municipal building at Dongo, where he was joined by his mistress Clara Petacci, who had been traveling in another group and had been recognized and captured. He signed a statement saying that he had been captured by the 52nd Garibaldi Brigade and had been treated correctly. They were taken to a farmhouse near Como. There they were given a large room and left alone to await the decision of the new authorities at Milan.

The committee could not make up its collective mind. However, the Communist members were determined to kill Mussolini, so Communist executioners went to find Mussolini and kill him before the rest of the committee could decide to turn him over to the Allies. He and Clara Petacci were taken from the farmhouse and driven toward the lake. Their escorts then stopped at the Villa Belmonte—a big house behind a stone wall—and put the two up against the wall and riddled them with machine-gun bullets.

Their bodies were then taken with those of 15 other Fascist leaders by moving van to Milan where they were hung upside down from a girder in a filling station as a final gesture of hatred. The bodies of the others were piled below them. That evening Mussolini was removed by the order of the Allied authorities and given a secret burial. Twelve years later, the body was released to his family and reburied in his home cemetery of San Cassiano in Predappio, the town of his birth.

Appendix A: Order of Battle as of July 10, 1943, D Day—Invasion of Sicily

ALLIED

Allied Force Headquarters—Mediterranean
      General Dwight D. Eisenhower
Fifteenth Army Group
      General Harold R.L.G. Alexander
Allied Naval Forces—Mediterranean
      Admiral Andrew B. Cunningham
Western Naval Task Force
      Vice Admiral Henry K. Hewitt, USN

American

Seventh Army
      Lieutenant General George S. Patton Jr.
            II Corps
                  1st Infantry Division
                  3rd Infantry Division
                  45th Infantry Division
                  2nd Armored Division
            Reserve (North Africa)
                  9th Infantry Division
                  82nd Airborne Division

British

Eastern Naval Task Force
>Vice Admiral B. L. Ramsay

Eighth Army
>General Bernard L. Montgomery
>>13th Corps
>>>5th Infantry Division
>>>50th Infantry Division
>>30th Corps
>>>1st Canadian Infantry Division
>>>51st Highland Infantry Division
>>Reserve (North Africa)
>>>1st Airborne Division
>>>78th Infantry Division

AXIS

Armed Forces Command—Sicily
>General d'Armata Alfredo Guzzoni

Italian

Sixth Army
>General d'Armata Alfredo Guzzoni
>>12th Corps
>>>26th Assieta Division
>>>28th Aosta Division
>>>3.3 Local Coastal Divisions
>>>2 Naval Base Garrisons
>>16th Corps (Rossi)
>>>4th Livorno Division
>>>54th Napoli Division
>>>2.6 Local Coastal Divisions
>>>3 Naval Base Garrisons

German

14th Panzer Corps
>15th Panzer Grenadier Division
>Hermann Goering Panzer Division
>3rd Panzer Grenadier Division
>16th Panzer Division

Appendix B: Order of Battle as of September 8, 1943, Salerno Landing

ALLIED

Allied Force Headquarters—Mediterranean
  General Dwight D. Eisenhower
Fifteenth Army Group
  General Harold R.L.G. Alexander

American

Western Naval Task Force
  Vice Admiral Henry K. Hewitt, USN
Fifth Army
  General Mark Clark
    6th Corps (U.S.)
      1st Armored Division
      3rd Infantry Division
      34th Infantry Division
      36th Infantry Division
      45th Infantry Division
      82nd Airborne Division
      3 Ranger Battalions

> 10th Corps (British)
>> 7th Armoured Division
>> 46th Infantry Division
>> 56th Infantry Division

British (Adriatic)

Eighth Army

> General Bernard L. Montgomery
>> 5th Corps
>>> 1st Airborne Division
>>> 8th Indian Division
>>> 78th Infantry Division
>> 13th Corps
>>> 1st Canadian Infantry Division
>>> 5th Infantry Division

AXIS

German

Commander in Chief—South

> Field Marshal Albert Kesselring
>> Tenth Army
>>> General Heinrich von Vietinghoff
>>>> 76th Panzer Corps
>>>>> 16th Panzer Division
>>>>> 1st Parachute Division
>>>>> 29th Panzer Grenadier Division
>>>> 14th Panzer Corps
>>>>> 26th Panzer Division
>>>>> 3rd Panzer Grenadier Division
>>>>> Hermann Goering Panzer Division
>>>>> 15th Panzer Grenadier Division
>>>> Reserve (Rome)
>>>>> 1st Parachute Corps
>>>>>> 2nd Parachute Division

Appendix C: Order of Battle as of January 22, 1944, Anzio Landing

ALLIED

Supreme Allied Command—Mediterranean
  Field Marshal Henry Maitland Wilson
Fifteenth Army Group
  Field Marshal Harold R.L.G. Alexander
    Fifth Army
      Anzio Force
        6th Corps
            1st Infantry Division (British)
            3rd Infantry Division (U.S.)
        Reserve
            1st Armored Division (U.S.)
            45th Infantry Division (U.S.)
      Main Force
        II Corps (U.S.)
            34th Infantry Division (U.S.)
            36th Infantry Division (U.S.)
        French Expeditionary Force
            2nd Moroccan Infantry Division
            3rd Algerian Infantry Division

> 10th Corps (British)
>> 5th Infantry Division
>> 46th Infantry Division
>> 56th Infantry Division

> Eighth Army
>> Lieutenant General Sir Oliver Leese
>>> 5th Corps (British)
>>>> 1st Canadian Infantry Division
>>>> 8th Indian Infantry Division
>>> 13th Corps (British)
>>>> 4th Indian Infantry Division
>>>> 78th Infantry Division

AXIS

German

Commander in Chief—South
> Field Marshal Albert Kesselring
>> Tenth Army
>>> 76th Panzer Corps
>>>> 1st Parachute Division
>>>> 26th Panzer Division
>>>> 334th Infantry Division
>>>> 305th Infantry Division
>>>> 3rd Panzer Grenadier Division
>>> 14th Panzer Corps
>>>> 5th Mountain Division
>>>> 44th Infantry Division
>>>> 71st Light Infantry Division
>>>> 15th Panzer Grenadier Division
>>>> Hermann Goering Panzer Division
>>>> 29th Panzer Grenadier Division
>>>> 94th Infantry Division
>>> 1st Paratroop Corps
>>>> 90th Panzer Grenadier Division
>>>> 4th Parachute Division
>>>> 92nd Infantry Division
>> Fourteenth Army
>>> Adriatic Command
>>>> 162nd Turcoman Infantry Division
>>>> 16th Schutzstaffel Panzer Grenadier Division

51st Mountain Corps

> 362nd Infantry Division
> 278th Infantry Division

76th Corps

> 356th Infantry Division
> 65th Infantry Division

Reserve

> 114th Jaeger Division
> 188th Mountain Division

Bibliographic Essay

The basis of this book is the records of the U.S. Army in the Mediterranean Theater of Operations. For the Italian campaign, I used the three volumes of official army history (*U.S. Army History*) dealing with Sicily, Salerno to Cassino, and Anzio to the Alps. For the British story, I depended largely on the American records and W.G.F. Jackson's *The Battle for Italy*, which relates in very modest terms the basic quarrels between the British and Americans. *The US Army Air Forces in WW II*, vol. 2, was valuable as was Omar Bradley's *Memoirs: A Soldier's Story*. Winston Churchill's *The Second World War*, vols. 4, 5, and 6, described British activity and his own. Dwight D. Eisenhower's *Crusade in Europe* gave something of his point of view. Mark Clark's *Calculated Risk* tells his story. Dan Kurzman's *The Race to Rome* told the story of Mark Clark's bid for glory. Martin Blumenson's *Bloody River* tells of the crossing of the Rapido River. From my own works, I used *The GI's War* for the story of American soldiers in Italy; *War in the Balkans* gave some background on British Empire troops fighting in Italy as did *War in North Africa*. The story of the end of Mussolini is from my *Mussolini's Empire*.

Much of this book depended on two interviews: one with General Mark Clark at The Presidio, San Francisco, September 1949; and the other with General James M. Gavin in Washington, D.C., October 1957.

Additional sources include:

Della Rosa, Eligio. *Montecassino, Return of the Lost Madonna*, and *The Inside Story of the Bombing of Montecassino*. Glen Cove, N.Y.: privately printed, 1988.

Hoyt, Edwin P. *Hitler's War*. New York: McGraw-Hill, 1988.

Kesselring, Albrecht. *The Memoirs of Field Marshal Kesselring*. Novato, Calif.: Presidio Press, 1953.

Montgomery, Field Marshal Bernard L. *Memoirs*. Cleveland and New York: World Publishing, 1958.

Mussolini, Benito. *The Fall of Mussolini: His Own Story*. New York: Farrar Straus, 1948.

Notes

1. Churchill, vol. 4, p. 319.
2. General Mark Clark interview, September 1949, The Presidio, San Francisco.
3. General James Gavin interview, Washington, D.C., October 1957.
4. Ibid.
5. Mussolini, p. 49.
6. Churchill, vol. 4, p. 685ff.
7. *U.S. Army History*, p. 47.
8. Bradley, p. 247.
9. Montgomery, p. 234.
10. *U.S. Army History*, p. 210.
11. Eisenhower, p. 187.
12. Churchill, vol. 4, p. 828.
13. Kesselring, p. 193.
14. Ibid.
15. Clark interview.
16. Clark, p. 296.
17. Ibid.
18. Hoyt, *Hitler's War*, p. 27ff.
19. Kesselring, p. 243.
20. Clark interview.
21. German propaganda leaflet at Cassino.
22. Kesselring, p. 265.
23. Ibid., p. 166ff.
24. Churchill, vol. 4, p. 318.

25. Hoyt, *Hitler's War*, p. 243.
26. Jackson.
27. American soldiers' song.
28. Hoyt, *Hitler's War*, p. 357.
29. Ibid.
30. Hoyt, *Mussolini's Empire*, p. 257.

Index

About the Author

EDWIN P. HOYT is an independent historian. He is the author of more than 150 books, mostly in the area of military history, including *The Last Kamikaze* (Praeger, 1993) and *Hirohito* (Praeger, 1992). Born and raised in Portland, Oregon, Hoyt turned his attention to journalism after service in the Pacific theater during World War II. He has written for the *Denver Post*, *Collier's Magazine*, and *American Heritage*, as well as for CBS news.